The Wonders Of Creation

The Wonders Of Creation

AN EXPLORATION
of the ORIGIN & SPLENDORS of the UNIVERSE

by Alfred M. Rehwinkel

Professor Emeritus, Concordia Seminary
St. Louis, Missouri

BETHANY FELLOWSHIP, INC.
Minneapolis, Minn. 55438

Library of Congress Cataloging in Publication Data

Rehwinkel, Alfred Martin, 1887-
The Wonders of Creation.
Includes bibliographical references.
1. Creation.
2. Bible. O. T. Genesis I-II—Criticism, interpretation, etc.
I. Title.
BS651.R39
213
74-8416
ISBN 0-87123-649-4

Published by Bethany Fellowship, Inc.
6820 Auto Club Road, Minneapolis, Minnesota 55438

Printed in the United States of America

DEDICATION

Dedicated to my children, Dorothy, Helen, and Eugene, and my grand and great-grandchildren, with the prayer that they may continue in the faith confessed and expressed in this book.

Acknowledgements

I wish to express my appreciation to the following:

The Philosophical Library, Inc., 15 E. 40th St., New York 16, New York, for permission to quote from their publication *"A Doctor's Soliloquy"* by Joseph Hayhin Krimsky.

E. P. Dutton & Co., 201 Park Ave. So., New York, N.Y. 10003, for permission to quote from their anniversary edition of Darwin's *"Origin of Species"* by Prof. W. F. Thompson.

To many individuals all over the world from whom I received valuable suggestions and information.

To Miss Norma Kramer who typed the complete manuscript.

To my daughter, Helen, for her valuable assistance in preparing the entire manuscript and the index for publication.

To David Jensen for his assistance in proofreading the manuscript.

To James Hanson for assistance in preparing the index.

The author, however, must take full responsibility for the final form of all statements in the book.

Contents

Preface

The title of this book is *The Wonders of Creation.*

This title is a concise summary of the content of this book. The underlying philosophy of this treatise is based on the premise that Genesis 1 and 2, and the rest of Genesis are factual and are history. The first basic principle I follow is that these chapters provide us with the only possible and reliable source of knowledge concerning the origin of the universe.

A second basic principle adhered to is the recognized fact that all knowledge is based on experience, either direct or indirect, and for everything beyond experience we are dependent upon revelation. Science is knowledge of facts, phenomena, and laws that has been gained and verified by exact observation, experimentation, and testing. Any claim beyond that is not science but mere speculation and theory.

The third principle followed is the axiom, "Every effect must have a corresponding cause." This is a universally accepted truth. Nothing cannot produce something. From this it follows inexorably that the origin of matter, of life, or forms and designs, and the laws of nature presuppose a Creator, a great Creator, a superintelligent Designer and Law Giver.

I believe that this Creator, Designer and Law Giver was the omnipotent and all-wise God as revealed in the first two chapters of Genesis and in all the rest of our sacred Bible.

The aim of this book is threefold:

1. To arouse in the reader the emotions of awe, reverence,

and adoration for our God, who created all the wonders of heaven and earth in His infinite wisdom and by the omnipotent power of His word.

2. To show that the most effective refutation of the absurd theory of evolution is to direct the honest seeker after truth to the wonders of nature and to the laws by which all things are sustained. No person in his right mind can honestly believe that a world so complex, so cosmic in its expansion, and so wonderful in all its details could possibly have happened by accident or by itself without a superior intelligence to design and create it.

Every house requires a builder; every machine, whether great or small, a maker. And so, this wonderful universe requires an omnipotent and an all-wise Creator. Every effect must have a cause. Nothing cannot produce something. Our common sense, as well as our human experience, tells us this is true.

3. A third aim of this book is to confirm the Christian—especially the young, inexperienced Christian—in his conviction that the interpretation of the riddle of the universe, as stated in the First Article of the Apostolic and the Nicene Creeds of our Christian confession, is the only interpretation that does not do violence to the intelligence of a normal human being, and to show that not we, but the evolutionists, are on the defensive. Our Christian cosmogony is based on divine revelation, which alone can lift the veil from the mystery of the beginning of all things because only God was there when this happened.

The evolutionist has no demonstrated scientific proof for his claims. He accepts his theory by a faith based on human speculation.

For a Christian, Genesis 1 and 2 provide the only possible answer to the question of the "whence" of all things.

But the tragedy is that not all men accept Genesis as a reliable source of knowledge. The number of those who still believe in a six-day creation, as revealed in Genesis, has become a dwindling minority in the civilized world of today. The majority of men, and especially of those who shape and influence public opinion in this matter, who write the textbooks for our students—and that includes many theologians—have relegated Genesis to the realm of myths and legends, and have reverted back to the pagan philosophy of the Greeks by assuming that all this came out of nothing and by itself.

And now, to show that Genesis is not a myth and that the evolutionary theory is an impossible assumption, I would like to invite the reader to examine with me, verse by verse, the first two chapters of Genesis, and there observe God in His creative work as He calls the things of this universe with its manifold creatures into existence during the six days of creation week by His omnipotent, "Let there be."

But while we examine the work of creation in this manner, we of necessity must enter the field which the scientist commonly claims for his own exclusive domain. And because of that, for many this will eliminate me as competent to discuss this subject. I am a theologian and not a professional scientist, and for many it is taken for granted that what a theologian, and especially a fundamental theologian, has to say on this subject is inconsequential.

In reply to these objections I would like to say that the problem concerning the origin of the universe is beyond the possibility of human observation and experimentation and therefore, outside the scope of science. This knowledge can be attained only through revelation and accepted by faith. The question of creation is, therefore, a question of theology and not of science.

1.

The Book of Genesis and Its Enemies

The heart and soul of our Christian religion is expressed in the words of the Second and Third Article of the Apostles' and Nicene Creeds, which can be summarized in the words of Luther's explanation where he says, "I believe that Jesus Christ, true God, begotten of the Father from eternity, and also true man, born of the Virgin Mary, is my Lord, Who has redeemed me, a lost and condemned creature, purchased and won me from all sins, from death, and from the power of the devil, not with gold or silver, but with His holy, precious blood and with His innocent suffering and death that I may be His own." And this is followed by the Third Article, which speaks of the work of the Holy Spirit, and the other great articles of the Christian faith in which we confess, "And I believe in the Holy Ghost; the holy Christian church, the communion of saints; the forgiveness of sins; the resurrection of the body; and the life everlasting."

These two articles express the essence of the Christian religion. There is no salvation outside of this faith.

However, there is also the First Article which deals with the work of the First Person of the Trinity, God the Father. And in this article we confess with all of Christendom, "I believe in God, the Father Almighty, Maker of heaven and earth."

This First Article, too, is an essential part of our Christian religion and must not be neglected or surrendered. And so, we shall now turn our special attention to the part of the Bible on which this First Article is based.

This First Article, dealing with creation, is based on Genesis 1 and 2, but is supported by many other references in the Old and New Testaments. To understand it we must study Genesis thoroughly, especially the first two chapters.

Genesis is the first book of our Bible. In many respects, Genesis must be regarded as the most important book of the Bible. The loss of some books of either the Old or the New Testament would not seriously affect our faith; other parts of the Bible could supply what would be missing. But it is not so with Genesis. There is no substitute for this book. Genesis is altogether unique. Without Genesis the rest of the Bible is all but impossible. Everything begins with Genesis.

In Genesis we have God's first revelation concerning himself. In Genesis we have the only record of the origin of the universe, the origin of man, the beginning of sin, the consequence of sin, the first gospel, the first death, the first record of human civilization, the first city, the end of the first world, the emergence of a second world from the wreckage of the Flood, and the beginning of the race from which the Messiah was to come. In fact, in Genesis we have the beginning of all things. Genesis answers a thousand questions for which we would have no answer were it not for this book. Genesis is the very foundation of our Bible, and all that follows has its roots deeply embedded in this first revelation of God to man.

But the very importance of Genesis has made it a special target for bitter attacks on the part of the enemies of our Bible. And these attacks date back to the very beginning of the history of the Christian Church.

Satan and his human agents soon realized that if Genesis could be undermined by creating doubt and skepticism concerning its reliability, all that follows would become equally uncertain. Once Genesis becomes doubtful, all the rest of the Bible becomes uncertain.

The earliest attack on Genesis and on the absolute authority of the Bible dates back to the time when a philosophy known as Gnosticism first appeared to disturb the church. This peculiar form of philosophy had its beginning at the time of the apostles. Paul warned the Christians of Asia Minor against this false philosophy in his Epistle to the Colossians, chapter 2, verse 8.

With the fall of the Western Roman Empire, all or most of Christendom gradually sank into ignorance and superstition.

This period of history is commonly known as the Dark Ages. No special attacks on Genesis or on the Bible as a whole were especially made during this period to confuse the faith of the Christians. There was not much left to confuse.

But when Luther again gave the Bible back to the people in their vernacular, it was not very long before errors and heresy of every description began to raise their ugly heads, so that one of the Reformation hymn writers cried out, "Viel' Sekten und viel' Schwaermerei auf einem Haufen kommt herbei." (Out of the same pile came many different sects and enthusiasms.)

But the most vicious attack on the Bible and its inerrant authority has come in modern times, beginning in the latter part of the 19th century and continuing in one form or another to the present date. The modern opposition to the Bible has chiefly found an expression in varying shades and degrees of the following four theological theories and philosophies: rationalism, higher criticism, neoorthodoxy, and evolution.

We shall examine each of these briefly:

1. *Rationalism*

The word 'rationalism' is derived from the Latin word *ratio*, which means reason.

Rationalism is the assertion of the supremacy and sufficiency of reason in all realms of human experience. It is the view that human reason is the only source of truth, that it alone is the judge as to what can be accepted or must be rejected. It is opposed to supernaturalism, divine revelation, and the miraculous element as sources for religion.

Rationalism, as a dominant philosophy, followed the period of pietism in German Protestantism, but its roots go back to the 5th century when it appeared in the sectarian movement known as Pelagianism (Pelagius, 410 A.D.). Pelagianism rejected inherent evil in man and believed in the perfectibility of human nature.

Rationalism appeared as a philosophical trend in Europe about the middle of the 17th century. It was nurtured by prerevolutionary naturalism in France and deism in England. In Germany it reached its most extreme manifestation in the period of enlightenment of the 18th and early 19th centuries. Men like Lessing, Professor Wolff of Halle, Emanuel Kant of Koenigsberg in Germany, John Locke and John Stuart Mill in England, Voltaire and the Encyclopedists in France, and Thomas Paine in America, lent their tremendous influence to this movement. Rationalism still continues in many forms of liberalism, humanism, and agnosticism in the thought-world today. All liberals in modern theology are essentially rationalists.

Rationalism influenced every area of human thought, but its baneful effect was especially disastrous on theology. It denied supernatural revelation; thus the Bible was reduced to the level of other ancient human books, and the Christian religion was regarded and treated as any other form of religion among many. It rejected the miraculous element in religion, regarding all forms of religion as the product of the human mind and equally good in their respective spheres. Jesus became a mere man; His miracles were natural phenomena; the Bible was regarded as a collection of ancient myths, legends, allegories, poetry, and possibly some history. It was subjected to the same treatment as any other human document. Genesis, in particular, was rejected as being of no historical significance.

Rationalism exalts man above God and makes human reason the measure of all things. It arrogantly denies all truth as revealed in Scripture and forever insinuates Satan's original diabolical tempting question, "Yea, hath God said . . . ?" and "Your eyes shall be opened, and ye shall be as gods" (Gen. 3:1, 5).

2. *Higher criticism*

Higher criticism was a movement in theological circles in the early part of the 19th century which resulted in casting doubts on the authenticity of individual books of the Bible, and especially in denying that Moses was the author of those books commonly ascribed to him.

This movement is called higher criticism in contrast to lower criticism.

Lower criticism deals with the text of the Old and New Testaments, its transmission and condition. It might also be called textual criticism, and in that respect renders a valuable service to theology.

Higher criticism, on the other hand, occupies itself with the study of the date and the authorship, the place and the circumstances of the composition, the purpose and character of the individual books. In general, however, the term higher criticism has come to mean an approach to the Old and New Testaments that denies the absolute trustworthiness of these books and their authorship, and arrogates the authority to discard such portions of Scripture which do not fit into its preconceived theological system.

This hostile attitude toward the Old Testament appeared during the early period of the Christian Church. It was especially true of certain leaders among gnostic sects and men such as Marcion, Celsus, and Porphyry, who were hostile opponents of Christianity and opposed the Old Testament from the then current philosophical point of view.

There were also those among the liberal Jews who raised questions about the authority of certain Old Testament books.

In modern times, this critical approach to the Bible dated back to the philosopher Spinoza (1632-77) who has been called the father of higher criticism. Spinoza denied the Mosaic authorship of the Pentateuch (*pente*, the Greek for five, and *teuchos*, the Greek for book), and thought it might have been the work of Ezra. A German theologian by the name of Witter (1711) held a view that there were two parallel accounts of creation in Genesis, distinguished by the use of different names for God. Others followed him and developed this idea still further. This principle of documentary analysis was adopted by Eichhorn (1780). He denied that Moses was the compiler of Genesis. He propounded the idea that there were many original sources for Genesis. He called one the "E" document because the Hebrew name for God, Elohim, is found in this portion of Genesis. Another he called the "J" document because Jehovah or Yahweh was used for God.

During the 19th century, other views appeared, growing out of these theories. One was the so-called development hypothesis which was popularized by Wellhausen (1876). His position was that Israel's religious institutions had gradually developed in the course of their history. According to his views, religion was not the result of divine revelation but arose from natural impulses in man. The patriarchs, in his view, were not historical figures, and Genesis did not present any accurate historical picture of the patriarchal times. It was not until Deuteronomic reforms of 622 B.C., under Josiah, that worship at a single sanctuary was required. The Levitical system was even regarded as belonging to a much later period.

Advocates of this theory denied also the Davidic authorship of those Psalms which are commonly ascribed to him, and they denied the unity of the book of Isaiah and the authorship of Daniel to the book that bears his name.

The general effect of this new theology was that it undermined the trustworthiness of Scripture in all its parts and created doubt and suspicion in the minds of Bible students and of the people in the church as a whole.

And then there were also those who supported this negative attitude toward the Bible by insisting that Moses could not have written the books commonly ascribed to him because they said the Hebrew alphabetical script did not even exist before the 8th or 9th centuries B.C. But thanks to archeological discoveries made during the past half century, these claims have been exposed as the false and unscholarly imagination of these enemies of the Bible.

In an article in *Christianity Today*, June 21, 1968, p. 926, Dr. Siegfried H. Horn, Professor of Archeology at Andrews University, Berrien Springs, Michigan, writes, "In 1917, Alan Gardiner, noted British Egyptologist, made the first decipherment of the Proto-Semitic inscription found at Mount Sinai by Flinders Petrie more than ten years earlier. These inscriptions, written in pictorial script by Canaanites before the middle of the second millennium B.C., prove that alphabetic writing existed before the time of Moses. Numerous other inscriptions in the same script have since that time come to light in Palestine and near Mount Sinai, showing that the art of writing in an alphabetical script was already widespread in the patriarchal age."

And then Professor Horn continues to show how many other archeological discoveries in these lands, dating back to the earliest period in Bible History, prove that the culture, customs, and laws described in the Biblical account of the patriarchs are in complete harmony with the culture, customs, and laws of the times in which they lived, thereby proving that the Biblical record presents an accurate picture of that period. Its original source must go back to the very times in which these events happened, and it is absurd and most unscholarly to assume that this portion of our Bible could not have been written until about 1400 years after the events described.

In view of the overwhelming evidence brought to light by modern excavation for the historicity of Genesis, Professor W. F. Albright of Johns Hopkins University, the foremost Orientalist of our times, wrote this significant statement in *The Christian Century*, November 19, 1958, p. 1329:

> Thanks to modern research, we now recognize its (the Bible) substantial historicity. The narrative of the patriarchs by Moses and the Exodus, of the conquest of Canaan, of the Judges, of the monarchy, the exile and restoration have all been confirmed and illustrated to an

extent that I should have thought impossible forty years ago.

3. *Neoorthodoxy*

Neoorthodoxy[1] is a modern movement in Protestant theology. It had its origin in a reaction to the liberalism of the 19th and 20th century theology in Germany. When it first appeared it seemed to be an honest return to a sound Biblical theology, and it was regarded by many as a new approach to a proper understanding of the Scriptures. The movement is also known as Barthianism because Karl Barth, a Swiss theologian, apparently gave the initial impetus to this new trend. Barth had been trained in German liberal theology and his new theology was a reaction from this. He soon found many like-minded followers. Prominent among them are such names as Emil Brunner, also of Switzerland, Reinhold Niebuhr of Union Theological Seminary of New York, Bultmann of Germany, Aulen of Sweden, Cullmann of Switzerland, and many others throughout the Protestant world. In fact, it may be said that today, most theological seminaries in America and theological faculties in Europe are in the stream of this new theology, or at least have been greatly influenced by it. Some have already gone beyond it. But it must be added that the Barthian School is not completely united. In general it may be said to consist of two main trends: the one has been called more "neo" than orthodox and the other more orthodox than "neo." Among the former may be counted men like Tillich, Bultmann, possibly even Niebuhr. Among the latter are Barth himself, then also Emil Brunner, Cullmann, and others of lesser prominence.

But while this movement began as an apparent reaction from the old threadbare liberalism and rationalism of German theology, it soon reverted back to the same old rationalism that it intended to replace—the rationalism which had had such a baneful influence on the theology of the many preceding decades. It now reappeared in a new garb and with a new vocabulary. As before, so now, much of Genesis is being relegated to the realm of poetry, allegory, or myth, and most

[1] For more detailed information on neoorthodoxy see the following: *Christus und Adam* by Karl Barth, a commentary on Romans 5; *Some Neo-orthodoxy Voices on Anthropology* by H. Hamann, The Australian Theological Review, Vol XXVI, Sept. 1955, No. 3; an article by Ernest Wright in *Journal of Bible and Religion*, Vol. XIV, Feb. 1946, No. 1, p. 87.

of the supernatural elements are regarded as unhistorical or as mere folklore. And these new orthodox theologians openly and frankly confess that they "owe a great debt of gratitude to science for having made the traditional view impossible. "For," they say, "as long as we can see the fall of man as an event in the remote past, we fail to think existentially. The Fall is something not in the past but something which we all commit. Let us not push the blame off on Adam. When God says to Adam, 'Where art thou?' He is speaking to each of us."

This new theology has a subtle appeal to the piously naive by speaking much about its Christo-centrality. It pretends to give all honor and glory to Christ. Every part of the Bible, including the creation chapters of Genesis, is viewed and interpreted in reference to Christ. Creation itself is the external basis of the covenant of God with man in Jesus Christ. And Jesus Christ is the embodiment of this covenant. He is the inner meaning of creation (whatever that may mean). Even the fall of man is regarded by Barth as an event that occurred within Jesus Christ and that it has its ultimate meaning, its ultimate resolution in Jesus Christ.

According to neoorthodoxy, the first two or three chapters of Genesis are not history, but a projection of Israel's understanding of its own creation as a people of God. God's creation of the world and man's fall into sin are the knowledge that came to Israel through self-knowledge concerning themselves as a people created and redeemed by God. This creation is understood in terms of redemption, which is to say, in terms of Jesus Christ, all of which sounds very profound and pious but is a foggy and an arrogant perversion of the clear words of divine revelation.

Orthodox Lutheran theology has always been a Christo-centered theology, but Christo-centered in the sense that Christ appears in Scripture, and the redemption of mankind has been revealed in the Gospel. It is the Scriptures one must rely on and not the theories of theologians who arrogate the right to change the clear language of Scripture and super-impose their own fanciful speculation, thereby distorting the simple, unsophisticated words of divine revelation into hazy allegories and myths. From one side of their mouth they speak piously about the Scriptures as the Word of God, and from the other side, they destroy its meaning and rob it of its power.

A writer in the Catholic *St. Louis Review* of November 10, 1967, exposes the absurdity of this fanciful method by applying it to the nursery rhyme, Jack and Jill. The article is titled

"How Theologians Might Explain Mother Goose" and then continues, in part, as follows:

> An English Professor at the University of Connecticut has given us a tongue-in-cheek preview of what we might expect by offering a close reading of the nursery rhyme about Jack and Jill:
>
> We are far from dealing with a folk rhyme, but with a highly sophisticated myth, narrating the tragedy of the fall of man. According to Arthur Deagon, an Associate Professor of English Education, writing in "The Teacher's Guide to Media and Methods"—
>
> The symbolical implications in this seemingly simple folk rhyme are rather startling when it is subjected to close scrutiny, wrote Professor Deagon about the which goes, "Jack and Jill went up the hill to fetch a pail of water; Jack fell down and broke his crown, and Jill came tumbling after."
>
> When the tools of scholarly research are employed towards the end of fuller exegesis on these four lines, he commented, "It can be seen that when Jack and Jill go up the hill, obviously they are involved in the myth of the Quest, the drive for Nirvana, the New Jerusalem, the road to immortality."
>
> The hill represents disappointments, frustrations, the slings and arrows and other such outrages which Dame Fortune bestows unsolicited during the life of man.
>
> They go to fetch a pail of water. Possibly, their quest is for the Grail, the goal, an ideal of the medieval era. However, because Jill, a woman—Eve, Pandora—temptation—the symbol of evil, accompanies Jack, his failure, his fall from grace is inevitable.
>
> And when Jack does fall down, the breaking of the crown may be interpreted as the destruction of potential immortality in man. Jack falls, breaking his god-head crown, and Jill, who will forever remind him of his disaster, comes tumbling after.
>
> And then the article concludes,
>
> At this rate, any Gospel according to Mother Goose is certain to lay an egg.
>
> To interpret a simple nursery rhyme by such a fantastic method is obviously ridiculous and absurd. But, when this sort of method is applied to sacred theology it is regarded as profound scholarship. But this is not theology. It is sheer blasphemy.

4. *The theory of evolution*

The theory of evolution is an attempt on the part of man to account for the origin of the universe and all things in it, including man, without the direct creative act of God. It assumes that matter is eternal, that life sprang by itself from dead matter, and that there has been an automatic and steady upward development of all things. It is complete denial of the Genesis account of creation. Man becomes nothing more than a higher form of animal life. The image of God in man is erased. What the Bible calls sin becomes an inevitable by-product in the process of an upward struggle, for which the individual cannot be held responsible. Eternal life is to live on in the memory of those that follow our own generation. Evolution has no place for Christ the Savior. Jesus is at best a noble martyr and a martyr for an idealist cause. The Gospel of Salvation, as presented in the New Testament, becomes altogether meaningless.

The theory of evolution attempts to present itself as a scientific explanation of the origin of all things. But evolution is not science. It is not based on a scientific demonstration of the facts upon which it claims to be built. Evolution is a theory, an assumption that must be accepted by faith just as the creationist must accept the Biblical doctrine of creation by faith.

"Through faith we understand," says the writer to the Hebrews, "that the worlds were framed by the word of God, so that things which are seen were not made of things which do appear" (Heb. 11:3). If the evolutionists were intellectually honest, they should make a similar confession.

The believers in evolution can be classified as atheistic, deistic, or theistic.

The atheistic evolutionist denies the very existence of God and therefore denies all divine influence in the origin of the universe. He believes that matter is eternal and will continue to evolve new forms forever, and that it was by the fortuitous coming together of the atoms of matter that the forms which now exist came into being.

The deistic evolutionist accepts the idea of a higher guiding intelligence in the formation of the universe, but rejects all special design and creation by a personal God.

The theistic evolutionist asserts that he believes in a personal God and in the Bible as the inspired Word of God. He claims to believe that God created heaven and earth but not as recorded in Genesis nor within the time limit given in the Biblical creation account. He accepts the theory of evolution and believes that all creatures, including man, evolved from some lower existence; but in distinction of other evolutionists, he believes that all occurred under the guiding and creative influence of a supreme architect or god, but not as reported in Genesis. Many theistic evolutionists are found in the orthodox churches and even in theological faculties.

The theory of evolution is commonly ascribed to the English biologist Charles Darwin (1809-1882) and is claimed to be based on science. But neither assertion is correct. Darwin was not the first to propound the evolutionary theory; he merely popularized it and gave it its modern form. And evolution is not a science based on scientific demonstration. It is a theory or hypothesis, or it may be called a philosophy, but it is not science. Just because so many men of science accept this theory does not make it a science any more than a group of Catholic scientists would make Catholicism a science.

It is natural for man, endowed with curiosity, to inquire whence he came and how all things about him had their beginning. The early Greek philosophers wrestled with this problem. They did not have the advantage of God's revelation as the Jews did, and so they resorted to speculation, and each evolved his own peculiar theory.

One of the first to center his speculation on the problem of origin seems to have been Thales of Miletus in Asia Minor, one of the seven wise men of Ancient Greece (640-546 B.C.). He might be called a philosopher, astronomer, and geometer. Thales regarded the ocean as the mother of all things and considered water the element from which all things had their origin. But he did not account for the origin of water nor of the sea.

Another of the Greek philosophers who speculated with the origin of things was Anaximander (611-547 B.C.), also from Miletus. Anaximander believed in the transformation of the aquatic into terrestrial life through a process of gradual development, and he believed that man originated from some fishlike being. He evidently took the mythical mermaids quite seriously.

Still another of these speculating Greek philosophers was Anaximenes (588-524 B.C.). He suggested the idea of spontaneous generation of life from primordial terrestrial slime under the influence of the sun.

Empedocles of Sicily (490-430 B.C.) is often considered the real father of evolution. He regarded fire, water, air, and the earth as the basic physical elements from which all other things sprang. He believed in spontaneous generation and in the development of life as a gradual process. He also held that plants evolved before animals and that the imperfect forms were gradually replaced by the perfect, or in other words, he foreshadowed the idea of the survival of the fittest.

It was the great Aristotle (384-322 B.C.), however, who is credited with having expressed nearly all fundamental ideas generally found in the theory of evolution. And Aristotle dominated natural philosophies from ancient times through the Middle Ages and nearly up to our own times. But Aristotle was great and honest enough to realize that the marvelous diversity and the beauty and order of existing forms and the laws that govern them could not have happened by mere chance. "Nothing," he said, "which occurs regularly can be the result of accident." Aristotle, therefore, might well be classified with the theistic evolutionist.[2]

Aristotle was followed by lesser lights in the ancient philosophical world, among them the school of the Epicureans. Epicurus, the founder of this school, has left only a few fragments of his writings, but one of his disciples was the Roman poet Lucretius (99-55 B.C.). In his poetic work *De Rerum Natura*, Lucretius sets forth the Epicurean view regarding the origin of all things. He regarded matter as eternal and the manifold forms of creation as they now appear as being the result of the fortuitous coming together of the atoms, which again in the course of time dissolve and disintegrate to reunite into new forms. This continues in an unending cycle without any supernatural influence from without.

And so we see that the idea of evolution is much older than Darwin. Every normal human being has a natural desire to know where he and all things came from. But no man can penetrate into this mystery without revelation. The greatest minds of antiquity groped around in their blindness and became contradictory, foolish, and absurd in the solutions they offered.

But even in the age in which Darwin lived and wrote, he was not alone in holding the view of evolution. Before him were such men as the great Linnaeus (1708-1778), Buffon (1707-1788), Erasmus Darwin, the grandfather of Charles Darwin, Lamarck (1744-1829), the great poet Goethe (1749-1832), and Alfred Russell Wallace, the contemporary of Darwin, and many others. The age of rationalism, deism and the so-called enlightenment had destroyed the faith of many in the Bible and in supernaturalism. Like the ancient pagan philosophers, they resorted to speculation in their attempt to find a rational explanation for the origin of the universe. The spiritual and philosophical climate of that age had prepared an environment in which men like Darwin and his associates would find a ready hearing.

In 1859, Darwin published his epoch-making book, *The Origin*

[2] From *The Greeks to Darwin* by Henry Fairchild Osborn (Osborn ScD). London: The Macmillan Co., pp. 43-57.

of Species, which made him the recognized leader in this movement, now often called by the name Darwinism.

The publication of *The Origin of Species* was a turning point in the intellectual history of western civilization. It introduced a new approach to the study of astronomy, geology, biology, psychology, philosophy, sociology, ethics and even religion. In fact, there is not a field of human thought that has not been affected by this theory.

An example of the enthusiasm and the high regard with which the evolutionary theory as presented by Darwin in *The Origin of Species* is accepted, even today, is found in Dr. John T. Bonner, Professor of Biology at Princeton University, who writes: "When Darwin published his book, *The Origin of Species*, it created a tremendous sensation. It seemed to be the key for which the whole world was waiting. —In the hundred years since the publication of *The Origin of Species*, our opinion of Darwin was never so high as it is now." [3]

Today the idea of evolution is presented as an absolute truth in school textbooks on all levels, from the kindergarten to the graduate school, and is presented in magazine articles, newspapers, on radio and TV programs and even in religious literature as a demonstrated fact.

And yet it has been shown time and time again by experimentation and research that the basis on which Darwin built his theory was false and untenable.

One of the most devastating analyses of Darwin's theory of evolution is found in the introduction to the anniversary edition of *The Origin of Species* published in Everyman's Library Series, Dent & Sons, 1959, by Professor W. R. Thompson, F.R.S. Professor Thompson is a world renowned entomologist and the distinguished director of the Commonwealth Institute of Biological Control in Ottawa, Canada. When he was asked by the publisher to write this introduction, he declined at first because of his complete disagreement with the theory of evolution as presented by Darwin. But when he was assured complete freedom for his treatment of the subject, he accepted the offer and wrote the most devastating analysis of the book that once made history and still serves as the Bible for the worshipper of the modern Baal of science. And because of his recognized status in the world of science, no honest man of science can ignore what he says.

For lack of space I can only select a few quotations from

---

[3] Dr. Henry M. Morris, *The Twilight of Evolution*, p. 13.

this fascinating treatise, but I trust that the few selected will be sufficient to show that the evolutionary theory is not science as is so boldly claimed, but rather the subjective assumption and the product of the very active imagination of men who do not want to know God and who refuse to see in the universe the hand of an all-wise and omnipotent Creator.

After explaining briefly why he had hesitated to accept the invitation to write the introduction to this publication as stated, Professor Thompson continues, "*The Origin of Species*" convinced the world that he [Darwin] had discovered the true explanation of biological diversity, and had shown how the intricate adaptation of living things developed by a single inevitable process which even the most simpleminded and unlearned can understand. But I am not satisfied that Darwin proved his point or that his influence in scientific and public thinking has been beneficial."

And aware that he is out of step with the views commonly accepted by the scientific world, he continues, "I am, of course, well aware that my views will be regarded by many biologists as heretical and reactionary. However, I happen to believe that in science, heresy is a virtue and reaction more desirable than in the evolutionary theory."

Then further on he continues with the following statement, "Since he [Darwin] had at the time *The Origin of Species* was published no body of experimental evidence to support his theory, he fell back on speculative arguments. 'The argumentation used by evolutionists,' said De Quaterfages, 'makes the discussion of their ideas extremely difficult.' Personal convictions, simple possibilities, are presented as if they were proofs, or at least valid arguments in favor of the theory. . . .

"The facts and interpretation on which Darwin relied have now ceased to convince. The long continued investigation on heredity and variation have undermined the Darwinian position. We now know that the variations determined by environmental changes, the individual differences regarded by Darwin as the material on which natural selection acts, are not hereditary.

"Darwin himself considered that the idea of evolution is unsatisfactory unless its mechanism can be explained. I agree, but since no one has explained to my satisfaction how evolution could happen, I do not feel impelled to say that it has happened. I prefer to say that on this matter our information is inadequate."

And then pointing to the argument about the succession of fossils, Professor Thompson has this to say, "The chronological succession of the fossils is also open to doubt, for it appears, generally speaking, that the age of the rocks is not determined by their intrinsic characteristics but by the fossils they contain; while the succession of the fossils is determined by the succession of the strata."

And then finally, to use one more concluding quotation from this interesting treatise, Professor Thompson continues, "That plants, animals and man can be distinguished because they are radically different is the common sense conviction, or was at least until the time of Darwin. Biologists still agree on the separation of plants and animals, but the idea that man and animals differ only in degree is now so general among them that even psychologists no longer attempt to use words like 'reason' or 'intelligence' in an exact sense.

"This general tendency to eliminate by means of unverifiable speculation the limits of the categories nature presents to us is the inheritance of biology from *The Origin of Species.* To establish the continuity required by theory, historical arguments are involved even though historical evidence is lacking. Thus are engendered those fragile towers of hypothesis based on hypothesis where facts and fiction intermingle in an indiscriminate confusion. That these constructions correspond to a natural appetite, there can be no doubt. It is certain, also, that in *The Origin of Species,* Darwin established what may be called the classical method of satisfying this appetite. We are beginnign to realize now that the method is unsound and the satisfaction illusory."

The selections quoted from Professor Thompson's work were chosen at random and represent only a meager sampling of this penetrating analysis of the evolutionary theory. Let the disciples of Darwin refute what this eminent scientist has to say on the subject and prove their theory with demonstrated facts. Of course they will not because they can not. But that will not cause them to give up their naive faith nor their opposition to the Biblical account of creation. Meanwhile, their unproven theories will continue to be accepted by the learned and the illiterate alike as absolute truth, and will be defended with a fanatic intolerance that has a parallel only in the bigotry of the darkest Middle Ages. If one does not accept evolution as an infallible dogma, implicitly and without question, one is regarded as an unenlightened ignoramus or is merely ignored as an obscurantist or a naive, uncritical fundamentalist. Such a man will have difficulties finding a publisher for a manuscript presenting a view contrary to this theory, and if published his book will not be recommended for a textbook in schools or colleges. It will not be easy for him to secure a position in the science department of one of our leading universities. Anyone who does not join in the modern "Baal worship" is a heretic and is treated accordingly.

But these wise men ought to know and also ought to be honest enough to admit that they are attempting to answer a question which cannot be answered by scientific demonstration. Knowledge concerning the origin of the universe is outside and beyond the sphere of scientific investigation. Such knowledge can be known only through another source.

All knowledge is based on one of three sources: direct experience, indirect experience, or revelation. Let us examine each one:

1. *Direct experience*

Direct experience is the knowledge that is acquired directly through the sense organs from one's environment. Without our sense organs—that is, without the ability to see, hear, smell, taste and touch—an awareness of our environment and even of our own physical self would be impossible, and hence the mind would remain an absolute *tabula rasa*.

But even knowledge gained by this method is not always absolutely reliable because our sense organs are subject to error. The laboratory method in our schools is an organized form of teaching and learning by this method of direct experience.

2. *Indirect experience*

Indirect experience is the learning process by which we accept the experience that others have had and have passed on to us in the form of an organized body of learning, such as is contained in institutions, laws, the arts, books, and written records that men have left behind. The libraries and museums of the world are the depositories of such experiences. By consulting these sources, we learn from others and increase our own knowledge by borrowing from their experience, and hence this is called indirect or vicarious experience.

3. *Revelation*

All knowledge, whether derived from direct or indirect experiences, presupposes an existing environment in which experiences can be acquired through the sense organs. No one can see, hear, smell, taste, or touch anything in a vacuum.

Man can have experiences only in an existing universe. He can examine matter, life, and the laws that govern them only after they have come into existence. No experimentation can solve the mystery of their origin. That can be known only from a third source of knowledge and that is *revelation*, defined in the dictionary as "an act of revealing." The writer of the Epistle to the Hebrews is, therefore, not only expressing a profound theological truth, but also a profound psychological and philosophical truth when he says, "Through faith we understand that the worlds were framed by the word of God, so that things which are seen were not made of things which do appear" (Heb. 11:3). Revelation is God giving man knowledge that can be known or discovered in no other way than through the Author of that knowledge, the only One who can solve the mystery of the origin of all things.

2.

The Testimony of the Old and the New Testaments and of the Lord Jesus and His Apostles for the Historicity of Genesis

"Through faith we understand that the worlds were framed by the word of God," says the writer to the Hebrews. That is the only possible source for such knowledge. And this faith by which we know and accept this truth has its roots in the first and second chapters of Genesis.

But Genesis, as we have already seen, has been subjected to very severe criticism on the part of the theologians and other scholars and has, in fact, been eliminated as a reliable source for our knowledge concerning the creation of the universe. And so it becomes necessary for us next to turn to this problem and inquire what evidence is available in support of Genesis as a trustworthy historical record and a reliable source for our faith to rest upon.

In every civilized country, an accused person on trial is permitted to testify in his own behalf and in his own defense. And normally, his testimony is regarded as of primary importance.

We shall apply this principle here in the trial of Genesis, and call upon Moses and other writers of the sacred Scriptures to testify in defense of the most disputed and the most maligned book of our Bible. And for the first witness we shall call upon Moses himself, the recognized author of the Pentateuch (also called "the Torah" or "Law of Moses"), of which Genesis is a part. But as we begin our examination of Moses and his authorship of Genesis, we discover to our surprise that nowhere in Genesis itself does Moses claim to be the author. On the contrary, we find that Genesis is rather a collection of a number of separate records which evidently were written at different times and by different individuals, long before the time of Moses. There are ten such separate sections, each specifically distinguished as a separate record by the recurring phrase, "This is the generation of," which means "This is the history of." Such separate sections are Genesis 1, Genesis 2:4, Genesis 5:1, Genesis 6:9, Genesis 10:1, Genesis 11:10, Genesis 25:12; 25:19, Genesis 36:1, Genesis 37:2.

Each of these sections deals with some specific event and apparently was written on a separate tablet at the time or near the time of the event described. These records were then passed on from Adam to Noah and after the Flood from Noah to Abraham and from Abraham through the succeeding generations to Moses, who then, upon God's command, incorporated them into the book now known as Genesis.

We know that some form of writing was known to man at least as early as a thousand years before Abraham. That would take us, at least, as far back as Noah. And when we consider the remarkable inventions and the high level of civilization described in Genesis 4:20-24, achieved by the generation of Adam, it is not unreasonable to assume that they also had learned to record their achievements in some form of written record. The opening line of a song which Lamech composed, referred to in Genesis 4:24, would seem to presuppose that. But even more convincing are the long and detailed genealogical tables of the antediluvian and the postdiluvian patriarchs from Adam to Noah and then from Noah to Abraham. It would seem impossible to have preserved these with such accurate details over a period of more than 2,500 years without some written form. And when we consider the remarkable table of nations and their location as recorded in the 10th chapter of Genesis, the existence of some written form becomes even more evident.

That Moses had before him some written sources when he compiled the history of Genesis is clearly evident from the occasional explanatory notes he inserts in the text in connection with some names, places, and events. For example, in Genesis 14:3 we are told that a number of kings from the East made war upon Sodom and Gomorrah and the other cities in the

Jordan Valley. And then we read: "All these were joined together in the vale of Siddim." But the Vale of Siddim was no longer there when Moses incorporated this story into the record of Genesis. Between the event referred to and the time of Moses, the destruction of Sodom and Gomorrah had occurred and the Dead Sea, also known as the Salt Sea, now covered the area which had formerly been the Vale of Siddim, and so Moses added the explanatory note "which is the salt sea."

In verse 7 of the same chapter, we read, "And they returned and came to En-mishpat." And the explanatory note follows, "which is Kadesh." At the time of Moses, the original name was no longer known but had been replaced by "Kadesh," and so Moses added this note to identify the place for his readers.

In Genesis 16:14 we read, "The well was Beer-la-hai-roi." And the note is added, "Behold, it is between Kadesh and Bered," again indicating that by the time of Moses, this information was not at that time sufficient to identify the place.

In Genesis 23:2 we read, "And Sarah died in Kir-jath-ar-ba," and the explanatory note is added, "The same is Hebron," which means that this place was not yet known as Hebron when Sarah died.

Similar explanatory additions in the record show that Moses must have had these records before him when he compiled Genesis and then added these explanatory notes where they had become necessary for the reader.

But while the name Moses is not mentioned as the author or compiler of Genesis, the fact remains that the Pentateuch, called the *Torah*, always included Genesis, and that at all times the *Torah* is consistently ascribed to Moses. This is true of the Old Testament as well as of the New Testament. Jesus and the New Testament writers often quote from Genesis and the other books of the Pentateuch merely by saying "as Moses says" or "as is written in the law."

Beginning with Exodus, the name of Moses is always explicitly mentioned as the author of the books that follow, which together with Genesis constitute the *Torah.*

In Exodus 3 we have the account of the Lord's appearance at the burning bush in the wilderness. There God appointed Moses as His messenger and at the same time equipped him with the necessary credentials to become His spokesman to Pharaoh and the people of Israel. But there we read that God spoke to Moses, and Moses then delivered the message of God to Pharaoh and his own people.

Again, when God gave the Law on Mount Sinai we read that he spoke with Moses (Ex. 19:19-21). And in Exodus 34:27, Moses was commanded to "write thou these words: for after the tenor of these words I have made a covenant with thee and with Israel."

In Leviticus, the phrase "Jehovah spake unto Moses and Aaron" occurs thirty-five times.

In the book of Numbers, the phrase "The Lord spake unto Moses" is repeated at the beginning of nearly half of the chapters of that book.

Deuteronomy consists very largely of discourses on the Law and these are ascribed to Moses. And in chapter 31, verse 9, we are told that Moses wrote the Law into a book.

And what is said of the Law also applied to the historical portions of the Pentateuch. For example, we read that Moses was commanded to write God's judgment upon Amalek (Ex. 17:14).

In Numbers 33:1, 2 we read that the Lord commanded Moses to write an account of the journey of Israel out of Egypt.

In fact, the whole account of Exodus and of all the books of the Pentateuch that follow is unthinkable without Genesis. Everything in the Pentateuch, beginning with Exodus, presupposes Genesis.

Josephus, therefore, is quite correct when he writes, "Of the sacred books of the Jews, of these, five belong to Moses which contain the Law and the traditions of the origin of mankind until his death." Moses is the towering figure of the Old Testament, and especially in the Pentateuch where his name occurs more than 500 times from Exodus to Deuteronomy. In fact, there is no character in the entire Old Testament who can be compared in prominence and greatness with Moses. To deny his claim as author of the Pentateuch is to commit historical vandalism.

This positive self-testimony of the Pentateuch is confirmed by other books of the Old Testament. Such confirming testimony we find in some fourteen of the Old Testament books, especially in Joshua, Judges, in the two books of Kings and Chronicles, in Ezra and Nehemiah, and in the Psalms. The prophets only occasionally mention Moses by name, but refer very frequently to the Law and that always means the Law of Moses or the *Torah*. For example, see Joshua 1:17, 8:31, 23:6, 24:26; I Kings 2:3; 2 Kings 14:6, 18:6, 12, 21:8, 22:8; 2 Chronicles 25:4, 34:14, 30, 35:12; Nehemiah 8:1; Psalms 1:2, 19:8, 40:8, 103:7, and 119.

In fact, the whole Old Testament form of worship is inconceivable without the Pentateuch early in the history of Israel. And the Old Testament theocracy and the political organization of the Jewish state and of the ministry of the Old Testament prophets are based on or presuppose the *Torah* of Moses.

But in addition to the testimony of the Old Testament showing Moses to be the author of the Pentateuch, we also have the testimony of the traditions and other extra-Biblical sources.

In the Apocryphal book of Ecclesiasticus, the most profound of the intertestimental literature written about 180 B.C., we read, chapter 49 verse 5, "He [Jehovah] made him [Moses] to hear His voice and brought him into the dark cloud and gave him commandments before His face, even the law of life and knowledge that he might teach Jacob His commandments and Israel His judgments."

In II Maccabees 7, we have an account of the martyrdom of the seven brothers and their mother by Antiochus. In verse 30, one of these brothers is quoted as saying, "I will not obey the king's commandments but I will obey the commandments of the Law [that is the Torah], that was given unto our fathers by Moses."

Philo, a Jewish philosopher, and contemporary of Jesus and St. Paul, attached such an importance to the books of Moses that he assigned the Pentateuch a unique place among the Old Testament books.

In the *Talmud*, the body of Jewish civil and canonical law, it is declared that any departure from the teaching that Moses wrote the Pentateuch would be punished by exclusion from Paradise.

The Testimony of the New Testament

We also have the testimony of the New Testament. Here the Lord Jesus himself, and after Him the inspired apostles of the Lord, bears witness to the authenticity of the writings of Moses.

For example, the Lord Jesus says to the Jews who would not believe in Him: "Had ye believed Moses, ye would have believed me: for he wrote of me" (John 5:46).

To the Pharisees who had argued with Him about divorce and marriage, Jesus said, "From the beginning of creation, God made them male and female," quoting the words from Genesis 1:27.

In the story of the rich man and poor Lazarus, Jesus has Abraham say to the rich man in hell, "They have Moses and the prophets; let them hear them" (Luke 16:29).

On several occasions Jesus indicated that He recognized the division of the Old Testament as later defined by Josephus. In Luke 24:27 we read, "And beginning at Moses and all the prophets, he expounded unto them in all the scriptures the things concerning himself."

Other references showing that Jesus and the apostles recognized Moses as the author of the *Torah* are found in Matthew 8:4, 19:7, 8; Mark 10:3, 12:19-27; Luke 16:29; John 1:45, 5:46; Acts 3:22; Romans 10:5; 2 Corinthians 9:9.

At the great event of the transfiguration of our Lord on the mountain, where God the Father glorified His Son before His disciples, Moses and Elijah appeared to Jesus in the presence of these three disciples. If the things which the Jews and the disciples believed of Moses—namely, that he was the first great prophet, that the *Torah* had been written by him, and that he was the founder of the Jewish nation—had not been true and were merely myths or legends, this whole display of divine glory would have been a deception and Jesus and God the Father himself would have been partners in the deception. The very thought of that is blasphemous.

However, someone may object and say that all these quotations from Jesus are words spoken when He was in the state of humiliation, and that in this state He was like any other Jew—limited in His understanding by the age in which He lived. But the objection is not valid because Jesus also recognized Moses and the Old Testament writings after His resurrection. When He walked with His two disciples from Jerusalem to Emmaus on the first Easter Day, we read concerning Him, "And beginning at Moses and all the prophets, he expounded unto them in all the scriptures the things concerning himself . . . which were written in the law of Moses, and in the prophets, and in the psalms . . ." (Luke 24:27, 44).

And when we turn to Acts and the Epistles of Paul and the other New Testament writings, we find that they are unanimous in recognizing the writings of Moses as their Sacred Scriptures inspired by God.

Seeing that we have the testimony of Jesus and of all of the New Testament writers, we have a solid foundation for the authenticity of the writings of Moses, and thus for the first chapter of Genesis.

To assume that the Lord Jesus was in error in this matter, or that He accommodated himself to the erroneous understanding of the Jews of His day, is nothing short of blasphemy.

And likewise, to assume that the apostles and the other holy men of God who wrote and "spake . . . as they were moved by the Holy Ghost" (2 Pet. 1:21), who accepted the entire *Torah* as from God, wrote in ignorance or confirmed the erroneous views of the Jews, would also be nothing less than a blasphemous assumption. The Psalmist says, "Thy word is a lamp unto my feet, and a light unto my path" (Ps. 119:105). If Genesis 1, 2 and 3 and the rest of the eleven chapters of Genesis are a myth or an allegory, as a whole or in part, they are not a "light" to guide us or a "lamp" unto our feet, but only a useless torch with a dead battery.

3.

Some General Observations About the First Two Chapters of Genesis

The first chapter of Genesis is the most remarkable chapter in the whole Bible and is unique in all the literature of the world.

Here we have in simple and beautiful language the only answer to the question how we and the world came into being. To appreciate the literary beauty of this chapter it must be read slowly and aloud, in order to expose the ear to the melodious rhythm and cadence of its lines. Here is dignity, simplicity and beauty. In a crisp, telegraphic style the drama of creation is unfolded day by day, beginning with the majestic lines, "In the beginning God created the heaven and the earth. And the earth was without form, and void: and darkness was upon the face of the deep. And the Spirit of God moved upon the face of the waters. And God said, Let there be light: and there was light" (Gen. 1:1-3).

There is no vagueness or uncertainty here, no bombast or meaningless verbage. There is no grotesque description of the creating gods as found in the pagan mythologies. The Eternal God was, He speaks, and things are. Every word is a flash of creating power. Here God reveals His majesty, power, and wisdom in actions that are beyond human comprehension; yet they are described in a language so simple that a child can understand it.

The entire chapter of 31 verses is composed almost exclusively of words of one and two syllables. There is not a single abstract noun or an abstract concept found in the chapter. There are no descriptive adjectives or adverbs. It is a chapter of nouns and of verbs, of concrete objects and of creative action.

To appreciate more fully the beauty and simplicity of the language in this chapter, it must be compared with the grotesque cosmogonies of pagan nations or even with the fantastic assumptions of the modern evolutionary theories. Or, it might also be suggested that the reader try to write an account of the construction of some building that he has observed or some other account of an event that he has witnessed and try to do this in the space equal to the length of the first chapter, and write it in such a style that people 4,000 years hence will still be able to understand his language and get a reasonable impression of what this structure or this event was like.

But this chapter is not only unique in its brevity and literary beauty: its content has stood the test of time. It has withstood the vicious attacks by the enemies of the Bible throughout all the ages—like the granite mountain peak calmly defying the raging storms and ravages of weather. But the pretentious Lilliputian critics of the past, who arrogantly attempted to undermine this Rock of Ages with their toy picks and shovels, have been forgotten and their ever-changing theories are remembered only by the professionals as antiquarian theological curiosities. The same will be true in the future of those who assume the role of critics now.

Higher critics have based the Genesis account on a Babylonian myth concerning their gods and the creation of the universe. But this Babylonian mythology is crude and grotesque and has no remote similarity to the Genesis account of creation. The Babylonian mythology represents the forces of nature as gods and ascribes all the evil characteristics found in the human race to them. They quarrel among themselves, they murder, they make wars, they fill their bodies with intoxicants, and they indulge in gross immorality. To say that these myths are the basis of the Genesis account is farfetched and absurd. Anyone who has actually examined these myths can find no possible connection between them and the first chapter of Genesis.

The divisions of chapters, we know, are man-made. The first chapter should really continue into the second chapter, which properly begins with verse 4. "These are the generations of" means, "This is the history of the creation of heaven and earth." Hostile critics of the Bible have tried to point to the difference between chapters 1 and 2 and claim that there is a conflict between the two because the creation account of the second chapter does not follow the same order as chapter 1. Their purpose, of course, is to discredit the creation account of Genesis. But this is a shallow interpretation of this apparent conflict. The unbiased reader will have no difficulty in harmonizing these two chapters. This second chapter must be examined in its proper context; it must be connected with the events recorded in the two chapters that follow.

It is very obviously not the purpose of chapter 2 to give another account of creation in general, but rather, to supplement it and to describe in greater detail the creation of man, the crown of all creation. To introduce or lead up to this intended subject, the chapter begins with a brief review of the creation events and then continues with a more detailed account of the creation of Adam and Eve, a description of the Garden of Eden, man's first abode, and the establishment of the institution of marriage. There is nothing in this chapter which is in conflict with chapter 1. Its purpose is not the same.

Only man, of all the creatures, is consciously related to his Maker. Only he was created in the image of God, was made a moral being, and was endowed with lordship over all the rest of creation. Hence, all that which follows, not only in this chapter but in all the rest of the Bible, deals with this relationship of man to his Creator. And this relationship affects all the rest of creation, as indicated in Genesis 3:17-19, Genesis 6 to 9, and Romans 8:19-22.

But chapter 2 also serves as a bridge between chapter 1 and chapter 3. Chapter 1 speaks of the creation of a perfect world which had received the verdict of "very good" from its Maker.

In chapter 3 we learn of the ruin of this perfect world and of the curse that was brought upon it by the Fall. To show how this could have come about, chapter 2 was necessary to supply the background.

And a further examination of this portion of Genesis will also show that chapters 2, 3, and 4 constitute a unit, and evidently were originally recorded on one tablet. That this is so is indicated by the introductory phrase "These are the generations of." It then continues until the end of chapter 4. In chapter 5 we have again a repetition of the same introductory words, "This is the book of the generations of," thereby showing that with chapter 5 another section in the early history of man is begun.

And it must also be noted that the second tablet, which contains the record of chapters 2, 3, and 4, must have been written much later than chapter 1. The different events recorded in these three chapters presuppose the lapse of considerable time.

For example, the detailed geographical description of the Garden of Eden, with the mentioning of four distinct rivers and each with a specific name, presupposes the exploring of this region and the selection of a name, which again would imply the passing of some time.

Then the reference to the land of Havilah, with the additional note that gold and precious stones were found there, also presupposes that this territory had been explored and, therefore, some time must have elapsed.

Even the sojourn of Adam and Eve in the Garden of Eden probably was much longer than is commonly assumed.

The story of Cain and Abel, as recorded in chapter 4, requires on the very face of it the lapse of considerable time. Both have grown to adulthood and both have an occupation, which means that a considerable number of years must have passed.

The references in chapter 4:19-24, to the important developments in the early civilization, such as the making and playing of musical instruments, both string and wind instruments; the workmanship in brass and iron which presupposes the discovery and the mining of minerals and the art of smelting these ores; the evidence of poetry and song, as found in verses 23 and 24; the building of a city by Cain and the fear expressed by him "that everyone that findeth me shall slay me," both of which point to a considerable increase in population, are a clear indication that considerable time is required for the events recorded in these three chapters. It is, of course, impossible to determine how much, but it is reasonable to assume that at least many centuries or more are involved.

To summarize, then, concerning the dispute over chapters 1 and 2 of Genesis, we can confidently say that there is no conflict or duplication between these two chapters because their purposes are not the same.

The first chapter was evidently directly revealed by God to Adam as to how this world and all that is in it came into being. And Adam, then, passed this on to his children, possibly even in some written form.

The second chapter is an account of the events which followed creation and of what man did in and with the wonderful world that God had given him as his royal domain.

4.

The Beginning of all Things

"The first day of creation, the beginning of time, the origin of matter, the creation of light" (Gen. 1:1-5).

Only God can know the beginning of all things, and His revelation of these events opens with these simple but majestic words: "In the beginning God created the heaven and the earth. And the earth was without form, and void; and darkness was upon the face of the deep. And the Spirit of God moved upon the face of the waters. And God said, Let there be light: and there was light. And God saw the light that it was good: and God divided the light from the darkness. And God called the light Day and the darkness he called Night. And the evening and the morning were the first day."

In the beginning God created. That beginning was when God began to create. Time began with creation. Before creation there was no time, only eternity. God was. God always was. His existence is here presupposed. God was from eternity. He is without time, without a beginning, and without an end. The concept of eternity is incomprehensible to finite man. The human mind is limited by time and space and cannot reach out beyond time.

The creation mythology of the South African Bantus gives a vivid description of their primitive comception of the absolute emptiness of infinite space before the world had come into existence. While this is the mere mythology of a primitive people, it nevertheless serves to show that the inconceivable emptiness and absolute nonexistence of anything before creation are as incomprehensible to the human mind as the concept of eternity.

The following is a section of the African creation myth, as reported by the Zulu witch doctor Vuzamazulu Credo Mutwa in *Indaba, My Children*, page 3, where we read:

> No stars were there—no sun,
> Neither moon nor earth—
> Nothing existed but darkness itself—
> A darkness everywhere.
> Nothing existed but Nothingness,
> A Nothingness neither hot nor cold,
> Dead nor alive—
> A Nothingness far worse than nothing
> And frightening in its utter nothingness.
>
> For how long this Nothingness lasted,
> No one will ever know;
> And why there was nothing but Nothing is something
> We must never try to learn.

God created heaven and earth—that is, the upper and the lower regions of this universe. The Hebrew language has no word for universe. Heaven, therefore, means the upper region of our universe. It does not mean the heaven of glory or the abode of God and His holy angels. The creation account deals only with our material heaven and earth. The Lord Jesus spoke of heaven and earth in a similar manner when He said, "Heaven and earth shall pass away" (Matt. 24:25). He was not speaking of the heaven of glory but the heaven created in the beginning. The heaven of glory will not pass away.

Some believe there might have been a long interval of time between the events of verses 1 and 2 of this first chapter. That means they assume two creations. And verse 1 is the creation account of the first world while the chaos and darkness mentioned in verse 2 refer to the ruins of that first world. That chaos was brought about by the angels that had rebelled and were cast out of heaven; and in revenge for this punishment they destroyed that first world created by God. The ruins that were left were the chaos out of which God subsequently created the second world.

The purpose of the insertion of an interval between these two verses is to find time for the creation of angels and the subsequent rebellion of the fallen angels, but also to build a bridge between the Biblical creation account of the six days and the evolutionary theories of geology which require eons of time for the formation of rocks and minerals, the accumulation of salt in the sea and for the explanation of the many fossils and the existence and disappearance of those grotesque prehistoric monsters whose fossil remains are found in all parts of the world and have excited the interest and imagination of man in all times.

But there is nothing in the language of these two verses which would warrant such an interpretation. These verses belong together and deal with one and the same event. Verse 2 is a logical sequel to verse 1.

But this theory also becomes untenable when the two verses are considered in the context of the entire chapter. According to this view, the sacred writer devoted a single, ambiguous sentence to account for the creation of the first world, then added part of another, even more obscure, to describe its destruction. He then continued with an entire chapter to describe the creation of the second world, and later devoted four chapters to account for the destruction of that world in the great flood of Noah.

The idea of a possible preexisting world before the present has given rise to a number of difficult questions for which there are no satisfactory answers. Among these are such questions as the following:

1. When were the angels created?
2. When occurred the rebellion of the fallen angels which caused them to become devils?
3. What did God do before creation if He was from all eternity?
4. When did God create the heaven of glory?

The answer to all of these questions is that God did not see fit to lift the veil that hides these mysteries from our cognition. And so, we have no answer. But the Bible does tell us a great deal about angels, these mighty spirits surrounding His throne, and also something about the mystery of the devils.

Both the Old and the New Testaments tell us that angels exist, they exist in great numbers, they are spirits in their being like God himself, they are very powerful and have great knowledge, and their activities consist of serving God and man. But we know nothing of the time when, or the manner in which, they were created. There is, however, a somewhat cryptic statement in the book of Job, pointing to their possible creation before the rest of the world: Here again God describes creation, saying that at that time ". . . the morning stars sang together, and all the sons of God shouted for joy" (Job 38:7).

In the entire chapter God reminds Job of the wonders and the powers revealed in the words of creation, and then in verse

7 adds these significant words about the stars of the morning and all the sons of God shouting for joy when they witnessed the wonderful manifestation and the glory of their God when He called this universe into being by the onmipotent power of His word. The term "stars of the morning" and "sons of God" can in this connection refer only to the angels in heaven. They were the only rational beings, besides God, in existence at that time, and we know that the Scripture elsewhere has used these terms to identify the angels. (Cf. Isaiah 14:12 and Job 1:6, 2:1.)

But if the angels witnessed the creation of heaven and earth, they could not have been a part of that creation. They must have been in existence before then.

But even this poetic reference to the possible existence of the angels does not tell us when they were created. The commonly accepted view of conservative theologians has been that the angels were created some time during the six days of the creation week. They base this assumption on the erroneous identification of the heaven mentioned in Genesis 1:1 with the heaven of glory, the abode of the angels. (See Graebner, *Doctrinal Theology*, p. 58.)

But the heaven of the angels must not be confused with the heaven of this world, as was pointed out before. The fact remains that the Bible does not reveal the time when or the manner in which the angels were created. But when we consider all that has been revealed to us concerning their exalted position, their power and glory, and their great numbers (the Bible speaks of ten thousand times ten thousand, Rev. 5:11), we might well assume that the creation of these exalted heavenly hosts and their heavenly abode must have been an event even greater than the creation of our material world, described in Genesis 1. This present world was created as an abode for man: though he was created in the image of God, yet "he was made a little lower than the angels" (Ps. 8:5). That world was created for the exalted spirits which surround the throne of God and, therefore, must be even greater than our present wonderful world.

But if the creation of the angels is shrouded in mystery, the fall of some of these angels is even a greater mystery. The Bible tells us that this tragic event happened, but it does not tell us when nor does it explain the cause of their rebellion or how it was possible that evil could arise in a sinless heaven and how holy angels could become fiendish devils.

However, in Isaiah 14:12 we have a cryptic reference to this awful tragedy, which might be regarded as a faint glimmer of what happened: "How art thou fallen from heaven, O Lucifer, son of the morning." And in 2 Peter 2:4, we get a further glimpse into this mystery when he writes: "God spared not the angels that sinned, but cast them down to hell." In Jude 6, the curtain is lifted just a little more when he adds, "And the angels which kept not their first estate, but left their own habitation, he hath reserved in everlasting chains under darkness unto the judgment of the great day." And St. John in the Book of Revelation adds this bit of additional information when he writes: "And there was war in heaven: Michael and his angels fought against the dragon; and the dragon fought and his angels, and prevailed not; neither was their place found anymore in heaven. And the great dragon was cast out, that old serpent, called the Devil, and Satan, which deceiveth the whole world: he was cast out into the earth, and his angels were cast out with him" (Rev. 12:7-9).

But aside from these few references concerning the origin of Satan, we know nothing of this fearful tragedy in the history of the universe. In *Paradise Lost*, Milton has dramatized these events in the following lines:

> The infernal Serpent: he it was whose guile,
> Stirred up with envy and revenge, deceived,
> The mother of mankind; what time his pride
> Had cast him out from heaven, with all his host
> Of rebel angels; by whose aid aspiring
> To set himself in glory above his peers,
> He trusted to have equaled the Most High,
> If he opposed; and with ambitious aim
> Against the throne and monarchy of God
> Raised impious war in heaven, and battle proud,
> With vain attempt. Him the Almighty Power
> Hurled headlong flaming from the eternal sky,
> With hideous ruin and combustion, down
> To bottomless perdition, there to dwell
> In adamant chain and penal fire,
> Who durst defy the Omnipotent to arms.
>
> —Book 1, lines 34-49

There are other questions belonging in this category of unexplainable mysteries: What did God do before the creation of time? Was He idle or was He active? And if active, what did He do?

God is from eternity. He was before time. "Before the mountains were brought forth or ever thou hadst formed the earth and the world, even from everlasting to everlasting, thou art

God," writes Moses in the 90th Psalm. The eternal existence of God, without having a beginning or an end, is incomprehensible to man, and hence, the thought of His eternal activity without the existence of a material world is likewise beyond our understanding. Finite man cannot comprehend the infinite God, and this is a part of His infinite incomprehensibleness.

And yet, when we apply the knowledge we have of God from His own revelation concerning himself, it would not seem irreverent or presumptuous to assume that He was active then as He is now, but in some other sphere of which we know nothing. The very nature of God would seem to demand this. God is life and the source of all life and energy. That means activity. And so we might assume that it was in this period of eternity, preceding time as we know it, that He created the world of His holy angels and the heavenly abode for these angelic spirits. And then, when God in His own council resolved to call into existence another world, our present material world, these heavenly hosts were so overawed, they were prompted to shout their songs of joy as they witnessed a new revelation of the glory and power of their own Creator and God, as is recorded in the 38th chapter of Job.

Now let us return again to the first verse of Genesis 1, where we read, "God created the heaven and the earth." Let us first especially note the word "create."

The Hebrew word used here for creating is *bara*, which means to make or to create something out of nothing, a word ascribed only to God. There are two other Hebrew words meaning "to create"; they are *yatzzar* and *asah*, but in distinction from *bara* these words are used for making something from material already in existence.

God created the *heaven* and the *earth*, says our text, and what does that mean? In view of what occurred on the six days of the creation week, the heaven and the earth in this connection can only mean that on the first day God began by the creation of matter out of which He formed the things that were made on the days that followed. God began the creation by first providing himself with the material out of which all other things were formed. Matter is not eternal, as the ancient Greek philosophers and the modern evolutionists assume. Matter had its beginning with God; He created it out of nothing; He first filled the absolute vacuum of nothingness with raw, unsystematized matter. There is no other possible source for the origin of matter. Dead matter could not have created itself.

But that raises the next important question: namely, What is matter? What is the essence of the substance out of which heaven and earth were made?

On the one hand, matter might be defined as a combination of a number of chemical substances which combined according to very specific laws to form that something which we call matter, but that leads to the next question: that is, What is the origin of the individual chemical substances which are combined to form matter? How did the laws come into being which cause them to combine in a given order? Science has isolated over a hundred separate substances which are basic or simple and do not consist of combinations of other substances, but how did they come to be just what they are? Why is gold, gold, and silver, silver, and uranium, uranium, and why are all the other isolated elements what they are, and why are they separated from one another? Why are they found where they are found and what accounts for their peculiar qualities?

Scientists thought they had succeeded in breaking down matter to its last ultimate unit: that is, the atom. In an article which appeared in a national magazine, a writer on this subject was introduced by the editor of that magazine as "one of the nation's foremost interpreters of modern science." This modern authority on science then wrote that the Greeks knew the atom but they did not know what we know about the atom nor of its infinite smallness. Then this writer continues by making a startling statement asserting that a teaspoonful of water contains a million billion trillion atoms. We can repeat these figures, but no one can comprehend what they mean. And this writer then says, "We now have learned that this infinitely tiny atom is composed of still smaller parts which form a microscopic universe in which there is action, energy and motion similar to that of our own solar system."

In everyday language we speak of dead matter, and, of course, it is dead in the sense that it does not have in it what we call the germ of life, nor can it propagate itself. But it is not dead in the sense that it is inactive or absolutely static. In a lump of so-called dead matter, there are countless billions of atoms, each one an active universe, a bundle of energy and force beyond all comprehension, as we have learned since the atomic bomb has come into existence.

The telescope reveals the infinitude of "bigness" of God's creation, and the microscope the infinitude of "smallness."

But whether great or small, all of these things bear an eloquent witness to the infinite wisdom and power of the almighty Creator of heaven and earth.

But we do not need to penetrate into the incomprehensible mystery of the atom to recognize the mysterious power in matter. It is all about us—in the soil, in the air, rocks and water. And so, let us first take a glance at the soil under our feet.

Soil consists of fine, ground-up particles of rock mixed with remains of plants and animals. We distinguish ordinarily such forms of soil as sandy soil, sandy loam, silt loam, clay and humus. But soil is so common that people pay no attention to it or are unimpressed by it unless it has been converted into dust to annoy them or into mud to cling to their shoes and interfere with the progress of their travel. And yet, what wonders are concealed in a mere handful of soil or dirt! For six thousand years and more the soil of our world has produced grains, fruits, and vegetation of every kind and has supplied mountains of food for billions upon billions of human beings and for countless trillions of animals that have lived on the face of the earth since the beginning, and yet, the bulk of this earth has not been destroyed or diminished and continues to produce food for all living creatures to the present day.

Consider for a moment the miracle that occurs on our farmland every year. Take, for example, an acre of good Iowa farmland: We know that it will produce one hundred or one-hundred and fifty bushels of corn in one season. And when that crop has been harvested and taken from the acre, the original soil is still all there and has not been noticeably diminished. If the one hundred and fifty bushels of corn, together with their giant stalks, would be gathered together into one great pile, it would represent a fair-sized hill of solid matter. Then consider that all of it was derived from the soil of this acre of land on which it grew, and then remember that this process has been going on year after year and decade after decade, and yet the amount of soil on that acre has remained the same. The hills are as high and the valleys no deeper. If changes have occurred in the general topography of the soil, these changes were not caused by the crops that were grown on them and taken from them, but by the erosion of wind and water.

And then consider that the farmland of the United States in 1967 produced more than four billion bushels of corn and three billion bushels of wheat; then add to this the thousands of bales of cotton, the millions of bushels of beans, the mountains of sugar beets, the millions upon millions of crates of apples, peaches, pears, and other fruits, the train and shiploads of fiber, lumber, and pulpwood, all taken from the land, and gather all of these products of one year together into one great heap and we would have a mountain as high as Pike's Peak. And all of this came from the farmland of our country, and yet, all the land is still all there and continues to repeat the same process year after year. How wonderful all this is, but we pay no attention to it. We merely take it for granted because it is such a common occurrence.

The disciples of the Lord Jesus and the multitude in the wilderness were overawed once when Jesus fed five thousand people with a few loaves of bread and a few fishes, and were ready to proclaim Him their King. But every year a greater miracle than this is performed by God when the humble earth produces food, not for five thousand but for three billion people and for all the other living creatures that are upon the face of the earth.

But even that is not all. We must also consider other important services rendered by Mother Earth. Gently and tenderly the earth takes to her bosom her children—the plants, the animals, and last of all man—when they have fulfilled their purpose in the world. When they have disintegrated, the earth receives them and assimilates them. She purifies the corruption of death, and then out of death and decay, phoenix-like, rises again a new life, a new form, and a new abundance of food for all living creatures that will follow. And this process continues in rhythmic regularity year after year until He, who in His infinite wisdom set in motion this cosmic operation, will himself call a final halt.

Rocks

Another form in which matter appears are the rocks.

Rocks as they are found on the surface of the earth are divided into three classes: the igneous, the sedimentary, and the metamorphic rocks.

Igneous rocks, also called primitive or crystalline rocks, are the foundation rocks of the earth. They are the oldest rocks and have their origin in original creation. They are massive in structure, not stratified, and contain no fossils. Granite is the best known example of this class of rock.

The sedimentary rocks are a younger rock. They originated from materials that were laid down by the action of water, wind or ice; hence, they are also called stratified rocks, from the Latin word *stratum*, meaning "that which has been spread out." The most common of the stratified rocks are the limestones, sandstones, and shales.

By metamorphic rocks are meant the rocks that were changed into another kind of rock by pressure, heat, or chemical action, such as limestone changed into marble, or shale into slate.

Each of these categories of rocks has its own individual place and purpose in the general economy of God's creation order. They vary greatly in structure and basic material.

1. *The igneous and metamorphic rock*

The igneous rocks are massive conglomerates composed of a variety of mineral crystals, closely cemented together to form the hardest and the most enduring of all rocks. Their color is determined by the predominance of some individual mineral. The igneous rocks form the core of our planet and probably also that of all the other planets. The most remarkable characteristics of these rocks are the mineral crystals of which they are composed.

The igneous rocks are not what they may appear to be to the casual observer, a mere conglomeration of a variety of minerals cemented together into a solid mass. Instead, they consist of countless minute, clearly defined particles of matter in a definite crystalline form. And a crystal may be defined as a chemically homogeneous, solid body of a definite structure and with geometrically arranged cleavage planes, always retaining a fixed pattern. Some minerals crystalize in the hexagonal, others in an octagonal, form. Some appear in cubic patterns; still others are diamond shaped. Quartz, for example, generally appears in the form of a hexagonal prism, terminated in a six-sided pyramid.

The corundum crystal always occurs in hexagonal shape, but often with a swelling in the middle to give it a sort of barrel-shaped appearance.

Pyrite and salt crystalize in the cube form.

The crystal of the garnet is of a rhombic dodecahedron form, and so we could continue with other minerals. Each mineral has its own peculiar pattern and always retains the same. In fact, the constancy of these patterns is so reliable that petrologists and mineralogists are guided by them to recognize and classify the different minerals.

The reason for calling special attention to these unique characteristics of the minerals at this place is to show that even in the structure of these hard and forbidding igneous rocks, there is nothing haphazard or accidental, but there are a definite plan and fixed laws to govern them. Theoretically it is conceivable on the basis of the law of averages, that the atoms of a given mineral might fortuitously unite to form a configuration similar to one of the crystals described, but that could occur only once in a million or billion of chances and then only as one occurrence and never as a fixed law; much less could this happen over and over again in the case of other minerals. The chances for that to happen would be about the same as when one would take the 26 letters of the alphabet, mix them together in some rotating container and then expect them to unite and form words and sentences and songs like "The Star Spangled Banner," "A Mighty Fortress," or "Oh Canada." And yet, that is precisely the absurd assumption of the evolutionist who will not accept a divine Creator.

But the igneous rocks reveal another aspect of the wisdom and the cosmic planning of the Creator, because with them we must also consider the minerals which are a part of the original basic matter created at the beginning. These minerals have been of paramount importance to man. They have enabled him to raise himself to the present high level of achievement. They exist in great abundance and are distributed over the entire earth but not with the same degree of plentitude in all parts. They are nearly as varied in kind and purpose as plant life and they have become the source 'of great wealth for nations' and people who have had the energy and ambition to search for them and use them. Without them man could never have achieved his present high level of civilization. And history shows that the most important of these minerals for man's material progress have been copper, iron, and those minerals necessary to combine with raw iron to form steel. These minerals provided man with the kind of material necessary for the creation of the advanced tools, implements, and machinery which enabled him to make himself the lord and master of the world, as God intended him to be.

But it is noteworthy that God also created gold, silver, and precious stones. Of all the minerals, these are the most costly and the most coveted by man. And yet, from a purely utilitarian point of view, they are the least important. The hills of our world might have consisted of solid gold or silver and the gravel pits might have been filled with emeralds and rubies, but without iron and steel they would not have been of great value to man. Bridges could not have been built with arches of silver, and the practical tools like hammers and saws or machines for farm and industry could not have been constructed of gold even if these metals would have been in sufficient supply. Gold and silver, rubies and emeralds are not essential for man's physical existence or survival. These precious gifts of the Creator have only a luxury value to serve man as ornaments, for the adornment of his body and the beautification of his home and immediate physical environment, and for the satisfaction of his innate sense of beauty. God endowed man with the ability to recognize and appreciate beauty in all its forms, which is one of the aspects that raises man above the animals. The animal shares with man the need for food, drink, and shelter, but the animal has no need for or appreciation of beauty. The ox remains absolutely stolid and unmoved at the sight of the most precious vessel of solid gold, and the hog prefers a bucketful of garbage to the most costly necklace of emeralds and rubies. But man was created to enjoy and be uplifted by beauty in all of its forms, and so the Creator provided him with objects of beauty for this higher and lofty aesthetic enjoyment in keeping with the dignity of man, created in the very image of God himself. Gold, silver, and precious stones belong to these gifts of a benevolent Creator.

But among the gifts of luxury provided for man, we must also include the gift of marble, a species of the metamorphic rock mentioned above.

Marble is not the most plentiful nor the most enduring building material, but it is the most beautiful. And civilized men in all ages have sought it for beautifying their dwelling places, their temples, and public buildings, or they have found it most attractive for carving out of it the great masterpieces of their art.

One need but see the temples and statues, or even only what is left of them, of ancient Greece and Rome that were built with or carved out of the purest of pure white marble, or look upon the pillars and monuments of renaissance Italy, or visit even our own public buildings, such as the national and state capitols, the luxury hotels in our wealthy tourist resorts, to be overawed, delighted and uplifted by the sheer beauty of this rock that the Creator in His goodness has provided for us and for our pleasure.

> "Lord, how Thy wisdom is displayed
> Where'r we turn our eyes,

Where'r we view the ground we tread
Or gaze upon the sky."

2. *The stratified rock*

When discussing the subject of matter in the form of rocks, we must also include the stratified or sedimentary rocks.

The stratified rocks are not as complex nor as glamorous as the other two classes mentioned; they differ from them especially in origin and in composition.

The stratified rocks are secondary rocks and were formed from the mineral debris that had previously existed in some other form or place. They were created by the action of running water, wind, and to some extent also by glaciers. They vary greatly in their mineral composition and in the degree of their hardness and are classified accordingly. They constitute the greater part of the outer crust of our earth today, which may differ in thickness from a few feet to the thickness that can be measured in miles. The greater part of the stratified rock now appearing on the surface of the earth came into existence as a result of the great flood of Noah. The magnitude of this world catastrophe and its fearful effect on the earth are beyond comprehension. A magnificent world, which had received the verdict of "very good" from its Creator, was destroyed, and a new world emerged from that wreckage; but it was stripped of its original glory. Mountains and hills had been leveled and new ones were born. Valleys and lowlands were filled with the debris of what had been and the relation of land and water segments altered on a diastrophic scale. Seas, lakes, and riverbottoms were raised and became dry land, and masses of dry land were submerged to become the bottom of the sea.

All vegetation and animal life was uprooted and then washed together into great heaps or floating islands to be buried by successive avalanches of sediments torn from the protruding mountain peaks and land masses and then laid down in layer after layer by the reoccurring tides and the storm-propelled waves of the swirling waters of the Flood.

By this fearful judgment God had destroyed the first world because of the wickedness of that generation. But while destroying in His anger, He mercifully preserved and reconstructed a new world out of the ruins of the old and converted the wreckage of its former grandeur into sources of unlimited benefits and blessings for the generation which was to repossess the new world. And the means by which God performed this miracle of a new creation were, in part at least, the stratified rocks.

First of all, these rocks themselves were a direct result of the Flood. And then God used them to create the great cosmic containers for the new benefits and blessings He had planned for the new race of men which was to occupy the earth. I shall not go into detail about all the wonders of this new creation, but limit myself particularly to three areas which have been of special significance for man's survival and progress. These are:

1. The subterranean reservoirs for storage of underground water.

2. The underground natural storage tanks for the world's supply of oil and natural gas.

3. The great basins for the world's coal deposits.

All of these services are of the greatest importance to man and without any of them his life on earth could never have become what it is today.

1. Let us direct our attention first to the problem of underground water and the mechanism by which it is carried and stored there.

Everyone knows the importance of wells; without wells life in many parts of the world would be impossible. But wells can occur only where underground streams or reservoirs can be tapped. But how did the water get there in the first place, and how was it stored? It is evident that this water could not have come from an underground connection with the ocean because if it had, its mineral content would make it unfit for plant, animal, and human use.

Some have held that God placed great basins of water in the interior of the earth at the time of creation. They base this view, in part, on a statement found in the Flood account, which says: ". . . the same day were the fountains of the great deep broken up" (Gen. 7:11). But that is a misinterpretation of the words "fountain of the great deep."

The fact is, the source of the underground water is the same as that of the lakes and rivers on the surface of the earth —namely, rain and snow. If rain and snow would cease only for a few seasons, all the rivers and lakes and all wells of the earth would dry up as we so often experience in longer periods of drought. By a mysterious process of the clouds water from the sea is carried over the land and there spread in the form of rain and snow. Some of that rainwater is absorbed by the soil and provides the necessary moisture for the sustaining of plants. Part of it is drained off and finds its way into brooks, creeks, and rivers, and ultimately into the sea from whence it came in the first place.

But some of this water is led to underground basins by natural conduits provided by the stratified rock. Without these formations, water could not have been carried there nor distributed as widely as it now is and could not have been stored in the earth. The igneous rocks, which form the core of the earth, are massive, impervious, and are not dissolved by the action of water. But the stratified rock can both carry and store water. The stratified rocks consist of layers deposited in succession, one after another. And by the action of the water, channels or conduits between the strata are formed, which then carry water to the lower-lying basins. The basins themselves consist of porous limestone, or shale, or are formed by beds of sand and gravel and sometimes even consist of large underground rivers or lakes.

In 1957, for example, oil drillers exploring for oil in southeastern Saskatchewan did not find oil but discovered, at a depth of nearly 3,000 feet, an enormous underground lake of water and quicksand 200 feet deep, and below that an enormous deposit of potash covering an area averaging 450 miles long and 50 miles wide. But before they reached the lake and the potash beds, they drilled through 2,726 feet of water-bearing shale and limestone and one hundred feet of solid rock salt.

It is well known when well diggers strike water, the water often rises very rapidly, sometimes even forming geyser-like fountains as in the case of artesian wells. This rising of the water is caused either by the pressure of the overlying strata or by the gravitational pressure from the higher-lying source of the particular stream that has been tapped. Water always seeks it own level; it is the same principle here that is followed by urban communities when building high water towers. They raise them so high to enable them to carry the water to the highest points of the city.

The pressure of the underground lake in Saskatchewan was found to be 470 pounds per square inch.

And so we see that even far down in the bowels of the earth there are fixed laws governing the forces of nature and the plain evidence of a guiding and designing hand of an omnipotent Creator.

2. Another important service rendered by the stratified rock is that it provides the underground tanks for the storage of oil and natural gas.

One of the wonders of our world is the great oil and gas resources found far down in the interior of the earth and in nearly all parts of the world.

The problem of the origin of natural oil has puzzled scientists since it was first discovered. The question is, what is its source, why is it found deep down in the earth, and how did it get there?

Various experiments and tests have shown conclusively that the original source of the oil in our earth was of an organic nature. But that leads to the next questions: what were these organisms and how and where could they have existed in such inconceivable numbers to account for the enormous oil resources in the world today? How did they get there? What destroyed them? How were they buried? Why did they not decompose as other organisms do immediately following death? And what force converted their remains into the rich petroleum as we now have it?

The most satisfactory answer to all of these questions was given by Dr. D. J. McFarlane, professor of botany at the University of Pennsylvania. According to his theory, fish were the source of petroleum, and he assumes that fish in prodigious numbers perished suddenly in some great, worldwide catastrophe somewhere in the early history of our earth and then were buried almost instantaneously by the upheaval of great land masses which crashed down upon them. And from the resulting pressure and heat, the oil in their bodies was distilled into the present petroleum.

A German scientist [1] confirmed this theory by subjecting animal fats to extreme heat and pressure with the result that he obtained artificial petroleum, as Dr. McFarlane had assumed.

There is only one world catastrophe known to us of a sufficient magnitude to have accomplished this, and that is the Biblical Flood of Noah. That catastrophe, according to the record, was world-wide; it destroyed all living things on the face of the earth, except those which were saved by Noah, and it was accompanied by a worldwide confusion of nature, including worldwide earthquakes and volcanic eruptions on land and on the sea bottom, which must have destroyed enormous masses of marine life as postulated by Dr. McFarlane.

And from Genesis 1:20-22, we know that the original seas of the first world did teem with an overabundance of fish of every kind, great and small, whales and leviathans, and countless other forms of marine life; and of course, great masses of these would have perished and would have been buried in the general upheaval on land and in the sea caused by the cosmic convulsion of nature in the universal flood, with the

[1] Der Reichtum der Erde, p. 432.

result, as assumed by Dr. McFarlane. The pressure of the debris that covered them and the heat that was generated by this pressure distilled the oil out of their bodies to form the petroleum as we now find it in the earth. And this was then preserved and stored in the great oil basins of the earth by means of the stratified rocks.

3. A similar service was rendered by the stratified rocks for the preservation of plant life in the form of the great coal deposits.

As the fish and other forms of marine life were destroyed and buried by the action of the great Flood and then converted into oil, so in like manner, the luxurious vegetation of that first world was uprooted, floated together into great heaps, and buried, and then converted into coal by the same process that had converted the bodies of the fish into petroleum.

Geologists are agreed that the source of all coal is some form of vegetable matter. Sir William Dawson, the famous Canadian geologist of the last century, writes: "Coal can, under the present constitution of nature, be produced only in one way, namely, by the accumulation of vegetable matter, for vegetation alone has the power of decomposing the carbonic acid of the atmosphere and accumulating it as carbon. Such vegetable matter, once accumulated, requires only pressure and the changes which come of its own putrification to be converted into coal."[2]

The coal reserves of the world are enormous. Coal has been found in every continent and on many islands of the sea and even way down in Antarctica. There is sufficient coal in the earth to provide man with power, heat, and light and all the other substances derived from coal for hundreds and thousands of years. It has been estimated, for example, that Nova Scotia alone can provide the world with 100,000,000 tons of coal for 15,000 years.

The coal resources of Alberta have been estimated at 673,000,000,000 tons. And the Russians claim that their coal reserves amount to 7 1/2 trillion tons. Add to this the great coal deposits of China, India, Australia, Europe, and of the rest of the world and the figures become truly staggering. And when we consider that all this coal was derived from the accumulation of the vegetation of the first world that perished in the Flood, the picture becomes even more overwhelming and hard to grasp with our limited imagination.

---

[2] Sir William Dawson, *The Historical Deluge in Relation to Scientific Research*, p. 253.

But equally awe-inspiring is the fact that God, in His merciful providence, also preserved, while destroying, by converting the ruins of that first magnificent creation into a thousand benefits for the generations that would follow in the form of coal, and stored these precious treasures in the great coal deposits in all the world, formed there by the stratified rocks.

Fire

The creation of matter also included the creation of fire, though it is not specifically mentioned in the creation account.

Fire is one of the most mysterious forces in the universe. That it was a part of God's original creation must be assumed, for it could not have originated by itself. But while it is not stated when and how God created fire, its origin is probably best associated with the creation of the igneous rocks, because these rocks have fire in them, or better, fire can be extracted from them by striking them with a flint or a piece of hard steel. The name "igneous rock" means fire stone.

Fire, a most perplexing and awesome force in nature, defies satisfactory explanation. The dictionary defines it as "the evolution of heat and light by combustion." But what does that mean? What is combustion and why does this process result in something we call flames, heat, and light?

The *Encyclopaedia Britannica* defines fire as "the process whereby the combination of one chemical element with another, when reduced to a gaseous condition, provides heat and flames." But that definition, too, is not very helpful. It does not explain the mystery of fire; it merely explains what happens when fire burns but does not explain why that process results in the peculiar characteristics that have been mentioned.

Fire separates inorganic and organic matters in the process of combustion. It reduces the inorganic into ashes and the organic into a gas in the form of smoke which is dispersed in the atmosphere. Fire does not destroy matter as such, but changes the form of its existence.

Fire, while producing heat, light, flames and smoke, consumes the very substance on which it subsists, but it consumes only the organic matter. It does not consume the inorganic, and in both cases the process is really simply a changing into a new form. Fire, applied to iron ore, separates the dross from the pure metal and converts the hard, brittle iron into a soft and malleable substance that can be rolled out into sheets, rods, and beams for the construction of buildings or bridges or for the manufacturing of tools, implements, and machinery. And fire will convert the hard substance of iron into a fluid that can be poured like a liquid and cast into any form desired. Clay when subjected to fire can be molded into bricks, tiles for roofs, or into beautiful porcelain and clay pottery.

Fire in the volcano reduces the hardest rock of the interior of the earth into flowing lava to form a river of molten rock.

Fire has made it possible for man to inhabit and subdue the coldest parts of our earth.

Fire is the means by which man bakes his bread, cooks his food, and changes inedible food into palatable nourishment.

But fire also enables man to create those horrible engines of war by which he has destroyed himself and is in the process of destroying civilization at the present time.

We are not told in Genesis when God created fire or when He introduced man to its awesome power. But it is safe to assume that as Adam was exploring the Garden of Eden and adjusting to his new environment, learning about the fruits and the grains, the birds and the animals that surrounded him, God also introduced him to the gift of fire and revealed its multiple use to him.

Very early in the history of the earth, we read that Tubalcain, a grandson of Adam, was a worker in brass and iron, which presupposes the knowledge of metallurgy and the use of fire (Gen. 4:22).

Fire is a most precious gift of the Creator to man. Without it he could never have raised himself above a near-animal existence. And it is no wonder, therefore, that primitive people in all ages have worshipped fire as a deity because of its awesome power for good and for evil. The Greeks had an interesting legend that Prometheus brought fire to man by lighting his torch on the chariot of the sun, the god of fire.

There is something strangely fascinating about fire, whether one is watching a frightful holocaust of a city on fire or the crackling sparks in the family hearth. Great public fires always attract curious spectators who will stand in awesome silence, watching the destruction of man's work. On the other hand, the glowing embers or lapping flames in the fireplace have a soothing effect upon the family that surrounds it. It produces a feeling of warmth and comfort and arouses a mood of silent meditation.

But fire has also been used as a most dreadful instrument of torture and punishment, and hell itself is described as a place of fiery torment.

While this mysterious force of nature is a wonderful and beneficial gift of God to man, it remains such only so long as it is contained and controlled by man. It becomes a frightful rampaging demon of destruction when out of control and freed of its fetters, devouring whatever happens to be in its path, whether that be the homes of people, cities, and forest, or other precious creation of man.

Schiller, the great German poet and dramatist, gave a vivid description of the beneficent and destructive force of fire in his famous poem "Die Glocke" (The Bell). A section dealing, in part, with the devastating power of fire reads in the translation [3] as follows:

Beneficent the might of Flame,
When man keeps watch and makes it tame.
In what he fashions, what he makes,
Help from this heaven's force he takes.
But fearful is this force of heaven,
When, having all its fetters riven,
It bursts forth, its own law to be,
The daughter, Nature, wild and free!
    Woe! when once emancipated,
With nought her power to withstand,
    Through the streets thick populated,
High she waves her monstrous brand!
    By the elements is hated
What is formed by mortal hand.

Water

Finally, when we think of matter, we must also include water.

Like fire, water is a mysterious creation, difficult to define. Ordinarily, we take it for granted because there is so much of it on the earth. Seven-tenths of the surface of our world is water. But just what is this mysterious creation we call "water"? Of course, everybody knows the chemical formula of H_2O, but why does the combination of these two gasses in this very exact mathematical formula produce this life-giving liquid, while these same elements combined in a slightly different proportion result in a deadly poison?

Water is a tangible substance. It can be touched and felt, has weight, and requires space, but is formless and has no body except when contained in a vessel or by the bank of a river or the shore of lakes or oceans.

---

[3] *The Poems of Schiller.* Completely edited and translated by Dr. Henry D. Wiseman, Philadelphia. I. G. Kohlen, No. 911 Arch St., 1879.

Water is tasteless, colorless, transparent, liquid, and buoyant. It is life-giving but frightfully destructive when out of bounds. Nothing is more refreshing than a cold drink of pure water when one is famished with thirst, and nothing is more deadly when foul. Neither plant, animal, nor human life can exist or survive very long without water. The most fertile land without water is a desert and produces nothing.

Running water, when falling over a precipice as in waterfalls, creates power, unlimited power, by generating electricity which then can provide power, light, and heat for cities and farmsteads hundreds of miles away.

Water is an efficient agent for transportation. Water carries the logs from the forest on the mountainside to the sawmill. Water carries the waste material of our cities to the rivers and seas and carries the nations' products in ships to the ends of the earth.

Water removes dirt, cleansing our homes, utensils, clothes, and bodies. Water supplies the liquid for all our beverages and provides the real protection against the ravages of fire. The water in rivers, lakes, and seas provides the habitat for the myriads of fish and other forms of aquatic life which constitute an important element in man's food supplies.

But water may also become a frightful destructive power when out of control in a rampaging flood. Floods have wiped out whole cities, uprooted trees, and changed the topography of a region. There is no force on earth that can stop a rampaging flood.

Water when subjected to a temperature below freezing will solidify into ice and become as solid as a mineral, and water converted into ice can form a bridge over rivers and lakes capable of carrying many tons of weight without the support of pillars or suspension cables. Water frozen into ice expands and breaks the vessel that contains it. We are told, for example, that Hannibal when crossing the Alps to invade Italy had no explosives to blast the rocks for the construction of a road across the mountains, and so he instructed his engineers to drill holes into the rocks on the mountainside and fill them with water. The frost did the rest and Hannibal built his road.

Frozen water forms a surface as smooth as glass and provides a magnificent playground for winter sports. Ice, three or four inches thick, will carry hundreds of young frolicking youths for their skating enjoyment.

Ice forms on the surface of the water, though cold water is heavier than warm and sinks to the bottom. But by a strange law of nature, when changed into ice, it rises again to the surface.

If it were not so, all the rivers and lakes in the northern climates would ultimately freeze into a solid mass of ice and the fish and all other forms of aquatic life would perish.

Water, exposed to heat of 212° Farenheit or over, is converted into vapor or steam and floats away into the atmosphere. Water extinguishes fire and fire responds by destroying water. But water, when contained in a boiler and subjected to heat and formed into steam, becomes a powerful force capable of driving the engines of our industries or the locomotives of our railroads. But when overheated and not released, it becomes a force of fearful destruction in its explosive power.

Water, like fire, has a peculiar fascination for man. People will travel thousands of miles to see the awesome spectacle of masses of water tumbling over a precipice like Niagara in United States, or the Victoria Falls in Africa, or the Iguazu Falls in South America. And the erupting geysers of Yellowstone Park attract thousands of tourists every year from all parts of the world. The wealthy build their summer homes on lakes and seasides, and water sports are among the most exhilarating forms of recreation among all people.

Water is found only on our earth, the only place in the universe created by God as an abode for man and other living things. There is no water on the moon.

Water constitutes a part of matter which God created on the first day of creation, and like all matter, water too is a mystery, a mystery in its essence and a mystery in the laws that govern it. It could not have come into existence by itself and out of nothing without a complex and scientific plan of a designer. No man in his right mind can believe that and consider himself rational. The only solution for this mystery and for all other mysteries in the universe is found in the first chapter of Genesis.

Light

After God had created matter He next created light and with that He began to bring order out of chaos.

Light is another mystery of God's creation which reveals the infinite wisdom and power of the Creator beyond all comprehension.

Light is an energy that fills the universe.

Scientists describe light in terms of light waves which travel at the incredible speed of 186,000 miles a second. But what is the energy that gives rise to these waves? Whence the marvelous colors that are found in the light waves and revealed in the rainbow? Whence the life-giving energy that radiates from the different beams of light? Life on earth would be impossible without light. Every beam of light is a bundle of mysteries which filled the universe when God said, "Let there be light." (More will be said about light when considering it with the fourth day of creation.)

The Bible speaks of God as a "God of light," as being "wrapped in light" as in a garment, while hell is described as being a place of "utter darkness."

What a spectacle it must have been for the angels in heaven when God spoke that omnipotent word: "Let there be light." The Austrian composer Haydn caught a glimpse of this wonderful spectacle and reproduced the impressions which he saw in his imagination in the great Oratorio "The Creation," in which he paints in magnificent colors of instrumental and choral music the dramatic scenes in the history of our universe, when the Creator says, "Let there be light." At that moment the instruments and choruses rise in a thunderous crescendo, and one can almost see and hear the darkness of eternity driven into flight while the new creation of light rushes in with the triumphant shout of the victor.

> Now vanquished by the holy rays
> The gloomy shades of darkness vanish;
> The first of days has dawned;
> Now chaos ends and order doth prevail.
> Aghast the host of hell's black spirit fly.
> Down they plunge, engulfed in the abyss
> To endless night!
>
> —Second aria, Haydn Oratorio "The Creation"

The most fitting conclusion and review of the first day of creation would be a reverent meditation on Job's magnificent description and contemplation of God's creation as found in the 38th chapter of his book, where we read:

> Where wast thou when I laid the foundations of the earth? declare, if thou hast understanding. Who hath laid the measures thereof, if thou knowest? or who hath stretched the line upon it? Whereupon are the foundations thereof fastened? or who laid the corner stone thereof; when the morning stars sang together and all the sons of God shouted for joy? or who shut up the sea with doors, when it brake forth, as if it had issued out of the womb? When I made the cloud the garment

thereof, and thick darkness a swaddling band for it, and brake up for it my decreed place, and set bars and doors, and said, Hitherto shalt thou come, but no further: and here shall thy proud waves be stayed? . . . Hast thou entered into the springs of the sea? or hast thou walked in the search of the depth? . . . Hast thou entered into the treasures of the snow? Or hast thou seen the treasures of the hail, which I have reserved against the time of trouble, against the day of battle and war? By what way is the light parted, which scattereth the east wind upon the earth? Who hath divided a water course for the overflowing of waters, or a way for the lightning or thunder; to cause it to rain on the earth, where no man is; on the wilderness, wherein there is no man; to satisfy the desolate and waste ground; and to cause the bud of the tender herb to spring forth? Hath the rain a father? or who hath begotten the drops of the dew? Out of whose womb came the ice? and the hoary frost of heaven? who hath gendered it? The waters are hid as with a stone, and the face of the deep is frozen. . . . Knowest thou the ordinance of the heaven? canst thou set the dominion thereof in the earth? Canst thou lift up thy voice to the clouds, that abundance of waters may cover thee? Canst thou send lightnings, that they may go, and say unto thee, Here we are? Who hath put wisdom in the inward parts? or who hath given understanding to the heart? Who can number the clouds in wisdom? or who can stay the bottles of heaven, when the dust groweth into hardness, and the clods cleave fast together? Wilt thou hunt the prey for the lion? or fill the appetite for the young lions, when they couch in their dens, and abide in the covert to lie in wait? Who provideth for the raven his food? When his young ones cry unto God, they wander for lack of meat. . . .Doth the eagle mount up at thy command, and make her nest on high? . . . Shall he that contendeth with the Almighty instruct him? he that reproveth God, let him answer it . . .

—Job 38, 39, 40

5.

The Length of the Creation Days

The record of the first day of the creation closes with these words, "And God called the light Day and the darkness he called Night. And the *evening and the morning were the first day.*"

Here the question has been raised again and again: Was this day and were the succeeding days of the creation week natural days of 24 hours or was every day a long period of time, each possibly consisting of millions or even billions of years? Many theologians and scientists, who still regard Genesis as a historical and factual record, hold the latter view. And in support of their position they advance the following arguments.

1. The Hebrew word used for day, namely, *yom*, can mean a long period of time. They point to Psalm 90:4 and 2 Peter 3:8, and other passages like them.

2. The work of creation of the different days would have required more than 24 hours, especially the work on the third and on the sixth day of creation.

3. The sun was not yet created to measure and regulate time.

4. It would help to resolve the existing conflict between the Biblical creation account and the modern theories of geology and other sciences which require long periods of time for the

universe to have developed, and in that way would remove a serious stumbling block for many in their faith regarding the trustworthiness of our Bible.

5. With the exception of about 100 well-known American scientists who subscribe to the creation theory of Genesis, there are few universally recognized scientists in the world today who still accept the Biblical creation account of six days and each of 24 normal hours in our time. All standard textbooks for schools and colleges today assume long periods of time.

In reply to these arguments I would like to submit the following:

1. The language of the text is simple and clear. Honest exegetes cannot read anything else out of these verses than a day of 24 hours and a week of 7 days. There is not the slightest indication that this is to be regarded as poetry or as an allegory or that it is not to be taken as a historical fact. The language is that of normal, human speech to be taken at face value, and the unbiased reader will understand it as it reads. There is no indication that anything but a literal sense is meant.

2. The first and literal meaning of the Hebrew word *yom* means a natural day, and unless the context forces us to assume another meaning, we must accept that literal first meaning. And more than that. When the Old Testament associates *yom*, or day, with a definite numeral, a solar day of 24 hours is always meant; for example, Genesis 7:11, 8:14, 17:12 and Exodus 12:6. Only by doing violence to the first principle of hermeneutics is it possible to arrive at any other conclusion.

Dr. R. F. Surburg in *Darwin, Evolution and Creation*, p. 61, quotes a letter by Arthur C. Custance, sent to nine contemporary Hebrew scholars, members of the faculties of nine leading universities, three in Canada, three in the United States, and three in England. In the letter he asked them questions about the meaning of *yom* in Genesis. For example, he asked "Do you consider the Hebrew *yom*, as used in Genesis 1, accompanied by a numeral, to be properly translated as (a) a day as commonly understood, or (b) an age, (c) an age or a day without preference for either? Seven of the nine scholars replied, and all stated that it means "a day as commonly understood."

3. Moses specifically speaks of evening and morning and thus gives the termini of the day which were with the Jews the evening and the morning. The well-known work generally recognized as a standard commentary on Genesis by C. F. Keil and F. Delitzsch has this comment on the length of the

creation day: "If the days of creation are regulated by the recurring interchange of light and darkness, they must be regarded not as periods of time of incalculable duration of years or thousands of years, but simply earthly days." [1]

4. In Exodus 20:9, 11 we read, "Six days shalt thou labour . . . for in six days the Lord made heaven and earth, the sea, and all that in them is. . . ." And again in Exodus 31:17 we read: "It is a sign between me and the children of Israel forever: for in six days the Lord made heaven and earth, and on the seventh day he rested, and was refreshed." These words would be meaningless unless they have reference to the six normal days of creation. Besides that, the days were especially numbered as first, second, third, etc.

5. The meaning "God rested on the seventh day" is a translation of *shabat*, which means to cut off, to stop, to cease. On the seventh day God ended His work. There has been no further creation "ex nihilo, nihil fit" since the seventh day.

6. The view of long periods would also do violence to the laws of nature. On the third day God created plants and trees and grasses of every kind, and there was no sun. If the third day was a period of millions or possibly more years, these plants would have had to live without the sun throughout this period, which is impossible and contrary to the laws of nature.

Every close observer of nature and every scientist knows that all of creation is a unified system, all its parts interlocking like the individual parts of a complex machine; none of them could have existed or survived without the other. The laws of nature exclude all possibility of long periods between the different parts.

7. We do not call on geology or any other science to interpret Scriptures. Scripture must interpret itself, and the language of the text, as we have seen, is very clear. Nowhere in Scripture do we find any reference that would in any way indicate that it was not days of 24 hours and a week of 7 days. If we permit human reason or science to interpret this part of Scripture, what about other portions which are even more difficult to harmonize with reason than the works of creation? For example, the atonement through the death and the blood of the Son of God, the virgin birth, the divinity of Christ, the resurrection of Christ, the real presence in the Lord's Supper, the resurrection of all the dead on the last day, and all the other miraculous statements recorded in the Bible. And as to the scientists and their view,

[1] Vol. 1, p. 56.

it must be stated again, as was pointed out in the section on evolution, that their views are not based on scientifically demonstrated facts but are mere theories and assumptions.

8. Even if we change the six days of creation into long days or periods of millions and possibly billions of years, this would not solve the problem of the evolutionary theories. The process assumed for these theories cannot be measured by any standards of time, and hence, it is not surprising that additional zeros have been added from time to time to the astronomical figures projected by the evolutionists for the history of the universe. Sixty or seventy years ago the estimation stood at approximately 50,000,000 years. Now this figure has grown somewhere between 5 and 25 billion years, and the end is not yet.

It is futile and folly to try to harmonize Genesis with the evolutionary theories by such methods.

9. And finally, we have a right to ask, "Who is man to sit in judgment of God, and what right has he to set limits to His omnipotent power in the name of human science and insist that the universe could not have been created in six days, as it is reported in Genesis?" The problem with these men is that their god is too small. They have created their god in the image of man and have reduced his divine and omnipotent power and infinite wisdom to human potentials. But it is sheer arrogance on the part of little, finite man to set limitations to an infinite God, or to attempt to measure God by human standards. Finite man cannot comprehend God and His infinite, eternal power and wisdom. In fact, only when we contemplate the wonders of God's creation can we get a faint glimpse of the majesty, wisdom, and omnipotent power of God and learn to confess with awe, humility, and reverence the words of the First Article of our Creed: "I believe in God, the Father Almighty, Maker of heaven and earth."

6.

The Second Day: The Dividing of the Waters and the Creation of the Firmament

The works of God on the second day of creation are described in Genesis 1:6-8, where we read:

"And God said, Let there be a firmament in the midst of the waters, and let it divide the waters from the waters. And God made the firmament, and divided the waters which were under the firmament from the waters which were above the firmament: and it was so. And God called the firmament Heaven. And the evening and the morning were the second day."

On the first day of time God created light and matter, the substances from which all subsequent things were made.

From the second day onward, we observe a systematic upward unfolding of God's creation plan, bringing order and beauty out of chaos and forming matter into the myriads of kinds of creatures and of the individual wonders that filled heaven and earth at the end of the creation week.

The second step of the creation process was dividing original chaos into an upper and lower sphere by the creation of the firmament. The Hebrew word for firmament is *Rakia*, which means a spreading out like a tent or a canopy. By the creation of the firmament, God surrounded our planet with the atmosphere, which to the human eye appears like a majestic blue canopy in the heaven above us. The atmosphere is a belt of air surrounding the earth to a thickness of about 60 to 100 miles, or possibly even more, which consists chiefly of two gases, namely, 78% nitrogen and 20% oxygen, with 2% other gases.

In the creation of the firmament, God wrapped the earth in a thick blanket of air, making life on this planet possible. The earth is only an insignificant speck among the myriads of celestial bodies that fill infinite space, but so far as we know it is the only body provided with an atmosphere. God intended the earth as the habitat for man, the crown of His creation, and that makes the earth the real center of the universe. The sun and moon and the surrounding stars are the servants of the earth. The moon has no atmosphere and no life, and no life on it is possible. All attempts, therefore, to invade the moon seem costly experiments in futility.

The gases of which the atmosphere is composed form a very delicately balanced mixture. If, for example, the proportion of nitrogen should be enlarged by only a very small percent, human and animal life would become impossible. And if, on the other hand, the oxygen content should be increased to 31 or 32% instead of 20%, all combustible substances in the world would go up in flames at the flash of lightning or with a spark of fire from any other source.

This accurate balance becomes even more wonderful when we consider the law of nature by which it is maintained. Man and animals require oxygen to live, and they have been using up oxygen with every breath they have taken. Billions upon billions of human beings and countless trillions of animals have lived upon the face of the earth since creation, each using oxygen, continuously, and yet a safe and perfect balance of the gases has been preserved throughout the ages. The instruments by which God achieves this miracle are the plants. Man and animals require oxygen to live; but plants, on the other hand, require nitrogen to survive. When men and animals inhale the air that surrounds them, the lungs absorb the oxygen and exhale the nitrogen that remains, while the plants absorb the nitrogen and exhale the oxygen, and so this wonderful balance of nature is beautifully preserved. No evolutionary theory can account for this wonder of nature.

But there are other great and wonderful features about the atmosphere which ordinarily escape the attention of man. For example, though invisible, the atmosphere is a material substance; it is tangible, it can be felt; it has weight—14 1/2 pounds per square inch at the sea level—it is transparent unless laden with fog, smog, dust, or some other foreign substance; it is buoyant like water; and it pushes upward a balloon filled with gases lighter than the atmosphere, like water forces a submerged piece of cork to the surface. The atmosphere absorbs heat and cold; its temperature can be raised to a burning heat or lowered to a degree of unbearable cold; the air of the atmosphere flows like a river of water: sometimes it flows in the gentle stream of a summer evening zephyr, but sometimes it becomes a roaring blizzard or a frightful tornado.

Life without the atmosphere would be impossible. What water is to fish, atmosphere is to man and beast. Remove a fish from its element and it dies; shut off the flow of air from man and beast and they perish.

Without the atmosphere there would be no sound, no music, no communication of any kind. The heat of the day would be so intense that everything would be burned to a crisp, and the cold of the night would be like that of the Arctic.

And then there is the beauty of the atmosphere, the magnificent azure blue of the heavenly canopy above with the silvery moon moving in silent dignity among the stars like a shepherd among his sheep. Consider the rosy blush of the morning dawn, gently arousing all nature to a new day of life and activity to be followed by the golden glow of a setting sun, bidding a warm goodnight to a day it has blessed with its life-giving warmth and light, but also reminding thoughtless mankind that "Sic transit gloria mundi" (thus passes the glory of the world).

Who has not been thrilled or moved to wonderment by the spectacular display of nature's magnificent pyrotechnics in the aurora borealis of the northern sky, or the zigzag flashing of the lightning followed by the rumbling roar of the thunder as it rolled through the heavens, or the billowing clouds that like great mountains of snow float over his head? Everywhere around us are the traces of the divine artist. If we would but open our eyes and really see these beauties, we would again and again sing out with the Psalmist in songs of joy and praise, "The heavens declare the glory of God; and the firmament sheweth his handywork" (Ps 19:1).

Weather and Climate

When considering the atmosphere, we must also include the mystery of weather and climate.

Webster's dictionary defines weather as "the state of

air or atmosphere with respect to heat and cold, wetness and dryness, calm and storm, clearness and cloudiness, or any other meteorological phenomenon."

And climate is described as "the average weather of a place or a region over an extended period of time."

These are very carefully drawn lexicographical definitions, but strictly speaking they do not define, but merely enumerate some of the most common characteristics of weather. They are not very helpful in explaining the why and the how of the mysterious phenomenon, nor do they tell us anything about the laws that govern it.

Man is always in weather and no one can resign from climate. We talk a great deal about the weather but know little about it, or, as Mark Twain said, "Everybody talks about the weather, but no one does anything about it."

However, observant men in all ages have been fascinated by and interested in weather. They have tried to discover the laws that govern it and have been guided by it in their activities. Jesus said to the Pharisees of His day, "When it is evening, ye say, It will be fair weather: for the sky is red. And in the morning, It will be foul weather today: for the sky is red and lowering" (Matt. 16:2, 3).

Today the study of weather has become one of the major sciences, called meteorology. The marvelous development of all branches of natural sciences and the many important technological inventions of our day, such as the airplane, radar, radio, television, man-made satellites and global observation platforms in outer space have contributed much to a better understanding of weather. But even now we have only scratched the surface, and there remain many unsolved problems about weather for which we have no satisfactory answer. What Jesus said to Nicodemus, therefore, still applies to many phases of weather and climate today: "The wind bloweth where it listeth and thou hearest the sound thereof, but canst not tell whence it cometh, and whither it goeth" (John 3:8). And so it is still today with many of the mysterious laws that govern weather.

Weather includes winds of every description: the chinook, the zephyr, storms, blizzards, dust storms, the sirocco and the monsoon, tornadoes, typhoons, and also clouds, smog, rain, snow, and hail.

One characteristic of weather is that it does not remain the same for very long at one time. Weather is affected by its geographical location. The atmosphere is like a giant sponge: it absorbs some of the characteristics of the terrain over which it moves and so it is affected by the mountains, hills and valleys, prairies and forest areas, by cultivated land, barren desert, and even by the time of the day. Weather is, therefore, changeable; hence the saying, "Changeable like the weather." The atmosphere which we breathe today, or even this very moment is not the same as it was yesterday or last month. Not so long ago the air that surrounds us at present might have been hovering over the desert sands of the Sahara or over the frozen northlands of the Arctic. It was modified, cooled or warmed as it moved over the terrain over which it came to reach us. As we cannot step into the same river twice, so we do not inhale the same air with the second or third breath we take.

The laws that govern climate and weather are as complex and incomprehensible as other laws of nature that prevail in the universe. And no evolutionary theory can explain their origin or their unaltered continuation. The meteorologist can observe the weather, can discover by his observation some of the laws that govern it, can tabulate what he has observed for the benefit of others, but he cannot give us the reason why or the how of the underlying causes of what he has discovered. To assume that they just happened is no explanation. It is not a scientific answer but a naive attempt to escape from the agony of saying, "We do not know."

Take, for example, the strange phenomenon of the trade winds or westerlies forming a broad belt of moving air encircling the globe on both sides of the equator. Professor James G. Edinger, writing in *Watching for the Winds*, says:

> The belt of variable winds in the middle latitude is a broad, turbulent air current girdling the globe and flowing from west to east in both northern and southern hemispheres. . . . It is studded with giant whirls and meanderings. It is the passage of these whirls called cyclones and anti-cyclones that bring about the changing winds of the middle latitude. The cyclones may be 500 to 1,000 miles across and move with speeds of 20 to 30 miles per hour. The cyclone, normally, brings clouds and precipitations. These winds swirl around in the counter-clockwise sense in the northern hemisphere. And curiously enough, the cyclones of the southern hemisphere turn in the opposite sense. (p. 11) . . . The strong westerlies with their cyclones and anti-cyclones are found much farther north in the summer than in winter. They move north just as the sun does during that season. For example,

California gets no rain in summer because it is south of the seasonal storm track in the westerly. (p. 15)

Another remarkable phenomenon of weather and climate is the chinook winds which occur in southern Alberta and in northern Montana. The chinook is a warm wind which sweeps in from the Pacific Ocean over the mountainous terrain of British Columbia and Washington and crosses the snow-covered Rockies and then fans out over the prairies with a considerable violence, causing radical and very sudden changes in the weather. I have witnessed such a sudden change in these parts from a temperature of 40 and more below zero to a rise of 50 and more above zero, and that within a matter of a few hours. Sometimes the approach of such a chinook was indicated by the violent turbulence of the clouds in the nearby mountains and the roaring sound of the storm long before it arrived. And the questions we amateur prairie weather prophets again and again would raise were: What started these winds? What is the force behind them? Why are they not cooled by the glaciers and the snow fields of the Rockies over which they come? Where are they going? Why do they stop? We had no satisfactory answer for these obvious queries.

Closely related to the chinook, in the same region, are the strong, violent gales blowing with little interruption during the season from about the middle of September to the end of March. And again one is prompted to ask, "Why do they blow where they blow and whence do they come and whence comes the tremendous force that drives them on?"

And then there is the mystery of the weather cycle in certain regions of the world. In the prairie provinces of Western Canada and in the adjoining regions of the United States there occur at irregular intervals periods of extended drought with little or no rain, sometimes extending over three and four or even six and seven years in succession, to be followed during the next season by excessive rainfalls and damaging floods. The terrible drought years of the '30's with their devastating dust storms are still a frightful nightmare in the memory of those who lived through them. And the winter of 1969 with the pouring rains and landslides and destructive floods in Southern California will never be forgotten by those who lost everything they had.

And another question is, Why are some winters in the northern latitude so much longer and colder than others, while others are mild and pleasant? In Edmonton, Alberta, for example, I lived through winters with temperatures of 50 and even 60 below zero to be followed in the next season by a winter nearly as mild as those of St. Louis, about 1700 miles farther south.

Another phenomenon of weather are the hurricanes, typhoons, and tornadoes. Who can explain the source of the fantastic power generated in these frightful storms? Weather experts tell us that any one of these rampaging renegades of nature may develop a destructive force much greater than that of a large atomic bomb.

Hurricanes commonly occur off the Atlantic coast and in the Gulf region from about July to October. The typhoon, which is the counterpart of the hurricane in the Pacific, is confined very largely to the region of the China Sea. Why?

Tornadoes are cyclonic storms similar to the hurricane and typhoon, but are not as broad in their destructive sweep, nor do they last as long. Tornadoes occur most frequently from April to about July, but may also strike at other times and sometimes do. They are most common in the so-called "Tornado Alley," that is, the Midwestern states, but nearly all parts of North America have felt their fury. The worst tornado year on record to date was 1965.* In that year a total of 898 tornadoes were reported in the United States in which 299 people lost their lives and the property damage caused by them was estimated at $200,000,000. The states most severely stricken at that time were: Iowa, Wisconsin, Michigan, Illinois, Indiana and Ohio.

The fearful destructive force of a hurricane and the havoc it can create are vividly described by an eyewitness of such a storm that struck the New England States in 1815. In the section describing especially the devastation caused in the city of Providence, Rhode Island, he writes:

> Rhode Island felt the full force of this remarkable gale, Providence, suffering to the amount of millions of dollars, accompanied with a fearful loss of life, as in other places. This was owing to the wind blowing directly up the river on which the place is built, unbroken by the Cape or Long Island, and in sweeping over such an extent of water it accumulated a dreadful and most destructive tide so that the vessels were actually driven over the wharfs and through the streets.
>
> Early in the morning the wind was northeast, but at about 8 o'clock it shifted southeast and soon began to blow violently, continuing to increase until 10, when it became a hurricane. All was now confusion and dismay in the exposed region. The tide, impelled by the tempest,

* 1973 had 1,086 tornadoes or more.

overflowed the wharfs; vessels broken from the moorings in the stream and their fastenings at the wharfs were soon driven with dreadful impetuosity towards the bridge which they swept away without a moment's check in their progress and passed on to the head of the basin where they drove high up the bank.

> Every exertion to protect property was rendered futile by the violence of the wind, the rapid rise of the water, and the falling of trees; indeed, these, with the crushing of chimneys crumbling upon the houses and descending into the streets, together with tiles and railings from the tops of buildings and many other species of dangerous missiles flying through the air, rendered it perilous to appear in the streets. . . . The tempest raged with increasing violence.
>
> The flood was overwhelming in the lower parts of the town: Stores and dwelling houses were tottering upon their foundations and then plunging into the deluge. . . . It was an awful and terrifying scene. Every store below, on the east side, was either carried away or completely shattered; and every building on the opposite side and on the wharfs was swept from its foundation . . . so that all the space where an hour or two before were so many valuable wharfs and stores, crowded with shipping and merchandise, was now one wide waste of tumultuous water. . . . It was such a scene of widespread ruin and desolation as beggars description.[1]

This storm occurred more than 150 years ago. Much has changed since then and we have made tremendous progress in every branch of science and technology: We have been able to harness many of the great forces of nature and compel them to be our servants. We are able to send our missiles hundreds and thousands of miles and can protect ourselves against hostile attacks with our counter-missiles. We are even in the process of invading the area of outer space, but tornadoes and hurricanes are still the wild, untamed savages of nature, in the face of which man is still as puny and as helpless as he was 150 years ago. The only difference between then and now is that we now have means of forewarning people of their approach so that they can seek shelter before they strike.

These cosmic forces of nature were a part of God's creation of the second day. They were intended to be benign and beneficial forces for the service and the good of man. They were included

[1] *The American Progress of the Greatest Century* by Honorable R. M. Devans, p. 179 ff.

in the verdict which God pronounced over all creation when He said, "Very good." They became what they are because of man's rebellion against his Creator. Man's sin destroyed the perfect harmony that existed between God and man, and this disharmony brought equal disharmony into the universe (Rom. 8:20). As the drudgery of labor and the thorns and thistles of the field today are a result of sin, so these rampaging forces of nature are the result of the same cause. It is the curse of sin that produced them. Hurricanes and destructive storms are in the firmament what the dreaded cancer cells are in the human body.

And then, what about the fearful electrical storms that sometimes become so frightening? And what about the source of the electric energy released in a major thunder storm? On page 31 in the April, 1968 edition of *Natural History*, a magazine published by the museum of Natural History, New York, the writer described a thunderstorm he observed in Massachusetts. He estimated the electrical power required for the unusual display of lightning flashing as being equal to one hundred million kilowatts which, at that time, was equivalent to the total generating capacity of the entire United States.

And in the *Press Bulletin* of the University of Alberta of December 26, 1930, I found the following startling statement about thunderstorms. It read: "It may be surprising to people in a temperate climate to hear that there are on the average about 1800 storms in operation at one time, with about 100 flashes per second. The energy expended in these storms amounts to the almost inconceivable figure of 1,300,000,000 horsepower."

These are, indeed, inconceivable figures. But for the average person who is not a trained engineer or mechanic, the term "horsepower" is a rather vague concept for the measurement of energy. In order to translate this into a more comprehensible and concrete form, I inquired of a dealer in large road construction machinery how much horsepower one of these monster caterpillar bulldozers produces. I was informed that the largest one they had in their plant, which was easily capable of uprooting large oak trees or removing even more formidable obstacles, had a capacity of 419 horsepower and required 100 gallons of diesel fuel a day for operation.

Then the question occurred to me, where would the evolutionist get the fuel, or, in plain language, where would he get the source for the fantastic power displayed in a thunderstorm as described in the science article quoted? His answer, no doubt, would be that it is the electricity developed in the thunder cloud. And then I would follow with other questions, And what is electricity? What is the essence of this mysterious power? Where does it come from? Why does it behave as it does? And why does a cloud of fog and rain produce this power? And, of course, there could be no honest, scientific answer to these questions unless one admitted a first cause, a designer's plan. And for us Christians that first cause and Designer is God the omnipotent and all-wise Creator. He placed this mysterious power into the clouds and directs it. But the tragedy is that the wise ones of the world refuse to acknowledge Him as the source of all these wonders surrounding us and fail to honor Him. Ancient Job knew better. He knew the answer and said, "He [God] made a decree for the rain, and a way for the lightning of the thunder" (Job 28:26).

For the ancient people who knew not God and did not understand the wonders of His creation, the awesome spectacle of a thunderstorm was a frightful manifestation of the anger of their gods, and they viewed it with superstitious fear.

To the Romans lightning was the terrible weapon in the hands of Jupiter, their supreme god, who in his anger hurled his fiery bolt to the earth when impious men failed to render him the worship he demanded.

The Greeks ascribed the same to Zeus, their foremost god, and would set aside the spot where the lightning struck as sacred ground, dedicated to their god.

Thor was the chief god of the Nordics, and to them a thunderstorm was Thor riding in his chariot in a wild chase over the roaring clouds, hurling his mighty hammer in the form of flashing lightning to the earth to terrify man.

A Christian observes a thunderstorm with awesome wonderment and admiration. To him it is a dramatic demonstration of the immeasurable, omnipotent power of the Creator. At the same time, however, he realizes that the blight of man's sin has also affected this force of nature so that it is no longer only a beneficent and benign power, as it was originally intended, but can become a frightful, destructive force, killing men, women, children, and cattle, and setting homes and whole cities and forest reserves on fire.

But even now, a frightening thunderstorm is still a wonderful link in God's providential care for the preservation of His creation. Men and animals require food for their survival. The basic source for that food is the plant. The plant, on the other hand, requires certain chemicals for its nourishment, part of which are derived from the soil and part from the atmosphere. The important chemical absorbed from the atmosphere is nitrogen. But the nitrogen of the atmosphere must undergo a change before it can be absorbed by the plant. And here is where the thunderstorm provides the necessary link and brings about the required change.

The intense heat of lightning fuses the nitrogen into nitrogen-oxide. In that form, nitrogen becomes soluble in water. The rain which accompanies the thunderstorm then washes this new chemical compound out of the air to the earth and thereby provides the important nourishment for the plant. Again we say, how wonderful, how wonderful! And again we marvel at the close interdependence and interaction of the forces of nature in this magnificent mechanism of God's creation order. No evolutionary theory can explain the origin of this delicate balance in nature.

Another perplexing problem of weather is the contrary air currents at different altitudes of the atmosphere. Sometimes air pilots find a strong surface wind blowing in one direction, but upon reaching higher levels, another strong air current is moving in the opposite direction. And sometimes they even encounter winds with a violent downward pull. When this happens over a mountainous region, it frequently results in an airplane disaster.

For all these and other mysteries and wonders of weather and the laws that govern it, there is only one rational explanation, and that is found in the first chapter of Genesis.

Clouds and the Atmosphere

As previously indicated, the creation of the atmosphere also included the wonders of clouds, rain, and snow. A cloud may be described as a mass of visible vapor floating in the atmosphere. According to an international code, clouds have been classified according to their general appearance and the altitude at which they are found. The following are some of the chief categories into which they have been divided.[2]

1. The *cumulus*. This is the most picturesque of the clouds towering over us in the sky, chiefly during the summer months. Sometimes they appear as great mountains of snow or masses

[2] Adapted from several sources: 1) *Encyclopaedia Britannica*. 2) *New Physiography* by Albert L. Arey, C.E.; Frank L. Bryant, B.S.; Wm. W. Clendenin, M.S.M.A.; Wm. T. Morrey, A.M.; D. C. Heath and Co. 3) *Watching for the Wind* by James G. Edinger, Doubleday Anchor Book.

of fluffy white wool or, with the addition of a little imagination, as great cathedrals, or castles floating in the air. They do not retain their shape very long at one time but are constantly taking on new forms. They are the most fascinating of these wonders over our heads.

2. A second group has been called *cirrus*. These are the fibrous, detached, feather-like clouds in the upper strata of the atmosphere, and they usually travel at greater speed than the other clouds.

3. The *Alto-stratus* cloud. These are next to the cirrus in altitude and appear like a thin gray-blue veil through which the sun and the moon are faintly visible.

4. The *nimbus clouds*. These are the dark, lowring clouds, hanging low in the atmosphere. They are nature's magnificent irrigation system, bringing rain and snow to the forests, fields, and gardens.

In addition to these major categories, there are a number of sub-varieties containing some of the characteristics found in the major groups.

Clouds are really gigantic reservoirs of water floating over our heads. They are created by the energy of the sun. The heat radiated from the sun vaporizes the water of the ocean and of other basins and converts it into a gaseous form. And by a magic force, this is then raised into the atmosphere, contrary to the law of gravity. There the microscopic particles of water are collected, cooled, and condensed into clouds, and the clouds are then pushed over the land by the force of the wind which has its own mysterious origin. When the temperature and other atmospheric conditions reach a certain point, nature's "count-down" begins and God's waterwagons discharge their cargos of millions and billions of tons of water, not in one mighty Niagara splash, but in a gentle sprinkle of refreshing rain, tenderly washing the dust from the delicate petals of the drooping flowers and bringing the life-giving moisture to their roots at the same time.

But that is not all. The wonders of God's magnificent water-works system become even more wonderful when considering the miraculous process by which ocean water is demineralized and converted into fresh water at the same time.

As already mentioned, the ultimate source of all water on the earth is the ocean. But ocean water is saline—that is, it is laden with a mixture of mineral salts, making it unfit for drinking or irrigation purposes. Before this water can be used, it must be purified. The ingenuity of man has succeeded in accomplishing this but only on a very small scale and at a prohibitive cost. A few cities have succeeded in providing drinking water in that manner from the ocean for their citizens. But the process is still too slow and too expensive to make it applicable for irrigation purposes.

But what man is able to do only in a very limited way, God does on a worldwide scale in a shower of rain that falls on the dry earth, and He does that free of charge. Furthermore, all these complex operations are automatic. They have their own thermostat and their own self-starter. They create their own powerhouse and require no engineer to regulate them. There is no wear or tear in their mechanism, no cost for upkeep or repair. Their mechanism operates without ceasing and has never stopped since they received their first impulse from the Creator. They cause no annoying noises in their operation, and there is no clang or clatter in the functioning of their magnificent machinery.

And yet, the forces involved in the production of a single cloud or a spring shower of rain are so enormous and so cosmic in their scope that even this common occurrence is a miracle beyond all comprehension.

A number of years ago, a Canadian physicist at the University of Alberta, in an article in the *University Bulletin*, gave his readers some startling figures to describe the forces involved in a rain over a limited area of land. He wrote: "A rain of four inches over an area of approximately 10,000 square miles would require the burning of 640,000,000 tons of coal to evaporate enough water for such a rain. To cool again the vapors thus produced and cause it to condense into clouds would require another 800,000,000 horsepower of refrigeration working day and night for one hundred days in order to produce a rainfall equivalent in amount to that mentioned."

The figures quoted represent the forces required for a limited rain over an area of 10,000 square miles. On the basis of these figures, try to estimate the forces required to provide sufficient rain for an entire state or for the whole continent.

The State of Minnesota has an area of 84,668 square miles. An agricultural expert of that state has figured out that the average farmer of his state receives annually, free of charge and without the cost of the upkeep of irrigation ditches, 407,510 gallons of water for every acre of his land, and the average rainfall is only 24 inches per year.

The State of Missouri has an area of nearly 70,000 square miles. The average annual rainfall for the whole state is 38 inches. This total amount of water would be equal to a lake 22 feet deep and covering an area approximately as large as Lake Erie, which is 250 miles long and 60 miles wide. That is a lot of water! And the energies, the machinery, the horsepower, the fuel and lubrication that would be required to pump that much water from the ocean, demineralize it, and convey it in pipes to the land of the state are beyond calculation. And yet, that is precisely what the clouds and the rain perform every year. And there is no wearing out of the machinery, no consumption of fuel and oil, and no rusting or breaking of the pipes. And this enormous volume of water is not only brought to the state but, in addition, is gently spread over the land in the miracle of God's wonderful rain.

Consider all the water required to provide the necessary moisture for the rest of our country!

The annual rainfall in only the states of the Middle West would, by the same calculation, be about equal to all the water in our Great Lakes system. God performs this wonder every year for us to make life and prosperity possible. But only few people among us recognize this and ever say "thank you" to God.

And then consider the immensity of the wonder that God performs by providing the life-giving moisture for the entire planet!

It has been estimated that the total annual rainfall on all the earth amounts to about 24,000 cubic miles. And what makes the wonder even more wonderful is the fact that this process is regulated by definite laws, so that the average rainfall in a given area remains essentially the same year after year.

All these figures, facts, and calculations are so stupendous that they are altogether beyond comprehension, but we never even give them a thought. We take them for granted because rain is a common, normal phenomenon.

St. Paul proved to the superstitious people of Lystra that his God was the only true God and had manifested himself as the omnipotent Ruler of the Universe by reminding them that God "gave us rain from heaven, and fruitful seasons, filling our hearts with food and gladness" (Acts 14:17).

To make the enormity of this wonder of God even more dramatic, I would suggest that the reader stand at some point on the bank of the Mississippi River, or, for that matter, on the bank of any other great river, and watch the muddy waters of this majestic river rolling down to the sea. Then let him try to measure in his imagination the amount of water that is passing him every hour at that point. Let him calculate what that would amount to for every hour of the day. Then, let him consider that this water of that river has been passing that point every hour of every day and of every year since this mighty river found its course down to the sea.

Add to the water of the Mississippi the water of all the great rivers of North and South America and of the rest of the world: the Columbia and the Colorado, the Hudson and the St. Lawrence, the Saskatchewan and the Mackenzie, the Amazon and the Parana, the Congo and the Nile, the Yangtze and the Yellow, the Indus and the Murray, the Volga and the Rhine, and all the fresh-water lakes and all the wells and springs in the world. All that water originally came from the great oceans of the world and was carried over the land by the wonderful waterworks of the clouds.

The clouds over our heads, the showers of rain, and the rivers and lakes of the world—what a magnificent wonder of our God's creation!

The eternal God revealed His majesty in the works of His creation that all men might recognize, worship, and glorify Him as God. St. Paul, writing to the sophisticated Romans, says, "Because that which may be known of God is manifest in them; for God hath shewed it unto them. For the invisible things of him from the creation of the world are clearly seen, being understood by the things that are made, even his eternal power and Godhead; so that they are without excuse: because that, when they knew God, they glorified him not as God, neither were thankful; but became vain in their imaginations, and their foolish heart was darkened. Professing themselves to be wise, they became fools" (Rom. 1:19-22).

Haydn, the Austrian composer, caught in his imagination a glimpse of the wonders that God performed when He created the firmament on the second day of creation. He expressed his emotions in verse and music.

> How now rage with fury, clouds and tempest.
> Like chaff in the whirlwind fly storm-driven clouds.
> The sky is cleft by fiery lightning,
> Tremendous, awful, the thunder roll.
> The floods give forth at His command
> The rains and showers, all refreshing;
> The hailstorms, all destroying;
> The light and fluffy snow.

—Third Recitation, Haydn's Oratorio, "The Creation"

Rainmaking

Here might be inserted an observation on attempts of rainmaking by man.

From times immemorial men have attempted to make rain in regions suffering from periodic drought. In the African jungle it has been the witch doctor; among the American Indians and other primitive people it was the medicine man or the priest. In modern America it has been the pseudo-scientific rainmaker who has tried to perform this miracle, exploiting, thereby, people facing disaster in a drought-stricken area.

About fifty years ago, one of these charlatans came to southern Alberta and promised the people, in a region that had suffered seriously during a long period of drought, so many inches of rain for a stipulated price per inch. The people were desperate and were taken in by this faker and paid the price. The man then set up his contraptions and his pots filled with some chemical substances while the people anxiously waited for the rain to come. And by a strange coincidence, soon after his false demonstration, a light rain actually fell. People became hopeful. But that was the end of that experiment. No more rain followed, and the rainmaker disappeared with his kettles and the money the people had paid him.

Since then similar attempts have been made again and again by various means, especially by seeding clouds with chemical crystals. However, the results have been the same as those of the rainmakers in the African jungle or the faker in southern Alberta.

The St. Louis *Globe-Democrat* of November 21, 1964, published an excerpt of the findings of The National Academy of Science, National Research Council, in which the editor of the progress report writes:

"It now turns out, after fifteen years of trying, at a cost running into many millions, that cloud-seeding has no significant positive effect upon rainfall. Indeed, it is possible that it may even decrease the precipitation.

"This is the finding of the National Academy of Science National Research Council in a just issued report on weather modification.

"A council panel headed by Gordon J. F. McDonald, a University of California weather scientist, suggests that farmers, businessmen, and taxpayers have been taken in by commerical cloud-seeders even if they are satisfied with the results. The whole argument for cloud-seeding, says the panel, is faith and hope of economic gain and that it cannot be substantiated anymore, scientifically, than the theories and the predictions in astrology.

"A British scientist declared 'All alleged rainmakers are frauds and that there is no hope that rainfall can ever be brought by artificial means in such quantity at least as to do any good. To produce the upward current of air,' he explains, 'which would result in a precipitation of one one-hundreds of an inch the expenditure of at least 10,000,000 horsepower for two hours would be required. Rain production,' he concludes, 'is like the tides and the winds, one of those natural phenomena which are on a scale altogether beyond man's power to control.' "[3]

And it is fortunate that it is so. When man arrogates power to manipulate the forces that belong in the realm of God's own omnipotent and all-wise providence, he will ultimately destroy himself.

One of the greatest tragedies in human history is the invention of the atomic and hydrogen bombs. Man now has created the instrument by which an evil man can actually blot out all life on our planet and annihilate the human race.

How terrible it would be if an enemy nation, ruled by an evil and an ambitious man, could control the weather and regulate rain and drought and hailstorms, turn them on and off as he saw fit for the annihilation of the people whom he would destroy!

Thank God the Creator of the universe is still in the heavens, and He will preserve what He has created. He has ordained as a permanent and a fixed law now, that "while the earth remaineth, seedtime and havest, and cold and heat, and summer and winter, and day and night shall not cease" (Gen. 8:22).

The Wonders of the Snow

Rain, as we have seen, is the most wonderful phenomenon of nature. Snow is a close relative of rain but adds form, design, beauty, and other wonders to it.

The dictionary defines snow as "precipitation taking the form of minute crystals of ice, formed from the aqueous vapor in the air when the temperature is below 32 degrees Farenheit."

In simple language, snow may be described as frozen rain, not frozen in solid particles of ice, but because of another law

---

[3] *Edmonton Journal*, July 22, 1925.

of nature, frozen into beautiful fluffy, white snowflakes, so white that nothing on earth surpasses them in whiteness. Every individual snowflake appears in a specific design and is a creation of exquisite beauty. Usually they appear in a star-shaped figure of the hexagonal system. Some twenty different forms have been recognized. The delicacy and beauty of these designs, as seen under the microscope, are beyond description. Goldsmiths have copied them to create unusual and attractive patterns in jewelry.

In the northern climates snowfalls are common and taken for granted. But every snowfall, in reality, is a most exciting experience and a joy to behold. Silently their fluffy, feathery, star-shaped icy crystals quietly and almost playfully float through the sky, decorating pines, spruce, and cedars with their sparkling whiteness and hiding all the unsightliness on earth created by man. After they have fallen, the individual flakes do not linger long to show off their beauty. Other flakes follow in quick succession, tenderly and quietly covering those that have fallen before, and in doing so they provide a protective blanket for the flowers and plants and other forms of life, wrapping all of nature in a shining garb of pure and innocent whiteness of indescribable beauty. Only the eyes of God have seen the beauty of each individual snowflake, but each of them is a magnificent glorification of the Artist that created it.

And then to think that there are some who assume and actually believe that those creations of beauty and wonder happened by chance and happened over and over and over again in every snowfall. For men and women with unperverted mental processes, it is too absurd to be taken seriously, if it were not that great men of learning actually believe this and propagate these absurdities as superior wisdom.

In the Arctic region of the North and in the high mountain peaks, the snow is gathered in the form of great icefields and glaciers. If it would permanently remain there, the moisture of the earth would eventually be gathered and stored in these forbidding regions. To prevent this, God provided a corrective law in creating the glaciers or moving icefields. By the law of gravity they are caused to move down the mountainside and from the Arctic regions into the sea, thereby returning the stored-up moisture to the sea, whence it originally came. Here, as we have seen before, we have the self-perpetuating cosmic forces constantly maintaining their balance in nature.

And so, as we consider the works of our God on the second day of creation, we are moved again and again to cry out with the Psalmist, "The heavens declare the glory of God; and the firmament sheweth his handywork"(Ps. 19:1).

7.

The Third Day of Creation

The creation of land and sea and the beginning of life on the earth.

The works of God on the third day are described in Genesis 1:9-13, where we read, "And God said, Let the waters under the heaven be gathered together unto one place, and let the dry land appear: and it was so.

"And God called the dry land Earth; and the gathering together of the waters called he Seas: and God saw that it was good.

"And God said, Let the earth bring forth grass, the herb yielding seed, and the fruit tree yielding fruit after his kind, whose seed is in itself, upon the earth: and it was so.

"And the earth brought forth grass, and herb yielding seed after his kind, and the tree yielding fruit, whose seed was in itself, after his kind: and God saw that it was good."

On the third day God separated the liquids from the solids of the original chaos and then formed them into the first planet, giving it a spherical shape; dividing it into continents, islands, and seas; dotting it with mountains and valleys, lakes and rivers, and covering its nakedness with a blanket of vegetation. Then He hung it in space without beams or cables and set it into a rotating motion, in which it has continued without interruption to this day and will continue until the Creator himself will call a halt.

What a spectacle the events of the third day must have been for the angels when they witnessed the birth of the first planet in the universe, and how they must have shouted for joy when they beheld the cosmic forces that were released when God said, "Let the waters under the heaven be gathered together unto one place, and let the dry land appear" (Gen. 1:9).

In the earthquake of Alaska on Good Friday, March 27, 1964, forces of incalculable magnitude were involved to bring about the widespread destruction in that great catastrophe. In a matter of two minutes the City of Anchorage, with a population of 100,000, and many other inhabited places were converted into heaps of rubble. The very foundation rocks on which the stricken communities were built were torn into great fissures; deep chasms were opened that swallowed up houses. A tidal wave on the Pacific was set in motion, 30 feet high, traveling at the speed of 500 miles an hour, wiping out everything in its path when it reached the mainland 2,000 miles away. And all that came from the forces released in one earthquake, confined to a limited area of one continent. and lasting only a few moments in time.

Now let us consider what incomprehensible forces were in action when the mass of original chaos was formed into a planet and when its liquid contents were separated from the solid, as when we squeeze the water out of a sponge, and all of it compressed into a gigantic ball, just as a baker might form a lump of dough into a loaf of bread. Then imagine what an awe-inspiring sight it must have been when the continents and islands rose from the deep with a mighty splash as if monster whales were coming to the surface, and when simultaneously trillions upon trillions of atoms united each with its own kind to form the rocks, the soil, the minerals of the earth, and when gold became gold and silver, silver, and all the metals and minerals became what they are and each was given its specific place in the mass of matter that was in the process of becoming a planet.

And what a tremor must have vibrated through infinite space when "all the waters under the heaven" were set in motion to gather into one place, rushing with a thunderous roar of thousand times ten thousand Niagaras to the basins provided for them, and then were there shut up as with a door, as Job describes it, chapter 38.

Haydn, in his *Creation Oratorio*, has attempted to portray by means of music and verse the great events that happened on the third day of Creation, when he writes:

Rolling in foaming billows,
Unceasing roar the boisterous seas,
Mountains and rocks now emerging,
Their summits soar above the clouds,
Through plains unmeasured and vast.
Broad rivers, sinuous, wind in flows majestic.
Gently murmuring, gleams and glides
Through peaceful vales the silver brook.

—Third Recitation

And after land and sea had been separated, God formed the dry land into a suitable habitation for man and for all other living creatures by providing it with an atmosphere and with water, without which life is impossible. To change the monotony of sameness, He created kaleidoscopic variations in the scenery by dividing the earth into climatic zones suitable for the character and nature of a variety of forms of life, and beautified its surface with the mountains, valleys and sparkling rivers. He replenished the interior with an abundance of minerals and chemicals of countless varieties for the practical use and enjoyment of man and then covered the sterile surface with a layer of fertile soil to make the life and growth of plants possible. And finally, when all this was done, He wrapped the new, infant planet, born into the infinitude of space, in a beautiful garment of vegetation varying from the lordly palm and towering sequoia to the humble mosses and lichens, and from the food-giving grains and grasses to the delicious and fragrant fruits and flowers, all of them of special design and enriched with beauty of form, taste, color, and aroma.

Compared with other heavenly bodies, the earth is a mere speck in the universe of millions and billions of stars, suns, and planets. The sun alone is a million times larger than the earth, and there are other bodies in the heavens which are even larger than the sun. The earth measures only 25,000 miles in circumference at the equator and 8,000 miles through its diameter. But though small in comparison, it is nonetheless an immense body of solid matter, with an estimated weight of 6,588,000,000,000,000,000,000 tons (World Almanac 1973), hanging in space, and whirling about its own axis at the incredible speed of a thousand miles an hour, thereby dividing time into day and night and providing the world with a clock of absolute precision, requiring no rewinding or regulation; at the same time it travels with all its load of creatures around the sun once a year in an orbit of 580 million miles at the fantastic speed of a thousand miles a minute, faster than any jet plane or man-made missile can fly. And that again it does with absolute regularity, requiring no replenishing of the energy that propels it on its course or recharging of any run-down batteries.

All the world was profoundly impressed by the achievements of our scientists when they succeeded in creating a vehicle in which they were able to conquer outer space and travel around the moon and even land on the moon. But this brilliant achievement was the result of many years of experimentation of many generations of the greatest scientists and required years to build at an astronomical cost, which only the wealthiest nation of the earth could afford. And when it finally was completed and got off the ground, every minute of its flight was carefully guided and supervised by an army of experts on the ground in all parts of the world.

No one outside of a mental hospital or home for the mentally retarded would claim or believe that this magnificent crown of human achievement, with all its complex instruments and mechanisms just happened and developed by itself without a designer or creator, but suddenly was there out of nothing. And yet, this man-made spaceship with all its marvelous scientific equipment is a mere toy compared with the planet spaceship of our earth, consisting of billions and trillions of tons of solid matter, traveling at a speed infinitely greater than that of the capsule which carried our astronauts around the moon, maintaining an absolutely accurate course in time and space and that without guidance or directions from a ground crew below or trained engineers within, and carrying not only three carefully selected and trained astronauts but a cargo of three-and-a-half billion human beings, men, women, and children, and billions and trillions of other forms of life, plus the great oceans, lakes, and rivers of the world with the atmosphere that surrounds it. And this God-created spaceship of our earth has not been traveling for two weeks or two months or two years, but ever since the third day of creation, some 6,000 or possibly 8,000 years ago. There has been no slowing up of its speed, no deviation in its course; it has retained with absolute accuracy the same distance from the sun and the moon and the other heavenly bodies that surround it; there have been no collisions, no refueling, no repairs, and no wearing out of parts.

This is our earth, the planet on which we live, which God set in motion on the third day. What an incomprehensible wonder of God's creative power! Who can fathom, understand, or measure the wisdom and the omnipotent power of our God who called this earth out of nothing into its marvelous existence?

And yet, while the people in all the world went into ecstasy in extolling the achievements of science for creating the little capsule in which men were able to circumnavigate the moon, they completely ignore the infinitely greater works of the Creator and refuse to give honor and glory to Him who made heaven and earth.

But that is the incomprehensible mystery of man's perversion. On the one hand he is so God-like in his creative genius that he is able to imitate the Creator himself, in whose image he was made, and then at the same time he can be so utterly blind and perverse and so stupified by his own conceit and pride that he is unable to see the obvious. And instead of humbly acknowledging his finite limitations and accepting what God himself has revealed concerning the origin of the universe, he will believe and accept as superior wisdom the most irrational and impossible fabrication of the perverted imagination of man.

Then to put, as it were, a premium on such absurd superstition, and give it a national blessing of the corporate wisdom of our country, the august body of the Supreme Court of the United States has solemnly ruled in "its wisdom" that teachers in our public schools must not be prevented from teaching these impossible theories as scientific truth, but that the reading of the Genesis account of creation, the only possible source of such knowledge, is unconstitutional and therefore prohibited. And hence, I say, the paradoxical perversion and blindness in man are a mystery for which there is no ordinary rational or psychological explanation. St. Paul in his first chapter of the Epistle to the Romans gives us the only answer to that mystery when he writes, "Because that, when they knew God, they glorified him not as God, neither were thankful; but became vain in their imaginations, and their foolish heart was darkened. Professing themselves to be wise, they became fools . . . wherefore God also gave them up to uncleanness . . ." (Rom. 1:21, 22, 24).

And again in 1 Timothy 4:1, 2 he writes, "Now the Spirit speaketh expressly, that in the latter times some shall depart from the faith, giving heed to seducing spirits, and doctrines of devils; speaking lies in hypocrisy, having their conscience seared with a hot iron."

And in 2 Thessalonians 2:11 he writes, "And for this cause God shall send them strong delusion, that they should believe a lie: that they all might be damned who believed not the truth, but had pleasure in unrighteousness."

And the lamentation of Jeremiah about his generation still applies today when he writes, "The heart is deceitful above all things, and desperately wicked: who can know it?" (Jer. 17:9)

It is God's judgment upon the unbelief of our generation that people are condemned to believe the lie rather than the truth, and in their blindness even glory in their folly.

To show what absurd theories these "men of science" have proposed in all seriousness, in place of the simple faith which we confess with all Christendom in the words of the Nicene Creed, "I believe in God the Father Almighty, Maker of heaven and earth and of all things visible and invisible," I shall add here a few quotations from their writings and let them say in their own words what irrational and unscientific substitutes they offer as a superior wisdom to the Genesis creation account.

I have before me two books dealing in part with the subject before us. The first is Volume II of *The World's Essential Knowledge* with a subtitle "Outline of Science," published by Funk & Wagnalls, New York. Note the words "Essential Knowledge" and "Outline of Science." Chapter III, on page 46, has this heading, "The Sun's Children Are Born." Then follows a description as to how the sun's children were born and is there presented as "essential knowledge." The author begins with the following three questions: Where did the earth come from? What was its origin? How long is it likely to be here?

These are all natural and legitimate questions for any normal human being to ask. The history of the human race shows that men in all ages and on all levels of culture have searched for an answer to these or similar questions. And, of course, there is only one reliable source for an answer and that is the revelation of the Creator himself because He alone was present when this happened. But the author of this "scientific" treatise simply ignores Genesis. He does not even mention it and does not even refer to it as a possible theory, though it had been accepted by millions and millions of people in all ages from the beginning of time. But instead he offers the wild and fuzzy speculation of man as "essential knowledge" in an "Outline of Science."

He admits, however, that in the past there have been many theories about the origin of the universe which were extremely fantastic and imaginative and had to be discarded, but then continues, "As science advanced, new *theories* were proposed." And he evidently regards these new theories as less fantastic because they are the result of a more "advanced science."

He proceeds to enumerate some of these theories, first mentioning the planetary ring hypothesis, which may also be called the Laplace theory, next, the star collision theory, then the nebular hypothesis theory, and finally the planetesimal theory advanced by the late Professor Chamberlin, who for many years was head of the Geology Department of Chicago University.

The author admits that most of the theories mentioned had to be discarded because they were proven inadequate, but he believes that the planetesimal theory of Professor Chamberlin has sufficiently wide acceptance to justify its appearance here. This means in plain language that the scientific truth concerning the mystery of the universe can be established by a sufficiently wide acceptance or by a majority rule of scientific theorists. And this, you must remember, is said in an "Outline of Science" in a book, *The World's Knowledge, Vol II.* He then proceeds to explain the planetesimal theory and says, "According to this theory, the planets are the offspring of the sun, the other parent having been a star which through 'chance' came into the gravitational field of the sun and which is now in all likelihood cold and exists only among the star wreckage. The parent star did not form the planets by directly hitting the sun, but being near the sun it had the effect of drawing out from the molten surface in cone-like protuberances that material which was to form the planet. The actual birth of the planet was due to the propulsive power of the sun, through eruption, light push, radiation, magnetism, and electrical discharges, forces almost equalling the gravitational attraction and the combined repelling and attraction of the other stars."

To the naive, the gullible, and those who are intrigued by the fanciful and the grotesque, all this might sound impressive and profound, just as the fables of Aesop and the fantastic exploits of Baron von Muenchausen arouse wonderment in the minds of children living in a world of make-believe and delighting in flights of fancy in their daydreams. But these ideas are proposed by men with an impressive reputation in the field of science and are accepted as truth and promulgated by the half-educated as absolute truth.

But note first that the author states quite frankly that many theories have been proposed as answers to the question which later had to be discarded because they proved untenable. And yet, while each of these theories was the current scientific answer to the mystery of the origin of all things, it was accepted as truth and as an absolute refutation of the Genesis account of creation. But a truth limited by time, only to be replaced by another, is not truth but a deception and a fraud.

In the second place, note that all of these theories really begged the basic question. They assume matter in the sun and the stars but do not account for its origin. They postulate some very mysterious forces already existing, such as gravitation, light, magnetism, electrical energy, the existence of the sun and stars, etc. They do not explain why our planet took on the spherical shape, whence came the mathematical balance of the gases that constitute the atmosphere which surrounds the earth and why these conditions are not found on the other planets. Nor do they account for the wonder of the rotating motion of the earth around its own axis and its fantastic flight around the sun. They do not explain the mystery of life and how it started on earth and why it is not found on the moon and the other planets. And so we could go on, asking a thousand questions for which none of these theories offers a rational answer. And yet this book boldly calls itself *A Source of Essential Knowledge*!

The second book before me is called "A Textbook for Geology." Its title is *Down to Earth*. It has two authors: Carey Croneis and William C. Krumbein, both from the Department of Geology of Chicago University. In many respects this is an excellent textbook for an introductory course in geology.

Chapter 31, page 275 ff., is devoted to a discussion of the subject before us. Under the title "Earth's Birth," the authors review the various theories that have been proposed, just as the previous author, but in somewhat greater detail. They accept the planetesimal theory of Chamberlin as the most plausible solution, but admit that other prominent geologists like Joseph Barrell of Yale and Sir James Jeans and Harold Jeffreys of Britain have proposed some major modification.

Then they continue:

> No matter how the earth originated, it *seems probable* that either it was once much smaller than at present and its principal growth was accomplished as a solid planet whose size was not so very different from the present dimensions. If our planet actually originated after the fashion postulated by the planetesimal hypothesis, the original earth's nucleus was relatively small in comparison to its present mass. In the very early stage, the nucleus mass may have been either molten or gaseous, but in any case it is considered to have cooled to a solid body, probably before there was a great deal of accretionary

growth. According to Chamberlin, general conditions favored an early accumulation of the heaviest planetesimals and thus the core came to have the present great weight and density. (p. 283)

And then, in attempting to account for the origin of the atmosphere, they continue:

> During the early period of the earth's growth the nucleus probably was too small to hold an atmosphere, but since it had grown to a diameter of something in excess of 2,000 miles, it began to retain a few gas molecules and as the planet grew in size, through the accretion of planetesimals from without, the capacity for holding an atmosphere also increased. Some of the gases of the emerging atmosphere were obtained through collision and disruption of large gas-containing planetesimals, also from early volcanism.

But they admit that it is a debatable question whether free oxygen existed from the early stages of the atmosphere. And they say that some scientists *feel* that primitive plant life originated before the earth achieved its present size and that these early plants then contributed to the oxygen in the atmosphere.

> And as the early atmosphere increased in size with the growing of the planet itself and through the increase of volcanism, it finally became able to hold water vapors. Finally, when locally the saturation point was reached, came that dramatic moment when water first fell to the earth as rain. The first of this early downpour evaporated very rapidly so that there was no great accumulation of water. But soon, the natural depressions began to have permanent pools, and the early work of running water had its crude and effectual beginning. Some sediments that the water carried, as well as the windborn sorts, began to accumulate. And as the hydrosphere increased in size, conditions became possible for the origin of life in spite of the fact that our planet was not yet full grown. (p. 285)

All this sounds like a newspaper account, reported by some prehistoric reporter, describing dramatically what he was witnessing from some favorite vantage point outside of the universe. To the naive and the unthinking, this may sound profound and much more impressive than the simple Genesis account. But whatever we may want to call it, whether poetry, myth, or sheer nonsense, it most certainly is not science, and there is not a thread of scientific truth in it. It conveniently avoids all the real difficulties involved in an honest discussion of the origin of our universe and blandly ignores the real basic questions. It presupposes the existence of matter in various forms, but does not explain where it came from. It speaks of the existence of gas, oxygen, vapors and water, heat and volcanism, rain and the atmosphere, wind and wind-born matters. It assumes the origin of plant life and its effect on the atmosphere, but says nothing about the origin of all of these things nor about the origin of the marvelous laws that govern them. All of the factors and forces mentioned are mysteries beyond comprehension, and to ignore them and naively assume that somehow they were there as ready building blocks from nothing, to create them into something, is not profound nor scientific, but a new kind of mythology.

Anybody is, of course, free to spin out of his own imagination whatever theory may appeal to him, reasonable or otherwise, about the mysteries for which neither science nor experience has a solution. But he must not call such theories science and expect people to accept them as truth.

We admire the genius of Dante for his imaginative description of the Inferno and his lurid picture of the condition of the damned in the place of torment, but no one would quote Dante to prove that there is a hell.

The fact that these cosmological speculations are proposed by scientists, even great scientists, does not make them science. They are nothing more than pure speculation and belong in the same category with astrology and the Delphic oracle.

And yet, strange to say, the great majority of people in our generation, including the wise and the learned, prefer to accept these absurd speculations rather than the sane creation account of Genesis. Genesis is an account of creation that is sane and reasonable because it begins with the first cause, as all logical thinking demands. That first cause is the Eternal God as we confess in the historic creeds with all of Christendom. We need not go to the Scriptures to prove the existence of God. His existence is demonstrated by the wonderful works of the creation, as St. Paul says in Romans 1:19, 20, so that all are without excuse.

Even when viewing the origin of the universe from a purely rational point of view, the Biblical account of creation is more reasonable and also more honest than the theories propounded by the evolutionists. It is more reasonable because, as stated, human reason requires a cause for an effect. No one can think of this universe coming into being without an author or a creator.

Reason and experience require this. We accept God as this first cause and as the Creator of heaven and earth. Belief in God is not a superstition but is universal. No nation or race of people has ever been found that did not have some form of belief in a god or gods. The natural knowledge of God is written in the hearts of all men. There are no real atheists. The wonders of creation and the infinite order in the universe and the laws by which it is sustained presuppose an infinite intelligence. The wonders of heaven and earth and the laws that govern them must have had a cause and an intelligent cause.

Also, belief in the creation by an omnipotent God is more honest. We believe that God created heaven and earth in the beginning of time, as revealed in Genesis 1 and 2. We accept these facts by faith. No man can know this in any other way. The evolutionists also accept their theories by faith because they cannot prove them by scientific demonstration. They are, therefore, dishonest when they call their theory "science." Theirs is also a belief or a faith. Our faith is based on the revelation of God as revealed in the Bible, which has proved its authenticity over and over again and was accepted in all its details by Christ himself. Their belief is based on the fantastic speculations of man which have not been demonstrated as truth and have no scientific foundation.

It is difficult to understand why so many otherwise intelligent and reasonable people can be so blind to simple and self-evident truths and even consider themselves of a superior intelligence by accepting the absurd.

The basic reason for this mystery of unbelief, of course, is the perverted heart of sinful man, as described by Jeremiah (Jer. 17:9). But the immediate reason for this attitude in different individuals may differ because of personality, character, and basic philosophy of life. In the case of the great masses of shallow-minded individuals, educated or illiterate, the chief reason seems to be sheer mental lethargy and a desire to be on the bandwagon with the crowd. Many of those who are most emphatic in their rejection of the Biblical creation account have not the faintest idea of the difficulties involved in the evolutionary theory they have accepted in its place. They are anxious to be with the crowd. Everybody shouts, "Great is Diana of the Ephesians" (Acts 19:34), and so they join the shouting crowd. It requires character and courage to swim against the stream and to be numbered with the minority, especially when that minority is branded with such labels as:

unscholarliness, unscientific, unprogressive, obscurantism or fundamentalism, etc. Labels like these alone are sufficient to cause many to wilt into abject submission, abdicating reason in order to follow the crowd.

But a more serious motive for the anti-Biblical attitude of many is the conscious or unconscious desire to get rid of God and thereby remove all accountability for what they believe, do, or do not do.

The idea of an omnipotent Creator of heaven and earth, to whom all men are responsible, is a disturbing thought to many, and so they try to get rid of Him by removing Him out of the universe from the very beginning. If this universe came into being without a divine Creator, and if it has been maintained by its own power and without any supernatural, outside assistance, then God is out, or at least has become completely irrelevant, and man needs no longer to worry about his responsibility towards Him.

This idea is not a discovery of the modern scientific man or the wise ones of our present enlightened age, but a mere revival of the ancient philosophy of Epicurianism. Epicurus, after whom this philosophy is called, was a Greek philosopher in Athens in the third century B.C. His philosophy may be characterized as enlightened self-interest. It is purely humanistic and completely godless. Pleasure is the highest good in life and is to be sought after, while pain is the greatest evil to be avoided. His slogan was, "Let us eat and drink; for tomorrow we die" (1 Cor. 15:32). Epicurus insisted that the chief reason for man's mental pain and unhappiness is the fear of god or of gods, and so genuine happiness requires one to eliminate the gods from human life by first eliminating the gods from the universe. His theory of the origin of the universe was in all essentials identical with the theories of modern evolutionists. Epicureans held that matter is eternal and the objects, as they now appear in the visible world, are the result of "fortuitous coming together of the atoms." These continue in that particular form for a while, then are dissolved to reunite again to appear in new forms of existence, and so this process continues "ad infinitum."

Epicurus also maintained that if gods do actually exist, they are so far removed from the mundane world of man that they are completely unconcerned about what he does here on earth, and so it is foolish on the part of man to worry about the gods and be frightened by the thought of them.

To anyone who knows the world today, it is evident that

this is the philosophy of the majority of men in the Western World in our age. The teachers of evolution removed God from the universe; they next abolished all absolutes and held that God had become altogether irrelevant in this advanced scientific age. As a result man has become his own god. He answers his own prayers. Man has become the measure of all things. Science has become the religion of men today. The scientists are the high priests and prophets.

But it is the ultimate in man's arrogance and stupidity to imagine that he can depose God. "He that sitteth in the heavens shall laugh: the Lord shall have them in derision. Then shall he speak unto them in his wrath, and vex them in his sore displeasure" (Ps. 2:4, 5).

And, "The fool hath said in his heart, There is no God. They are corrupt, they have done abominable works" (Ps. 14:1).

Some day all men, whether they believe in an existence of God or not, "must all appear before the judgment seat of Christ; that every one may receive the things done in his body, according to that he hath done, whether it be good or bad" (2 Cor. 5:10).

Other people are sometimes motivated in their unbelief either by pride or by naïvete or by both. They believe that great learning makes a simple faith in Biblical revelation impossible.

But such thinking is a camouflage of the devil and another device of Satan to delude men by appealing to their pride and their superior knowledge. The honest scientist and scholar knows that all human knowledge, including his own, is fragmentary and imperfect and the greatest among them will agree with the great Goethe, who lamented: "Das will mir gar das Herz zerreisen das man so wenig wissen kann." [1] Neither superior knowledge nor science is in conflict with revelation. In fact, revelation supplies what man cannot know by observation or experimentation, as the famous medieval philosopher and theologian, Thomas Aquinas, says:

> There is a point, however high it may be, beyond which the reason must confess its inability to understand; but it is just at this point that faith comes to the rescue of reason; the mind in matters of faith, gives its assent to truth upon the authority of God, manifested through revelation. And thus man completes the edifice of his knowledge with the

[1] Even the great Goethe confessed that it caused him great agony of the soul that his knowledge was so fragmentary.

structure of superhuman truth. The realm of faith, then, is not to be conceived in opposition to the realm of natural truth, but as a continuation, for in both reigns supreme the same Divine Intelligence.[2]

This delusion about great learning being in conflict with faith is the result of a complete misunderstanding of faith and of conviction. Faith and conviction are not matters of the intellect at all. If it were so, why is unbelief so common among the ignorant and the uneducated and so widely spread as among the learned people? Most people who reject Genesis and accept the evolutionary theory do so, not because they are intelligent or because they understand what they believe; much less are they able to explain what they have accepted as superior truth. They reject Genesis and accept the evolutionary theories because they want to believe them. Faith is not a matter of learning and enlightenment; faith is a matter of the will. People believe what they want to believe.

The Pharisees and Sadducees at the time of Christ witnessed His works and could not deny them. They saw His perfect, sinless life and could not refute His teaching, but they did not believe in Him because they did not want to. Jesus wept over their unbelief and said, "How often would I have gathered thy children together, as a hen gathers her brood under her wings, but ye *would not*!" (Luke 13:34). They willed not to accept Jesus as their Messiah.

The intellect and the emotions contribute to the total content of the mind, but it is the will that determines the course of action an individual takes. It is the will that makes the decision in forming man's attitude and determines his whole behavior. And the will always is the result of and in complete harmony with the totality of man's personality and character. Man decides, acts, and believes or disbelieves as he is. It is the nature of a tree that determines the kind of fruit it produces. And so it is the nature of man that determines his behavior. The fact that man prefers to believe a lie rather than the truth is the tragic effect of the deep corruption of human nature cursed by sin. It is sin that has darkened his intellect so that he prefers the lie to the truth and even considers himself, because of that, as having superior wisdom.

---

[2] Thomas Aquinas, *Marique History of Education*, pp. 168-69.

8.

The Creation of the Seas

And now let us next turn our attention to the seas of the earth, the great gatherings of water which also came into existence as a part of God's creative work on the third day, for we read:

> And God said, Let the waters under the heaven be gathered together unto one place . . . and the gathering together of waters called he Seas: and God saw that it was good.
>
> Genesis 1:9,10

Water, as we have seen, is a part of matter created on the first day. Like all matter, water, too, is a mystery that defies explanation. And this mystery becomes even more mysterious when considering water in the aggregate as now collected in the great seas.

The sea, which constitutes so large a part of our world of wonders, is itself a world of incomprehensible wonders, but is still very largely unexplored. We know something of its surface characteristics, but the great deep is still shrouded in complete darkness and probably always will remain the great unknown. Man has always been fascinated by the mysteries of the sea. Its immensity has filled him with awe and fear and has symbolized for him the incomprehensible, unlimited eternity. The mysterious unknown beyond its horizon has beckoned to him to venture out and explore the beyond. Its roaring billows and untamed forces have frightened him. When John the Evangelist described the New Jerusalem in his Book of Revelation he says, "And there was no sea there." The horrors of the sea would be incompatible with the new heaven and the new earth.

And when the Psalmist contemplated the wonders of God's creation, he included the sea and wrote, "O Lord, how manifold are thy works! in wisdom hast thou made them all: the earth is full of thy riches. So is this great and wide sea, wherein are things creeping innumerable, both small and great beasts. There go the ships: there is that leviathan, whom thou hast made to play therein" (Ps. 104:24-26).

And wise King Solomon, impressed with the wonders of the sea, wrote: "All the rivers run into the sea; yet the sea is not full; unto the place from whence the rivers come, thither they return again" (Eccles. 1:7).

The sea is a supreme wonder and at the same time a mysterious paradox. It fascinates man with its grandeur and beauty and at the same time fills him with terror. It is a barrier between lands and nations and yet provides a highway to unite mankind. It is a source of life but also a frightful force of destruction. It affects the atmosphere, climate, and weather in all the world and makes life possible on the dry land. The seas on our earth make this planet unique among the heavenly bodies. No other planet has a sea on it and, therefore, no life. But God created the earth as the habitation for man and for other living creatures to serve man. And so He divided this planet into land and sea. In fact, the greater part of our earth is covered by the sea.

The total area of our planet is 197 million square miles. Of this total area, 139 million square miles are sea and only 58 million square miles are land. Or to say it in other words, about three-fourths of the surface of the earth is water and only one-fourth is land, much of which is uninhabitable wasteland. There is enough water in the seas to cover the entire face of the earth with a mile and a half of water if all the mountains of the sea and the land and the plateaus were planed down and all valleys filled up to the same level.

Geologists have found evidence that the relation of land and sea on the earth has not always been the same as it is now. They believe that somewhere in the past history of the world the water level evidently was raised while large areas of the original continents were submerged and became a part of the sea. The so-called continental shelves off the coast of some of the continents seem to be conclusive evidence for this. In North America, for example, this continental shelf extends out into the Atlantic for about 100 miles, and even the submerged channel of the Hudson River on it can still be traced. The same is true of the Congo Canyon, off the coast of Africa. The most extensive shelf is found off the southern coast of Asia, which covers an area of approximately 1,000,000 square miles. A similar submerged land mass is found in the Far North, in the Arctic.

There are also reasons for assuming that originally all the continents of the earth were connected and that the large bodies of water now separating land masses from each other did not exist, or at least not in their present proportion. It is quite certain that North America and Europe were at one time connected via Greenland and Scandinavia. Asia and America were also united in the Far North by a land bridge, the present Bering Straits. Eastern Asia probably extended southward to include the East Indies and New Guinea and possibly even Australia and New Zealand. Evidence has also been found that the mythical continent of Atlantis described by Plato was not mythical at all, but actually existed between North Africa and America; but for some reason it has completely disappeared.

There is also evidence that the North Sea did not always fill the present basin where it now exists, but it, together with the British Isles and the Scandinavian countries, constituted a part of the European mainland. Nor did the present Baltic Sea occupy all of its present basin. The same is true of the Mediterranean. It is evident that Europe and Africa, at one time, were also connected by a land bridge.

Geologists offer a variety of explanations for these changes, but all of their theories require eons of time and this requirement alone rules them out as an acceptable solution. The most reasonable explanation can be found in the Biblical Flood. That event was so cosmic in proportion and so revolutionary in its effect that the world after the Flood was not the same as it had been before.

In Genesis 1:7, we are told that God created the firmament and "divided the waters which were under the firmament from the waters which were above the firmament." This was the creation of the atmosphere, as has been pointed out before.

The statement that the water of original chaos was divided so that part of it remained here on earth and part of it was absorbed by the atmosphere, would seem to warrant the conclusion that the original atmosphere had a much higher water content than it now has. Further evidence for that assumption seems to be the uniform, spring-like climate that existed in all parts of the world before the Flood. That such a uniform, mild climate did exist from pole to pole is established beyond doubt by the many and various fossils that have been found in all parts of the world, including the extreme polar region. We may conclude from Genesis 1:7 that the original atmosphere formed a sort of canopy surrounding the earth, and because of its high water content absorbed and retained a great amount of the heat of the sun. In that way it defused its heat equally to all parts of the earth and thus gave it a climate such as is described in Genesis 2:5,6. In the flood, these conditions were changed. In Genesis 7:11 we read that part of the enormous quantities of the flood water which engulfed the earth came from the "windows of heaven," that is, from the atmosphere. And when the flood waters subsided, not all of the waters that had come from the "windows of heaven" returned there, but remained below the firmament, and as a result, the original balance between land and sea was altered and large areas of the former continents were submerged and became parts of the sea.

To that must be added the fact that the Flood must have been accompanied by great cosmic revolutions caused by world-wide earthquakes, volcanic activity, and diastrophic movements of the earth. It is evident that the whole surface of our planet was radically changed as a result of this great world catastrophe, including the changes referred to.

Until fairly modern times, very little was known about the lower levels of the sea or the condition of the ocean floor. The enormous depth of the ocean and the tremendous pressure of the weight of its water made exploration of these regions impossible. But since the invention of instruments by which man can now measure even the deepest depressions in the sea, we have learned a great deal about the mystery of these lower regions and about the general condition of the ocean floor.

One of the things discovered was that the topography of the bottom of the sea is as varied in its general contours and as rugged, or even more so, as the topography of the different continents of our earth. There are mountain ranges, volcanoes, plateaus, valleys and deep canyons in the bottom of the seas. The deepest depressions in the seas were found to be deeper in comparison than the highest mountains on the continents.

The longest and highest mountain ranges on our planet are not on land, but in the sea. A mountain range was discovered in the mid-Atlantic, extending from Iceland in the north to the Antarctic in the south, about 10,000 miles long and 500 miles wide, with peaks higher than most mountains on land, reaching an altitude of 27,613 feet at the Azores, of which 20,000 feet were below the water level.

Similar mountain ranges, not quite as long, are found in the Pacific and in the Indian Ocean. The highest peak of the mountain range in the Pacific, 1600 miles long, forms the Hawaiian Islands, which are of volcanic origin. The highest peak of these Pacific mountains reaches an altitude of 31,000 feet compared with Pike's Peak in Colorado with 14,147 feet; Mount Rainier in Washington with 14,363 feet; Mount McKinley in Alaska, 20,314 feet; and Mount Everest in the Himalayas, 29,028 feet, the highest mountain on the continent.

The deepest depressions were found in the Philippine Trench, off the Philippine Islands, and in the Mariana Trench, off the coast of Japan. The greatest depth in the Philippine Trench was found to be 34,578 feet; and in the Mariana Trench, 35,640 feet. The average depth of the Pacific is 14,648 feet; of the Atlantic, 12,880 feet; of the Indian Ocean, 13,602 feet; and of the Arctic, 3,965 feet. The average temperature of the surface water in the polar region is 28 degrees Fahrenheit while it is 90 degrees in the Persian Gulf.

The sea is the habitat for countless forms and varieties of creatures, both of the plant and animal kingdom. In fact, it is claimed that the number and kinds of living organisms are far greater in the sea than on land. However, we will speak of this in greater detail later.

But there are other remarkable features about the sea which must be mentioned here. First among them is the mineral content of the seawater. Water is of the greatest importance for the maintenance of life here on earth, but seawater in its natural form is unusable for man and beast and is not even fit for irrigation purposes to maintain plant life. The average mineral content of the seawater is about 3%, but it is not the same in all seas or in all parts of the sea. For example, it is very high in the Red Sea, but in the Baltic it is low. It is highest in the inland lakes like the Dead Sea in Palestine or Salt Lake in Utah. Three-fourths of the mineral content in the seas consists of common salt. Other minerals are magnesium chloride, magnesium sulphate, calcium sulphate, potasium, and others in smaller quantities. It has been estimated that the mineral content of the oceans of the world would be sufficient, if extracted, to cover all the land masses of the earth with 120 feet of solid minerals.

For anyone who contemplates this strange phenomenon, the questions must arise, "Why is this so? Where do these minerals come from? How are they forever held in suspension and how were they so widely defused in this enormous volume of water? Was the sea created with saline water from the beginning or was this also the result of the Flood?" The answer commonly given by the geologists is that the minerals originally came from the earth and were carried into the sea by the rivers. But when one considers the immensity of the sea and the enormous quantity of minerals found in the ocean, this answer is not adequate to account for this mystery.

Another remarkable phenomenon of the sea is the tides—that is, the rhythmic rising and falling of the water with absolute daily regularity.

The ancients had observed this phenomenon, but of course had no explanation for it. The superstitious among them ascribed it to the breathing of some mysterious sea monster.

Herodotus, the Greek historian of the 5th century B.C., was the first to write about the tides. But it was not until Sir Isaac Newton discovered the laws of gravity that there was any scientific explanation for this mystery. As a result of this discovery, it was found that the gravitational pull of the moon and, to a lesser extent, of the sun, was responsible for this phenomenon. The moon is closer to the earth than the sun and therefore exerts a greater influence on the sea. And so it is chiefly the relation of the moon to the earth that accounts for the tides. And here again, as elsewhere, we notice a definite interacting relation between the various bodies in the universe and definitely fixed laws governing that relationship, thereby revealing the design and plan of a master builder. The distance between the earth and the moon is exactly in proper balance to account for the clock-like rhythm of the tides. If the distance were greater there would be no movement of the ocean waters. If it were closer, the tides would rise to such a height that the greater part of all the continents would become completely submerged at regular intervals, thus making life in any form on earth impossible.

There are other peculiarities about the tides which are not so easily explained. For example, it has been found that the tides are very sensitive to the changing phases of the moon.

On the Atlantic Coast of North America, for instance, the tides rise higher when the moon is full or in the new-moon phase than when in the first or third quarter. And there is also a difference with respect to the height to which tides rise in different parts of the sea. At Nantucket, for example, the tides rise only about one foot, while in the Bay of Fundy in Nova Scotia, they roll in to a height of 40 feet.

But while the gravitational pull of the heavenly bodies on the sea offers an acceptable explanation for the phenomenon of tides, it does not explain the real mystery involved here. This explanation is based on gravity and takes the laws of gravity for granted, but it does not explain the mystery of gravity itself. What is gravity? Where does it come from? What is the nature of its force? Why does one body of matter attract another body? And whence are the laws that regulate this force with such mathematical precision? In short, the sea is full of unsolved wonders. Our knowledge of the universe and even of our own planet is still very fragmentary and ought, therefore, to keep us quite humble.

Another very remarkable phenomenon of the sea is the ocean currents or rivers of water flowing within walls of water. This is another mystery that no theory of evolution can explain.

Just as the ocean of air which surrounds our earth in the form of an atmosphere is in constant motion, caused either by regular air currents moving out from the equator in permanently fixed directions or by winds, tornadoes and blizzards sweeping over the earth, just so it is with the ocean of water that covers so much of our planet. It, too, is not static as it may appear but is in constant motion and change. These changes are brought about, in part, by tides and by waves stirred up by winds and storms but especially by the great rivers of water flowing within walls of water in the sea from the equator to the poles and from the poles to the equator and other streams criss-crossing at different levels in every direction. There is nothing static or dead in the universe. All its countless elements and parts are united in one great cosmic system operating together in a perfect order, like the separate sections of a great industrial assembly line. The ocean currents are a mysterious part of this Creator's assembly line.

The best known of these ocean currents in the Northern Hemisphere are the Gulf Stream in the Atlantic and the Japanese Current in the Pacific.

The Gulf Stream, deriving its name from the Gulf of Mexico from which it emerges, is the largest river in the world. It is about 1500 feet deep, 50 miles wide, and over 4,000 miles long. It is larger than either the Mississippi or the Amazon. It is a river of warm water flowing within banks of cold water northward as far as Iceland, then turning eastward toward the continent of Europe and merging with another stream moving southward to the Bay of Biscay. It is this river of warm water that is responsible for the moderate and pleasant climate of northern Europe and of Iceland. If it were not for the Gulf Stream, the British Islands would be as sterile as Labrador, and Scandinavia would be as uninhabitable as Greenland.

This is another wonderful phenomenon of nature we take for granted but cannot explain.

We can understand the rivers on the land areas of the continents. They are caused by the runoff from the rain and snow that falls on the land, which then collects in the lower region of the land and moves there by the force of gravity. But what gives rise to the rivers of water in the water of the sea, where there is no runoff, where there are no hills and valleys to provide the force of gravity to cause it to move and cause it to flow in a fixed direction? Why doesn't the water of these ocean rivers merge with the water that surrounds them? How were these watery banks established in the first place? What causes these rivers to maintain a definite course? What force has established them? How is it possible for the Gulf Stream to maintain its warm temperature when flowing through thousands of miles of cold, and even in part through icy waters of the northern Atlantic? And how is it possible for the stream to exert such a remarkable influence on the climate of the northern and subarctic regions of our world?

I had an opportunity to observe this remarkable influence of the Gulf Stream on climate and weather when visiting Iceland and Greenland in the summer of 1969.

Iceland is located on the very edge of the Arctic Circle and far north of Hudson Bay, Hudson's Strait, and Baffinland in northern Canada, regions which are icebound for about nine months of the year. And naturally, I expected to find similar conditions here in a latitude even farther north than the Canadian regions, especially when looking across the sea to its nearest neighbor on the west, the glacier-covered subcontinent of Greenland. But I was most agreeably surprised at what I found. Iceland is far from being icebound and its name is a gross misnomer. Iceland has a very moderate and pleasant climate, similar to that of northern Europe, and the reason for this is the miracle of the Gulf Stream, which nearly surrounds it. The winters in this Arctic region are not colder than the winters in St. Louis or not even as cold, and the occasional snowfall in Reykjavik remains only for a very short time, while the summers are most delightful and pleasant.

There are other ocean currents in the Atlantic besides the Gulf Stream that are not so well known. In 1966 it was reported that Russian oceanographers had discovered an ocean current at a depth of about 9,000 feet below the Gulf Stream, flowing in the opposite direction at a rate of 8 miles a day. A similar ocean river was discovered under the Pacific Equatorial Current flowing in an easterly direction at a rate of 2 1/2 miles a day; under this current there was another current, again flowing in the opposite direction.

The Japanese Stream in the Pacific has a similar effect on the climate of southern Alaska and British Columbia as the Gulf Stream has on Iceland and northern Europe. Vancouver, for example, is in about the same latitude as Winnipeg in Manitoba, and while Winnipeg is known for its extremely cold winter, Vancouver and all of British Columbia enjoy a most delightful moderate climate, making it the California of Canada, so that fruit-growing in that province has become one of the important industries. The strange phenomenon of the warm chinook winds in southern Alberta and Montana also has its origin in the warm Japanese current of the Pacific.

And so, when considering this most remarkable phenomenon of the ocean currents, we should ask all those who refuse to believe in an omnipotent Creator to explain this wonder and give proof how these currents got started and how the laws came into being by which they are maintained and regulated.

There are still other wonders of the sea which are not yet understood or of which we have only a very fragmentary knowledge. The greatest unknown of our planet is still the sea, and this unknown ought to be the greatest challenge to the best minds among our scientists. God must have had a purpose when He created so much water. And no doubt there are still great treasures hidden in the sea which were intended for the benefit of man.

We are traveling in the wrong direction when we try to invade the moon and other heavenly bodies. God gave man dominion over this planet, which was created as a habitation for man. The moon or the other heavenly bodies were not intended for that purpose. Our problems are here on earth and not on the moon. These problems are increasing at a frightening rate, caused by the spectacular growth of population and by the senseless waste and destruction by man himself of the natural resources given to us.

We shall return to the sea and its wonders when we come to examine the works of God on the fifth day of creation. But these wonders already referred to are some of the wonders we ought to think of when we chant the words of our Sunday litany:

> For the Lord our God is a great God,
> And a great King above all gods . . .
> The sea is his and he made it:
> And his hands formed the dry land.
> Oh come, let us worship and bow down:
> Let us kneel before the Lord our maker.
> For he is our God;
> And we are the people of his pasture,
> And the sheep of his hand.
>
> (Ps. 95:3-7)

9.

The Creation of Plants and The Beginning of Life on Earth

Genesis describes the works of creation on the third day in three stages:

1. Separation of the liquid from the solid matter in original chaos.

2. The creation of the seas and the formation of the continents.

3. The covering of the dry land with a blanket of varied and luxuriant vegetation.

With the appearance of plants on earth, creation had moved a major step upward in the creation ladder. Something new and completely distinct from matter had come into existence, namely, the wonders of life.

Life is the mystery of mysteries. Its essence is incomprehensible and undefinable. It can be observed and explained only in its manifestations. And yet, our natural curiosity will prompt us again and again to ask, "What is life? What is its essence? Where is it located in the material body where it appears? Is science capable of reproducing life apart from the plant and animal forms in which it now exists?" The answers to all of these questions have remained a perplexing blank. With all of man's efforts and experimentations, no answer to this riddle has been found. The dictionary defines life as: "The state of being alive, that condition in which plants and animals exist, with capability of exercising their normal functions." A glance at this definition will show that it really is no definition at all but merely calls attention to some of the manifestations of life.

Life is a spark of some mysterious power, wrapped in some specific material form or body. It animates that body and makes it a living organism, functioning in and through this body, but remaining distinct from it. It is not possible to see or observe this spark of life, not even with a high-powered microscope, nor can it be isolated by chemical analysis. It can be destroyed with its material body, but when destroyed its body decays and returns to the original chemical substance from which it had been formed.

In some respects life can be compared with electricity. Electricity also is a mysterious force whose manifestation we are able to observe and experience, as in the light bulb or in the form of a shock which we might receive, but no one really knows what electricity is. We can produce it by different devices but its essence remains a mystery. And so it is with life. Life can never come from lifeless matter. That fact has been established over and over again. Only a living organism can reproduce a living thing. Only God, the source of all life, could have been the creator of life.

The current attempts of scientists to create life in a test tube have been heralded by *Popular Science* writers as a great achievement and as a possible key to the mystery of life. But what these experiments have achieved is only a peculiar reaction of certain chemicals in a given combination which seemed to behave as life, but are not actual life and lack the essential elements of life. It is a biological axiom that life cannot come by itself from chemical substances. No combination of inorganic chemicals can result in actual life.

Some of the basic elements of life that cannot be reproduced in a test tube are:

1. The mysterious power of reproduction of its own kind.
2. The mystery of growth.
3. The power to change inorganic matter into organic.
4. The infinite varieties and kinds and forms in which life appears.

Power of Reproduction

Life has within it the mysterious power of reproducing itself. It has this power in all its forms, but can only reproduce itself in the form in which it appears. It exists in an infinite number and a variety of kinds, but none ever crosses over to the other, i.e., a specific kind never gets mixed up or confused with another. Wheat will only produce more wheat, never corn. An oak will produce more oaks, never a pine.

The means by which life perpetuates itself is the seed. Every organism produces within itself seed and every seed contains within itself a variety of complex, submicroscopic elements we call genes, by which specific characteristics of the parent organisms are perpetuated. And such fertile seeds are produced only by the union of a male and female element in the parent organism which adds a further perplexing mystery to the wonders of the seed.

When we examine a seed, such as a grain of wheat, a kernel of corn or a poppy seed, we see and feel nothing but what appears to be dead matter. And when we analyze that seed in a chemical laboratory, we find nothing but a number of chemical substances in a carefully balanced combination which is not identical in the different seeds. Some contain important food elements for man and animals; others have a high content of fats and oils, and still others may contain medicinal or even poisonous substances for man. Some seeds are large, like the coconut; others are nearly microscopic, like the poppy. Seeds can be stored for a long period of time and nothing happens. In desert or near desert areas such as the extensive regions in central and northern parts of Australia, seeds might lie dormant for years for lack of moisture. But when an unexpected rain occurs, these dormant seeds suddenly come to life and the barren desert blossoms like a garden. It is claimed that wheat found in Egyptian tombs where it had been lying dormant for thousands of years, still germinated when exposed to sunlight and moisture. Seeds can be exposed to extreme heat or severe frost in winter and they remain unaffected by either.

A bin full of wheat and a pile of sand look very much alike. Both seem to be a mere accumulation of dead matter. But take that apparent dead matter from the wheat bin and place it into the body of mother earth and let heaven baptize it with its life-giving rain and the rays of sun warm its little body—then a miracle happens. Suddenly this bit of lifeless matter becomes very much alive. Some mysterious force begins to stir within it. A tiny sprout is pushed out of its little body to form what we call a root. This is followed by another and then by another. The first roots turn downward, anchoring the seed securely to the ground from which it sprang. Other roots follow and spread out in a network of roots to gather nourishment for the plant from its environment. Every one of these roots is a system of microscopic cells arranged in a very specific order and cooperating in a unified system like the organs in the human body for its growth and development. And while the first roots turn downward and spread out in the soil to gather food for the emerging plant, others soon follow, but this time turn upward to form a plant, breaking through the crust of the earth like a little chick breaking the shell of the egg in which it had developed.

"How can this happen?" every thoughtful person must ask when observing this mysterious process. How does that first undifferentiated cell, at the start of life, select its set of instructions to create, step by step, a complex organism containing thousands of varieties of cells, each performing a specialized function to reproduce the same kind of plant which had produced the seed in the first place? Why do these cells unite in such a way that in one case it results in a stalk of corn, in another a blade of wheat, a tomato plant, a watermelon, or a mighty oak or any other of the countless millions of plants that cover our earth?

Every cell of a root system is a marvelous laboratory which absorbs inorganic matter from the soil and by a miraculous process converts it into the same organic substance of a mature plant. And more than that. Everyone of these microscopic cells carefully selects from its environment exactly those substances which are essential to reproduce a perfect copy of the parent plant. A seed of a carrot and a seed of a turnip might be planted side by side and draw their nourishment from the same soil. But the one will metamorphose the inorganic matter it absorbs into the substance of a carrot while the other will produce a turnip. And when the plant has reached maturity the same life cycle begins all over again.

The chief function and purpose of the plants in God's overall creation plan was to provide food for man and animals who were to inhabit this earth. This is evident from the words which God spoke to Adam when He said, "Behold, I have given you every herb bearing seed, which is upon the face of the earth, and every tree, in the which is the fruit of a tree yielding seed; to you it shall be for meat. And to every beast of the earth, and to every fowl of the air, and to everything that creepeth upon the earth, wherein there is life, I have given every green herb for meat: and it was so" (Gen. 1:29-30).

To accomplish this purpose, God did three things:

1. He created an infinite variety of plants to match the needs of the infinite variety of living creatures that were to fill the earth.

2. He created an infinite abundance of plants so that there would always be a sufficient supply at all times for all creatures.

3. He provided the plant with a mysterious power to reproduce itself so that it would continue to provide food for all creatures and to meet the needs of the growing population of both men and animals.

The plants have fulfilled this function in a most marvelous fashion. They have supplied food for the billions and trillions of human beings and for the more billions and trillions of animals and birds that have existed upon the earth since the beginning of time. And the food supply has never become exhausted. The miracle of the feeding of the five thousand has been repeated over and over again on a world scale, not feeding only five thousand, but five thousand millions and trillions, so that the Psalmist who observed this was moved to say, "The eyes of all wait upon thee; and thou givest them their meat in due season. Thou openest thine hand, and satisfiest the desire of every living thing" (Ps. 145:15, 16).

The reproductive capacity of plants is truly tremendous, as a few examples chosen at random will show. Some plants reproduce themselves at the rate of thirty or sixty or even a hundredfold, while others increase at an incredible rate that can be measured only by the thousands and the millions.

Observe a bean plant or a pea plant or a watermelon in your garden and count the number of beans and peas and black watermelon seeds each plant produces in one season, in each case the result of one original seed. Your eyes will be opened to the wonders that God performs every year in your own little garden.

In October of 1967 I was lecturing on Genesis 1 and 2 at a Bible Institute in Yorktown, Iowa, in the very heart of the tall corn country that has made Iowa so famous. In the course of one of my lectures I inquired whether anyone in my audience, all of whom were farmers, had ever thought of counting the number of kernels a single cornstalk would produce in one season. No one there had ever thought of doing so. But the next day a young lad by the name of Kervin von Dielingen came to me and timidly reported that he had acted upon my suggestion and had counted the kernels of one stalk of corn produced on his father's farm, and he found that this one plant had produced 682 kernels—that is, one original grain of corn had multiplied itself 682 times in one season. This would mean that if these 682 seeds were planted again in the following year and they would increase at about the same rate, the offspring of that first original seed, in its second generation, would number over 900,000,000 new seeds, all capable of continuing the same process ad infinitum. A single poppy seed can produce as high as 30,000 new seeds in one summer. One mushroom plant can produce a billion spores—that is, seeds, each capable of reproducing itself at the same rate. A single maple tree will produce more than a million seeds a year. And so we could continue mentioning other examples, equally spectacular in their reproductive power.

But to maintain a balance in the plant world, automatic checks are also provided in nature in the form of parasitic organisms which check the unrestrained increase of any species of plant that might take over and threaten the survival of other plants. These also increase at a fantastic rate. When I was a student of botany at the University of Alberta, we were at one time working on wheat rust in the laboratory because that was the great menace to the wheat farmer of Western Canada at that time. Our assignment was to examine a microscopic particle of wheat rust under a high-powered microscope with the purpose of finding the reproductive potential of this dread wheat parasite. To do this we used a pointed instrument with which we were to puncture one of these microscopic particles of black dust to find out their reproductive potential. I had worked on my project unsuccessfully for a considerable time, when suddenly I succeeded. I will never forget the picture that unfolded itself before my eyes when this happened. The invisible specks of black dust burst open like a sack of beans and out of it rolled a mass of sub-microscopic blackness that could not be counted, but possibly consisted of millions of individual particles. And again each one of these microscopic particles was living seed that would reproduce itself in the same manner on another wheat plant as its host.

Even a casual observation of plant life in one's own immediate environment will reveal wonders upon wonders of nature which cannot be explained by reason and are as incomprehensible as some of the wonderful miracles recorded in the Bible. But few people even see or take note of them, merely taking them for granted, and some even believe that all of these wonders just happen and continue to happen by themselves.

Some unknown writer who evidently had caught a glimpse of God's wonders in a humble seed, wrote the following poem:

A Package of Seed

I paid a dime for seeds, and the clerk tossed them out with a flip,
"We got them assorted for every man's needs," he said with a smile on his lip,
"Pansies and poppies and asters and peas."
Now seeds are just dimes to the man in the store,
And the dimes are things that he needs.
And I have been to buy them in seasons before
But have thought of them merely as seeds.
But it flashed through my mind, as I took this seed,
"You've purchased a miracle this time for a dime.
You've a dime's worth of power no man can create,
You've a dime's worth of life in your hand.
You've a dime's worth of mystery, destiny, fate,
Which the wisest cannot understand.
In this bright little package, now isn't it odd?
You've a dime's worth of something known only to God!"

Another, also meditating upon the wonder of plants, of seeds and of the soil in which they grow, was moved to write the following beautiful lines:

The soil will nurture and will grow whatever kind of seed we sow.
If weeds are planted, rest assured that weeds we'll have when they're matured.
We cannot expect from weeds to rise a flowered vine of paradise.
The soil of life will likewise grow whatever kind of seed we sow.
Regardless of the plant we breed, the product rises from the seed
So, onward as through life we go, we must watch the seed we sow.

—Cosmo I. Dokos

An important stage in the life of some plants is the formation of their buds. Buds in their early stage appear as a mere swelling on the twig of a shrub or a tree, and like the seed, seem to be completely lifeless.

But when the winter sun begins to rise a little higher on the horizon as spring approaches, and its warm rays become more effective, something happens in those little swellings on the twig. They begin to swell and show signs of life, and then at the right time, when all danger of a deadly frost has passed, they suddenly burst open and vigorously unfold themselves like a proud peacock showing the beauty of his tail feathers. Some become new leaves just as the old ones had been which they had dropped when the winter approached. Others appear in a gorgeous robe of beautiful colored flowers that even Solomon in all his wealth and glory could not match.

A nature lover and writer for the St. Louis *Globe-Democrat* had observed season after season the wonders of nature as revealed in the humble budding of the trees and the shrubs around him, and was moved to share the wonderment and exuberant excitement of what he had experienced with the readers of that paper. He wrote the following beautiful tribute to the bud in the April 4 issue of 1966.

> Through the turning year nature offers its wonders to those with hearts that respond to the goodness and glory of the natural world. When Spring's climbing sun and warming air brings the first strands of green on southern slopes, along the meadow creeks the buds begin to swell rapidly.
>
> We take many of life's miracles for granted. Many think that the buds on branches and boughs grow in the spring. Buds now stirring with life juices were formed last summer.
>
> Layer upon layer, the tissue of leaf or blossom was folded and wrapped in an almost waterproof capsule. They have waited through an autumn and winter. Each meticulously padded bud has received just enough moisture and oxygen to maintain life.
>
> If you have never studied buds beneath a lens you have an experience in beauty waiting. The colors are many; there are reds and yellows, browns and pinks, bronzes and grays.
>
> Each tree species has its distinctive bud shape: red apples' buds are crimson and tridants. White oak has a bluish oval bud; the dogwood has a plump, pewter gray bud that may remind you of a shoe button. Elm buds are slender, pointed, and light brown; the high bush blueberry has a beautiful reddish-brown bud with lacy scales. Buds, some think, are common things. But to him who studies and watches as the miracle of spring gathers momentum, a bud is a sacred thing. For in those capsules that will produce leaf and flower is the essence of life itself.
>
> Buds waited through the blizzards of winter for the fulfillment of time; now the life forces are stirring and the

ancient plan is following the established pattern.

A bud on a bough is a small object, but in that humble package is stored the faith that helps man to glimpse the Grail.

Charles L. H. Wagner found a sermon in the lilies and wrote the following beautiful poem:

In the beauty of the Lilies
We can see the love of God.
They, without a conscious effort,
Rise supreme above the sod.
Clothed in tents of radiant glory,
Fed by springs sent from above,
Each a message of creation,
Each an emblem of His love.

O ye souls that doubt and falter,
Here is truth sublime that lives
In the flowers kissed by heaven,
Proving love divine He gives.
Are ye not of much more moment
Than the lilies of the field?
Ye, believe, and faith returneth
More than wishful hope can yield.

The Mystery of Growth

Another unique characteristic of a living organism is the mystery of growth.

Organisms grow. They begin with a submicroscopic spark of life, then develop through a process of carefully regulated stages from this microscopic beginning through intermediary stages to maturity. This process we call growth. A stone or any other inanimate object can increase its size only by accretion—that is, by adding something to itself from without. But the process of growth is something that occurs from within. Growth means that an organism absorbs, by means of an inherent power, a foreign substance outside of itself, and then converts that substance into its own body and grows to normal maturity.

This process is always specific in every individual organism. In some the period of growth is very short, while in others it is long. The growth of a tomato plant requires less than one summer season, while that of an oak requires many years. And every plant, absorbing a foreign substance from its environment, always converts that substance into the selfsame substance as that of the parent plant. A pumpkin seed grows into a pumpkin and never into a turnip, though the two might be growing side by side and drawing their nourishment from the same soil. A cucumber seed always grows into another cucumber and not into a cabbage head. And every species always perpetuates its own peculiar characteristics with respect to shape, size, color, flowers, and general appearance. A carrot is always yellow and never red like its neighbor the beet. A soybean is always black, never pink. The lichen always remains a very humble creeping plant, covering the sterile rocky soil of the Arctic region, while the Douglas Fir gracefully raises its royal crown high into the air, sometimes 250 feet and more, and proudly overshadows all its neighbors. A radish never grows to the size of a turnip, nor a pea to that of an apple. And a rosebush never becomes a lilac.

These are all familiar phenomena of nature, which we can observe all around us. But though they are so wonderful that no one can understand or explain them, we are not impressed by this miraculous process. We just take it for granted because it is so common. And yet, this common everyday occurrence is a most eloquent proclamation of the wisdom and the power of the Eternal God who made them that way.

The Power to Change Matter

Plants are the bridge between the inorganic and the organic, and unite the two in one magnificent system. Plants create food for man and animals. Without plants we could not exist. Neither man nor animal is able to absorb the inorganic and convert it into nourishment for itself. The plants perform this service for them. The mechanism by which this miracle is performed are the roots and the green leaves of the plant. These two, operating together, form a perfectly unified food-manufacturing system.

The roots absorb the mineral content of the plant from the soil; and the chlorophyll in the green leaves, acted upon by the energy of the sun in a process called photosynthesis, absorbs carbon dioxide and water from the air and converts these gases into basic food elements, such as carbohydrates, proteins and fats. All plant and animal foods, textile materials, lumber, rubber, fibers, organic oil, and other products essential for man's life, comfort, luxury, and general progress are produced by this mysterious process of photosynthesis. This is the most efficient manufacturing system known to man. And the wonder is that its operation is absolutely silent; there is no wear and tear on its mechanism; it replaces its own machinery; and it has continued its operation without interruption and with unfailing efficiency since it was set in motion on the third day of creation.

In addition, plants also maintain the delicate balance between the gases in the atmosphere by inhaling carbon dioxide which is exhaled by man and animals, and exhaling oxygen which again is essential for human and animal life.

Plants provide a protective covering for the soil and preserve it from wind and water erosion; they influence climate and beautify the landscape. They provide a shelter for animals and birds and make the earth a delightful habitation for man.

Plants are the source of all the coal on the earth. Without coal, our present industrial and economic progress would have been impossible. The great coal deposits in the bowels of the earth are the fossil remains of the luxuriant antediluvial plant life which was wiped away and buried in the Great Flood. Every plant, therefore, is a wonder of God's creation, and we ought to look at it with reverent awe as the poet does when he sings:

> There is not a plant or flower below
> But makes Thy glory known.
> And clouds arise and tempests blow
> By order from Thy throne.

Variety of Plants

A fourth remarkable aspect of plant life is the millions and billions of forms and species in which plants appear, from the microscopic diatom and plankton of the sea to the majestic giants of the redwoods of California. No two plants are exactly alike, whether shrubs or trees, flowers or weeds, grains or vegetables, and even the leaves of the same species are not mere duplicates one of the other. These marvels become even more spectacular when one compares the vegetation of one climatic zone with that of another, or the plants of one altitude and latitude with that of another, and desert plants with those of the rainy regions of our world.

This wonderful variation in the plant world is one of the things that makes traveling in foreign lands and climates so interesting. Every continent has its own unique kind of plant life. The magnificent vegetation of India and Ceylon is quite distinct from the equally fascinating vegetation of South America. And the native trees, shrubs, flowers, and grasses of Australia are quite different from those of Africa and North America.

I recall an exciting experience I had while traveling in Brazil. We were driving through a typical tropical rain forest and a new, wonderful world of God's creation was opened up to me. While we happened to be right in the midst of this tropical wilderness, our faithful Volkswagen suddenly developed tire trouble, causing a considerable delay. While my companions were busy correcting this problem, I used the time to examine more closely the vegetation surrounding us on all sides of our narrow trail. I was, first of all, profoundly impressed with the density of the vegetation. I found that the trees and shrubs and countless other varieties of plants were so closely knit together and interwoven that they formed a solid wall, so dense that neither man nor beast could penetrate them, except possibly a snake. And yet, I noticed that every plant had retained its own peculiar characteristics. None was confused with the other, and it was evident that even here every plant had propagated its own kind as the Creator had ordained it. Here the theory of evolution would have had a wonderful opportunity to prove itself, but there was no evidence of it anywhere. Every plant had remained strictly distinct from every other plant, though the roots, branches and flowers were closely intertwined. I had somewhat similar experiences in the jungles of India and Africa.

All plants are wonderful, and the more carefully one examines them the more mysterious they become. A student of botany in a well-equipped botanical laboratory has a wonderful opportunity to observe this when examining these wonders. If he has eyes to see, he will discover that it is utterly absurd and irrational to assume that these wonders could have just happened, when everywhere he finds careful design and meticulous laws to govern them.

The scope of this study does not allow us to observe nature on a broad scale, but we would miss a valuable opportunity to point out the wonderful wisdom of the Creator revealed in every plant, if we would fail to examine in somewhat greater detail at least one specimen of the vast world of plants around us. And so I would like to invite the reader to take a closer look at one of our best friends in nature, the beloved tree. To do this, examine some of the trees in your nearby park or forest and note some of the distinctive characteristics that all have in common and then how one differs from the other. Note the size, their form, spread of branches of the different species, the design of their leaves, the character of the bark, the quality and color of their wood, whether soft or hard, the kind of seeds, nuts, or fruits they produce, their commercial or aesthetic value, etc. In short, learn to know the trees that serve, enrich and beautify your own life and your community's, and you will learn to realize more fully that every tree is a wonderful creation of God and a precious gift of the Creator to the human race that could never have come about by itself.

And then think of the billions and trillions of trees in the great forests of the world. All have similar characteristics and yet are divided into thousands of species, all of them different. Of trees alone, a hundred and fifty thousand species are known to us today. Among these are 300 kinds of oaks and 90 different pines, and so thousands of other species, all different one from the other. Some are small and have a short life; others reach a height of over 300 feet and have attained an age of more than 3,000 years.

On the assembly lines of our great industries, automobiles roll off these lines by the thousands, but every one is exactly like the other; all are made on the same pattern and put together from standardized parts. But there is no assembly line in the forest. Every tree is an individual creation and not merely a collection of standardized parts. No two trees are exactly alike in all details, not even those of the same species. Each grows by itself and takes on its own peculiar form with branches equally distributed on all sides, gracefully coming to a symmetrical rounded or pointed crown, maintaining an erect position, held there by a sturdy central trunk and an extensive root system exactly commensurate with its size, and strong enough to withstand the blast of the winds and storms that beat against it.

Dr. Austerhout, of the engineering department of St. Louis University, graciously calculated for me the possible pressure exerted by a wind of 60 miles an hour on a tree 45 feet high with a 25-foot spread of branches. According to his estimates, the pressure exerted on such a tree when translated into horsepower would be equivalent to approximately 2,000 horsepower. That is a lot of power and tremendous impact for a tree to withstand. And yet, a healthy tree with its roots securely anchored in solid soil and not in sand will not be uprooted. It may lose some leaves and a few branches, but the quality of its wood permits it to bend and to twist in the battle against the storm, and when the storm is over, the tree will calmly again raise its crown, ready to challenge another antagonist. Consider also the heavy load the tender branches of some fruit trees carry without breaking down. I was informed that a normal apple tree, for example, may bear as many as 15 bushels of apples in one season. That is a very substantial load for tender branches to carry, and yet they do not break.

But even that does not account for all the wonders of a tree. Let us take a closer look at the body of the tree itself. We speak of the wood of a tree. But what is wood? How was it formed? Why did the substance which the roots absorb from the soil form into wood and not into the softer body of, say, a turnip or a strawberry? Why did it divide itself into trunk, branches, roots and leaves? Why is some wood hard and other wood soft? Why does some wood consist of longer and other wood of shorter fibers? Why is some white, while others are yellow, brown or red? Why do some trees bear fruit, others nuts, and still others only flowers and seeds? How will anyone explain without a divine Creator the great varieties of delicious flavors in the different fruits and nuts and the gorgeous display of colorful flowers in some trees? In short, how would the evolutionists explain all these mysteries? And we have a right to demand an explanation if they expect us to believe their theory.

And again, to the casual observer, the body of a tree has no special attraction. It is only just another something that happens to be growing where it is and provides us with some benefits, such as fuel, boards, pulp and other building materials, fruits, and refreshing shade. However, a closer examination will reveal that every tree is a complex living organism consisting of billions and trillions of cells, each designed for a specific function and all operating together in a wonderful system for the life and growth of that tree.

In some respects, the body of the tree may be compared with the human body and its various organs. We have noted that the body of the tree and all its parts are covered with a bark or the epidermis, as it is technically called, which serves as a protection against damages that might be caused by insects or other injuries from without, and which also retains the sap or the lifeblood of a tree as the veins do in the human body. Next, its cortex or the internal structure of the tree may be compared with the skeleton of the human body which gives it rigidity and strength. The vascular bundle, another internal part of the tree, provides a continuous circulatory system from the roots to the leaves, like the circulatory system in the human body. And the function of the root and the leaves might be likened to the other vital organs in the human body, such as the stomach, lungs and kidneys.

And then consider the rising of the sap in the spring, spreading to every part of the tree and receding again in the fall. What is the force that causes the tree to absorb tons and tons of water from the soil in which it grows, converting it into its own sap or lifeblood and then raising it and spreading it to all its parts, sometimes to a height of several hundred feet, and that contrary to the laws of gravity? Why do some trees shed their leaves in fall, remain dormant for a season, and then reproduce new ones in spring while others do not? Why do the different trees in some orchards, drawing their substance from the same soil, produce different fruits: the pear trees, pears; the orange trees, oranges; the walnut trees, walnuts?

How will anyone, denying a divine Creator, account for the different flavors, aromas, flowers and other peculiar qualities of the different fruits? How will the evolutionist explain the origin of the different colors? How could nothing produce a red, or a pink, or a blue, or a green, or any of the other wonderful colors found in trees and plants in the world? What explains the beauty of the Japanese cherry tree, the flowering crab, the gorgeous Jacaranda of South America, the beautiful wattle of Australia, or all the other wonderful flowering trees and plants in the tropics on all the continents and islands of the world? Yes, and possibly even more basic than all these questions is the question, How could evolution produce a simple green leaf with the mysterious chlorophyll without a plant, and how could a plant have originated, grown, survived without a leaf? In short, for a normal, honest human being endowed with reason and common sense, every tree is a most devastating refutation of the absurdities of the evolutionary theory which assumes that all these wonders just happened.

Even the pagan philosopher Cicero (106-43 B.C.) knew better, and in refutation of the evolutionary teachings of the Epicureans of his day, wrote:

> For we may now put aside the elaborate arguments and gaze, as it were, with our eyes upon the beauty of the creation of divine Providence, as we declare them to be. And first let us behold the whole earth, situated in the center of the world, the solid spherical mass gathered into a globe by a natural gravitation of all its parts, clothed with flowers and grass and trees and corn, forms of vegetation all of them incredibly numerous and inexhaustibly varied and diverse. Add to these cool foun-

> tains ever-flowing, transparent streams and rivers, their banks clad in brightest verdure, deep valuted caverns, craggy rocks, sheer mountain heights and plains of immeasurable extent; add also the hidden veins of gold and silver, and marble in unlimited quantity. Think of all the various species of animals, both tame and wild! Think of the flight and song of birds! of the pastures filled with cattle, and the teeming life of the woodlands! . . . Could we but behold these things with our eyes as we can picture them in our minds, no one taking in the whole earth at one view could doubt the divine reason. Then how great is the beauty of the sea! How glorious the aspect of the vast expanse! How many and how diverse are its islands! How lovely the scenery of the coast and shores! How numerous and how different the species of marine animals, some dwelling in the depths, some floating and swimming on the surface, some clinging in their own shells to the rocks. . . .
>
> Next the air, bordering on the sea, undergoes the alteration of day and night and now rises upwards, melted and rarified, now is condensed and compressed into clouds and gathering moisture and enriches the earth with rain, now flows forth in currents, to and fro, and produces winds. Likewise it causes the yearly variation of cold and heat, and it also both supports the flight of birds and, inhaled by breathing, nourishes and sustains the animal race.[1]

Everyone who has carefully looked at a tree, whether he be a scientist, technician or housewife, and whose appreciation for the wonders of nature has not been completely dulled by the clang and clatter of the mechanistic world created by man all around him, will agree with the sentiments expressed by Joyce Kilmer, in his simple little poem about the tree where he writes:

> I think that I shall never see
> A poem so lovely as a tree,
> A tree whose hungry mouth is pressed
> Against the earth's sweet flowing breast,
> A tree that looks at God all day
> And lifts her leafy arms to pray,
> A tree that may in summer wear
> A nest of robins in her hair,
> Upon whose bosom snow has lain,
> Who intimately lives with rain.
> Poems are made by fools like me
> But only God can make a tree.

[1] Cicero (106-43 B.C.). De Natura Deorum, 2nd section 39, LC, pp. 218-220.

10.

The Fourth Day of Creation

The creation of sun, moon and stars.

The works of God on the fourth day of creation are described in Genesis 1:16-19 where we read: "And God made two great lights; the greater light to rule the day, and the lesser light to rule the night: he made the stars also. And God set them in the firmament of the heaven to give light upon the earth, and to rule over the day and over the night, and to divide the light from the darkness: and God saw that it was good. And the evening and the morning were the fourth day."

God had devoted the first three days of the creation week to our planet, the earth. On the fourth day He went beyond and reached up into outer space surrounding the earth, and filled it with an infinite number of other worlds which were to serve the earth. The earth is only an insignificant speck when compared with the other heavenly bodies. But God in His own wisdom chose this speck for a habitation of man, the crown of all creation, and so all other worlds must serve this little planet.

On the fourth day God created the sun, moon, and stars. Some stars are small; others are of incomprehensible magnitude. Some are dim; others shine with great brilliancy. Some appear isolated and alone; others appear in clusters and form great constellations.

And all these heavenly bodies that were called into existence were at the same time set into perpetual motion, each moving in its own orbit and maintaining the same distance from each other and traveling through space at a speed far greater than that of an atomic missile. All have continued in their respective orbits without interruption or collision, each maintaining its individual timetable with an absolute and mathematical accuracy.

When observing and meditating on these wonders of the heavens, young David, the shepherd lad on the hills of Bethlehem, reached for his harp and sang: "The heavens declare the glory of God; and the firmament sheweth his handywork. Day unto day uttereth speech, and night unto night sheweth knowledge. There is no speech nor language, where their voice is not heard. Their line is gone out through all the earth and their words to the end of the world. In them hath he set a tabernacle for the sun, which is as a bridegroom coming out of his chamber, and rejoiceth as a strong man to run a race. His going forth is from the end of the heaven, and his circuit unto the ends of it: and there is nothing hid from the heat thereof" (Ps. 19:1-6).

The starry heavens have always fascinated the imagination of men. There is a peculiar mystery about a clear, dark night with the heavenly dome all ablaze with myriads of twinkling stars, and so it is natural that men in all ages have had a burning curiosity to know more about the mysterious wonders of the heavens above, of the sun, the moon and the stars, the source of their light and their heat and the force that propels them on their way and regulates their course.

The little nursery rhyme of our children,

> "Twinkle, twinkle little star
> How I wonder what you are,
> Up above the world so high
> Like a diamond in the sky,"

really symbolizes the yearning desire of every thoughtful person to understand more of the mysteries of the skies. He is overawed by the beauty of the heavens in the darkness of the night, or is thrilled by the rising sun as it welcomes a sleeping world to a new day of action and life, wondering how time can be divided into days and nights and the year into its seasons with the regularity of a gigantic clock.

Primitive people imagined the earth to be flat because it appeared that way to them, and the horizon they regarded as the end of the earth because they could see nothing beyond it. Some believed that the dome of the sky above was the roof of the world and that the stars were little lights attached to the underside of it. Or they believed that there was a lighted world above and that the stars were the lights shining through small holes in what they thought might be the floor of that world. The more poetic mythology described these heavenly bodies as deities, riding on fiery chariots through the sky, jealously watching over the activities of men.

However, the civilized nations very early in their history acquired a remarkable knowledge of the stars and their movements. They accurately predicted the eclipses of the sun; they recognized by name such stars as Arcturus and Orion and the Pleiades, a group of stars forming the constellation Taurus of which six or seven are visible to the naked eye (Job 9:9).

The early Babylonians seemed to have been the first to develop the study of the stars in the science of astronomy. They mapped out the heavens and located a great number of the most important stars and constellations. They established a calendar of 365 1/2 days on the basis of their astronomical observations. They accurately predicted the eclipses of the sun and the moon. In order to do this they probably had invented a primitive instrument similar to our telescope and also another instrument called the astrolabe for measuring the altitude of stars above the earth.

When Alexander the Great entered the City of Babylon, after he had conquered the Persian Empire, he found catalogs of tabulated eclipses covering a long period of years ahead. These early astronomers also introduced the practice of astrology. Their wise men attempted to map out the course of the future life of people on the basis of the position of the stars under which they were born. This strange superstition has again become a popular practice in our sophisticated age with many who consider themselves too wise and too scientific to believe the simple divine revelations of the Bible.

The Wise Men from the East who came to Jerusalem to seek the newborn King of the Jews no doubt were Babylonian astronomers (Matt. 2:1-12).

The Greeks followed the Babylonians. Their earliest philosophers were very much concerned about the mysteries of the universe.

Thales, of Miletus (640-546 B.C.), is generally regarded as the father of Greek astronomy. Among other things he taught the Greek sailors to steer their ships by Polaris, the North

Star, and besides that made many other important astronomical observations.

Pythagoras of Magna Graeca, in southern Italy (582-500 B.C.), made valuable mathematical contributions to Greek astronomy.

In 332 B.C., Alexander the Great founded the city of Alexandria in Egypt. The Ptolemies who followed him developed that city into the foremost center of Hellenistic learning and culture, which dominated the Mediterranean world for centuries after. And the University of Alexandria attracted the greatest scholars of that world during all this period. It was natural, therefore, that here, too, the study of astronomy would receive special attention.

Aristarchus (310-230 B.C.), one of the philosophers of that great seat of learning, had come to the conclusion that what seemed to be the movement of the stars was caused by the rotation of the earth on its own axis. He also maintained that the earth revolved around the sun and not the sun around the earth.

Aristophanes of Byzantium, another philosopher of the same period and the librarian of the famous Alexandrian library, taught that the earth was not a flat disc, as was commonly held, but a sphere. And he calculated the circumference of the earth at the Equator with almost perfect accuracy.

In the second century A.D., Claudius Ptolemy, also of Alexandria, promulgated his famous geo-centric worldview which after him has been known as the Ptolemaic System. This view was generally accepted by the astronomers following him, and throughout the Middle Ages was regarded by the church as being in harmony with Biblical astronomy.

But in the 16th century, a German-Polish monk by the name of Copernicus, a contemporary of Martin Luther, shocked all Christendom by claiming that the sun, not the earth, was the center of the universe, and that the earth revolved around the sun instead of the sun around the earth. For a long time his views were rejected as heretical.

Stimulated by this new approach to the problem of the universe, other astronomers continued their astronomical investigation with the result that the centuries-old Ptolemaic System was gradually replaced by this new approach to the mysteries of the universe, which is now known as the Copernicus System. Among the foremost astronomers that followed Copernicus and made notable contributions were such men as the Italian Galileo (1564-1642); the Danish Tycho Brahe (1541-1600), and his student, the German Johan Kepler (1570-1630); and the famous British Sir Isaac Newton (1642-1727).

A noted contemporary of Newton who made important contributions to the advancement of astronomy was Christian Huygens (1629-1695), the celebrated Dutch physicist, astronomer and mathematician.

In the early 18th century, James Bradley (1693-1762), the Astronomer Royal of England and the Herschel family, the father Sir William (1738-1822), his sister Caroline (1750-1848), and his son Sir John Herschel (1792-1871) made very important contributions to the advancement of astronomy.

Today we know a great deal more about the sun, moon and the stars than any previous generation before us did, and that is so because, first of all, we are the fortunate heirs of the accumulated knowledge of these great men who lived and labored before us, and we were able, therefore, merely to continue where they left off. But modern astronomy has also been greatly benefited by the advancement in modern times of other contributing sciences such as mathematics, physics and chemistry. However, the greatest contribution to the science of astronomy, no doubt, was made by the invention of the telescope and the spectroscope which followed in 1860.

The telescope was invented by the Dutch Hans Lippershey about 1608. It was developed to greater efficiency by the famous Galileo, and since then many others have contributed much to the perfection of this most important tool of the astronomer. The largest telescope in the world today is on Mount Palomar in California. It has a lens which is 200 inches wide in diameter, is three feet thick, and weighs 30 tons. It has increased the potential of the human eye by 640,000 times. It has brought the most remote heavenly bodies close to us and has opened up undreamed of vistas of the heavens and brought into view millions and billions of heavenly bodies which no one except God and the hosts of heaven had ever seen before.

But the most dramatic astronomical achievement of all times was made in our day when in 1969 our scientists succeeded in sending a spaceship with three men aboard to the moon and then landing on its surface. Two of these American astronauts actually walked on the surface of the moon; they took pictures of the moon's landscape, spoke by means of a radio-telephone with the President of the United States from a distance of 240,000 miles away, photographed the earth from the moon, and brought back some samples of rocks and minerals of which the moon is composed. This was a magnificent triumph of modern science and technology. These two men were the first, since the creation of these heavenly bodies, who actually came into physical contact with one of the celestial bodies and touched with their hands the substance of which God had created the moon.

The Sun

In Genesis 1:16 we read, "And God made two great lights; the greater light to rule the day, and the lesser light to rule the night: he made the stars also."

The sun is the greater light that rules the day. No human mind can fully comprehend the meaning of this brief statement: "God made the greater light to rule the day."

The sun is the center of our universe. Everything in infinite space revolves around it and is dependent upon it.

The sun is the lamp and the power plant of the earth. Life without it would be impossible.

The sun is a revolving sphere of glowing gases a million times larger than our earth, with a diameter of 866,000 miles compared with the less than 8,000 miles of our earth's diameter. It has been described as an atomic furnace producing a heat at the core estimated at 35,000,000 degrees of Fahrenheit, which is reduced to 11,000 degrees of Fahrenheit at its surface.

The heat of the sun is so great that a body of solid ice as large as our earth would be melted within two hours if the sun came closer to the earth, and if the earth itself would fall into the sun it would be completely vaporized in a matter of minutes.

The distance between the earth and the sun is 93,000,000 miles. Astronomers have estimated that if this distance were increased to 120,000,000 miles instead of the 93,000,000, our planet would be a perpetual frozen Arctic, and life on it would be impossible.

If, on the other hand, this distance were reduced to about 60,000,000 miles, the surface of the earth would be a glowing furnace, again making life on it impossible. But the wonder is that this ball of fire of incalculable heat is exactly 93,000,000 miles away, the exact distance to provide the earth with a balanced amount of heat and light to make life in all its forms possible, and also to divide the earth into climatic zones to make variation in plant and animal life possible. Here again we notice the perfect balance in nature, even among these remote heavenly bodies, and the perfect balance has been maintained with mathematical precision ever since this cosmic machine was set into motion.

There is no rational explanation for this supreme engineering achievement without a supreme, intelligent, and master Builder. And so I would like to quote Cicero again in this connection to show that reason and common sense alone are sufficient to recognize that these wonders of creation would not have happened by themselves but required superhuman, divine power to bring them into existence. Cicero had no knowledge of Genesis or other revelations of Scripture as we have, yet he writes as follows:[1]

> The most potent cause of the belief was the uniform motion and revolution of the heavens, and the varied groupings and ordered beauty of the sun, moon and stars, the very sight of which was in itself enough to prove that these things are not the mere effect of chance. When a man goes into a house, or a wrestling-school, or a public assembly and observes in all that goes on—arrangement, regularity and system—he cannot possibly suppose that these things come about without a cause: he realizes that there is someone who presides and controls. Therefore with the vast movements and phases of the heavenly bodies, and these ordered processes of a multitude of enormous masses of matter, which throughout the countless ages of the past have never in the smallest degree played false, is he compelled to infer that these mighty world motions are regulated by some Mind. . . . Now the heavenly bodies and all those things that display a never-ending regularity cannot be created by man; therefore that which creates them is superior to man; yet what better name is there for this than 'god.'

But we Christians will go even beyond Cicero because we know that our great and omnipotent God created heaven and earth, and we will therefore join the poet and sing His praises and say:

> We sing th' Almighty pow'r of God
> Who bade the mountains rise,
> Who spread the flowing seas abroad
> And built the lofty skies.
>
> We sing the wisdom that ordained
> The sun to rule the day;
> The moon shines, too,

[1] Cicero, De Natura Deorum, Bk. II, Sec. 4 ff. LC, p. 137 ff.

At His command
And all the stars obey.

We sing the goodness of the Lord
Who fills the earth with food
Who formed His creatures by a word
And then pronounced them good.

Lord, how Thy wonders are displayed
Where e'r we turn our eyes
Whene'r we view the ground we tread
Or gaze upon the skies.

There is not a plant nor flower below
But makes Thy glories known;
And clouds arise and tempest blow
By order from Thy throne.

On Thee each moment we depend;
If Thou withdraw, we die.
Oh, may we ne'r that God offend
Who is forever nigh! Amen.

Lutheran Hymnal,
1931 edition, page 293

The fire of the sun has been burning ever since the fourth day of creation. It has not consumed the substance on which it feeds. Its heat has remained the same, as though regulated by a gigantic thermostat. Its gases have not been dispersed into outer space, as would be in keeping with the nature of gases. It has been estimated that if the whole earth were a solid mass of coal and all of it became a furnace of fire at the same time, it would provide heat equivalent to that of the sun for only two and a fourth days.

The light of the sun consists of a variety of rays of different wave lengths which give rise to the different colors. Some are not visible to the human eye, such as the infrared and the ultraviolet. Newton, in his analysis of sunlight, found seven basic colors in its rays—namely, red, orange, yellow, green, blue, indigo, and violet. But there are infinitely more shades of colors caused by one merging into the other. We are told that each ray has a specific function for living things on the earth.

There are variations in the sun; they have been called sunspots. No one knows exactly what they are or what causes them. In size they vary from 500 to 150,000 miles across. They exert an influence on weather and possibly also affect other phases of nature yet not fully understood, and they are also sometimes a disturbing factor to delicate electrical instruments on earth.

Other strange phenomena of the sun are the vast eruptions called preeminences. They seem to occur near the sunspots. These eruptions of flaming gases shoot up to a height ranging from 20,000 miles up to 300,000 miles or even more. They seem to be caused by great explosions in the interior of the sun.

The sun is the source of all energy upon earth. Astronomers estimate that the sun's radiation of energy upon the earth is equivalent to 230,000,000,000,000 units of horsepower, and this is only a fraction of the total energy radiated from the sun, the greater part being dispersed into the universe and to the other planets at the fantastic speed of 186,000 miles per second. All these figures are incomprehensible in scope and no human mind is capable of understanding what they mean. Who, for example, can understand what a million horsepower actually means? And if we cannot understand that, how can we think in terms of billions and even trillions of horsepower, and of speed 186,000 miles per second? All these figures are altogether beyond the grasp of the human mind. Only an infinite and omnipotent God can operate in such dimensions.

The energy of the sun radiated upon the atmosphere of our planet is responsible for the climate and the weather and changes in the weather; it gives rise to the winds and storms on land and sea. It raises millions and billions of tons of water from the ocean, vaporizes and demineralizes it; collects the vapors into clouds, moves the clouds thousands of miles over land and sea by the energy of the wind, which is also produced by the energy of the sun; condenses the vapors, and then scatters them again on the dry land to make life possible. The energy of the sun activates the germ of life hidden in the seed and causes it to grow, to produce the plant and to reproduce itself. The green leaf, with its mysterious chlorophyll, would not be possible without the energy of the sun. There could be no forests on the mountainsides or green meadows for cattle and sheep, and there would be no flowers or fruit to delight the heart of man without the energy of the sun. Even the coal, deep down in the bowels of the earth, which has been warming our homes and providing the energy to turn the wheels of our great industries, is but the stored-up energy of the sun in fossilized remains of previous worlds of plant life.

Planets

The sun is surrounded by nine planets of which our earth

is one. The other eight planets are: Mercury, Venus, Mars, Jupiter, Saturn, Uranus, Neptune, and Pluto. These are all names of gods in Greek and Roman mythology, assigned to these celestial bodies by the early astronomers.

All planets revolve around the sun in the same direction, each moving in its own orbit and all retaining the same distance from one another. Each planet rotates around its own axis while traveling around the sun. Our planet, the earth, rotates at the speed of 1,000 miles an hour and thereby divides time into day and night. In its flight around the sun, the earth travels 580,000,000 miles each year, which means that we, on our spaceship earth, are traveling at the fantastic speed of 1,000 miles a minute. That exceeds by far the speed of the astronauts on their journey to the moon. Consider also the enormous load our spaceship is carrying. And then let us remind ourselves that all these mysterious powers and wonders of the sun are all implied in the brief statement, "And God made . . . the greater light to rule the day."

When the Psalmist looked up to the heavens and contemplated this sublime manifestation of God's majesty and power, he cried out in ecstasy, "O Lord, how excellent are all thy works, in wisdom hast thou made them all!"

Men of all ages and races have always been mystified by the solemn grandeur, the heat, energy, and movement of the sun; but they knew not God, the Creator, as the Psalmist did, and so they turned to the sun itself and worshipped it as god.

The oldest forms of idolatry in the history of the human race have always been the deification of the sun and other heavenly bodies. The sun has most dramatically symbolized to men the life-giving and the life-preserving power in the universe, and so they have worshipped it. There are still some sun worshippers in India. This form of idolatry at least had a semblance of rationale for its practice. They reasoned back from an effect which they could see to the cause which produced it. Reason told them that there could not be an effect without a corresponding cause.

They did not know the God who made heaven and earth, and so because they found the need for a god, they found one for themselves.

But the current idolatry in the civilized world today has no reason behind it. Scientists have deified a vague, impersonal, irrational, nonexisting force called evolution. This force operates solely on the principle of chance and accident, completely ignoring the law of cause and effect; it does not have even a semblance of reason or experience to support it. Yet they regard this "something," which is "nothing," as the creator of the universe with all its wonders. This new form of idolatry, compared with even the most extravagant and naive mythology of darkest heathenism, is more irrational and absurd. And so I would like to quote Cicero once more because he was a pagan philosopher and had not the advantage of revelation. This is what he has to say on this point:[2]

> Can any sane person believe that all this array of stars and the vast celestial adornment could have been created out of atoms rushing to and fro fortuitously and at random? Could any other being devoid of intelligence and reason have created them? Not merely did their creation postulate intelligence, but it is impossible to understand their nature without intelligence of a high order. . . .
>
> If any man is not impressed by this coordination of things and this harmonious combination of nature to secure the preservation of the world, I know for certain that he has never given any consideration to these matters.

Astronomically speaking, the sun, not the earth, is the center of the universe. Our earth is only a satellite of the sun and a mere speck in the infinite universe, compared with the millions and billions of other heavenly bodies. And yet God chose this little speck to make himself known to rational beings outside of His heavenly abode. Here, on this speck, He created life and all the requirements to maintain life. On this little planet He placed man, the crown of all creation. Here He revealed himself through Moses and the prophets. And above all, here on this planet, the Son of God, the Lord Jesus by whom all things were made (John 1:1), became man, to reunite the human race with their Creator from whom they had become estranged through their rebellion. And to this little speck in the universe God, the Creator and Judge of all the world, will return on the Day of Judgment to terminate the history of this present universe and create a new heaven and a new earth which shall abide forever.

And so it is true that our earth is, after all, the real center of the universe, and all the other heavenly bodies, great and small, were created to serve this little planet.

---

[2] Cicero, De Natura Deorum, Sec. 46, pp. 233-237.

11.

Creation of the Moon and the Stars

We read: "And God made . . . the lesser light to rule the night" (Gen. 1:16). The lesser light is the moon.

Of all the celestial bodies, the moon is our nearest neighbor. The average distance of the moon from the earth is 240,000 miles. In size, the moon is smaller than the earth, its diameter being 2,160 miles or about 1/4 of that of the earth.

The moon is a satellite of the earth, just as the earth is a satellite of the sun. It revolves around the earth in an irregular orbit at a speed of 2,288 miles an hour; that is about the same as the velocity of a bullet traveling from the muzzle of a high-powered gun. While the moon revolves around the earth, it also rotates around its own axis at a rate in harmony with its rotation around the earth, thereby always keeping the same side of its surface turned towards the earth. And so it happens that we on earth only see one side of the moon. One of the most remarkable aspects of the moon is the reoccurring changes in its shape and size, which are called phases of the moon. These changes are a regular, monthly occurrence, during which the face of the moon changes from a thin crescent until it becomes a full, round disc which we call the full moon. Once it has reached the stage of the full moon, the cycle immediately starts all over again.

It requires 29 1/2 days for the moon to "wax and wane" through its different phases from one full moon to another; thus it divides time into months and the months into subdivisions of quarters, halves, three-quarters, and full moons. It thus completes a systematic calendar of time which God ordained at the beginning (Gen. 1:14). And this time schedule has continued without interruption throughout all the ages with absolute accuracy, so that all calendars and clocks of the world are regulated by it.

The moon seems to grow and shrink in shape and size, but that is not so in reality; these changes are caused by the amount of light from the sun that strikes the surface of the moon while it rotates around the earth. The moon has no light of its own but only reflects the light of the sun and, of course, only those parts of the surface of the moon can function as a reflector that are directly exposed to the sunlight. All the rest of the moon remains in darkness and therefore invisible to man on earth.

I have already mentioned that the moon revolves around the earth in 29 1/2 days. It is, therefore, constantly changing its position in relation to the earth and to the sun. And so the shadow of the earth falling upon the surface of the moon will change accordingly, in that way causing the phases or changes in the moon. Only once every month, and then only for a very short time, the entire half of the moon's surface is exposed to the direct rays of the sun. This phase we call the full moon. Sometimes the earth completely blocks out the direct rays of the sun from the moon, and then we have a lunar eclipse, which occurs twice a year.

The substance of which the moon is made is essentially the same as that of the earth. This means that it is composed of the same matter that God created on the first day of creation. Astronomers had established this fact by means of the spectroscope long before the astronauts set foot upon the moon's surface. But what the astronauts found completely vindicated the astronomers and confirmed their previous findings.

The density and volume of the moon are less than those of the earth; and its gravity, therefore, will vary accordingly, being only one-sixth of that of the earth, which means that a man weighing 180 pounds on earth would weigh only 30 pounds on the moon.

The topography of the moon is barren and extremely rugged. Its mountains are higher than ours and their outlines can be seen even with the naked eye from the earth. The plains of the moon are scarred by many and deep craters of various sizes, some of them measuring from 60 to 140 miles across and one thousand feet deep.

The moon has no water or atmosphere. Life on the moon is, therefore, non-existent. Because of the absence of atmosphere on the moon, the rays of the sun striking it are not dispersed as they are on the earth. This fact causes the temperatures to be extreme, both as to heat and cold. And hence, while the rays of the sun are striking directly upon its exposed side during the long moonday, the temperature rises to a boiling point. During the long, dark night of the moon it falls about 100 degrees Fahrenheit below zero.

When these characteristics of the moon are considered, our invasion of this heavenly body can never result in any great benefit to mankind. Its climatic conditions are such that it will be forever uninhabitable. And though it were made of solid gold, the cost to get it would be so astronomical that it would not pay. Our effort to put a man on the moon was a tremendous scientific and technological achievement which gave a great boost to our national ego, and especially so because we beat the Russians in this great international contest. But the price of that game was so enormous that national common sense ought to cause us to ask whether the practical benefits derived from it were worth the cost. I cannot help but feel that when we consider the problems in all the world and also in our own country that are threatening to overwhelm us, the $24,000,000,000 spent on this expedition and the time and talents devoted to it would seem to have resulted in greater benefits to mankind if all that would have been devoted towards solving our problems here on earth. The world's problems are not on the moon but here on earth where man creates them and where he must solve them if he is to survive. However, that is only my opinion. Perhaps the spiritual impact of the astronaut's testimony to God is worth more to Him than the money expended.

The effect of the moon on the oceans of the world in causing their tides has already been referred to earlier in this discussion.

There seems to be some evidence, however, that the brilliant moon of the tropics sometimes may have a harmful effect on the physical and mental well-being of people exposed directly to its light. But the belief of some people that crops, and especially potatoes, when planted in a certain phase of the moon will do better, does not seem to have any real foundation and may be a mere survival of some ancient superstition.

There is something enchanting about the beautiful, mellow, harvest full moon which tends to stimulate an aura of sentimental romanticism in the lives of both young and old.

The Stars

The Genesis account continues: "he made the stars also" (Gen. 1:16).

Four crisp, one-syllable words connected to the preceding account by the conjunction "also" are all the sacred writer employs to complete the account of the creation of the heavenly bodies on the fourth day.

Perhaps these four one-syllable words constitute the shortest, most pregnant statement in all of written language. It would require an encyclopedia of many volumes to describe in detail what these four words imply. And yet, these four words are the only authentic account concerning the origin of the stars.

No human mind can fully comprehend the immensity of the worlds this little "also" includes. And even the most vivid and creative imagination grows confused and dizzy when trying to comprehend the vast number of stars created on the fourth day and the enormity of distances and sizes involved.

The starry heavens above on a dark wintry evening, with a sky not yet blurred by man-made pollutions, present a picture of such sublime grandeur that human language is inadequate to describe it. Even the philosopher Kant, whom no one would accuse of being sentimental, was so impressed that he was prompted to say, "I know of nothing more awe-inspiring than the starry heaven above and the moral law within us." [1]

When we speak of the stars we generally include all the heavenly bodies except the sun and the moon. And this includes the nine planets referred to above, the asteroids, the meteorites, the comets, and the galaxies.

The nine planets, of which the earth is one, are in reality not stars at all because they do not shine by virtue of their own light, but like the moon merely reflect the light of the sun. To the astronauts, in their rendezvous in outer space, our earth shone like the moon shines to us here on earth.

Of the nine planets, Mercury is the smallest in size and

---

[1] Kant. *Critique of Practical Reason*, in the conclusion (Beachluss) Reclam. Edition. Leipzig, p. 193.

nearest to the sun. It is a little larger than the moon, measuring 3,100 miles through its diameter, compared with the moon's 2,160 miles. Its distance from the sun is 36,000,000 miles compared with the 93,000,000 miles of the earth. Mercury has no atmosphere, and hence the rays of the sun beat down on it directly with an intensity much greater than that on the earth. Its temperature on its sunlit side is about 660 degrees Fahrenheit, while the opposite side is correspondingly cold, making life in all its forms impossible on this planet. Since the distance between the sun and Mercury is much less than that between the sun and the earth, its orbit is between the earth and the sun. And because of its nearness to the sun, it is not easily visible from the earth.

Venus

Venus is almost a twin of the earth with respect to its size and is, next to Mercury, the nearest to the sun, its distance being 67,000,000 miles. It is believed that Venus is enveloped by some kind of atmosphere but not the same as that on earth, for neither oxygen nor water seems to be present; and so life on this planet, as we know it, would be impossible. But Venus, like the moon, has phases and sometimes appears in the shape of a crescent.

Mars

The planet Mars seems to resemble the earth more nearly than any other planet. Mars was the Roman god of war, and because of the bloody-red color of this planet it was given that name. Mars is tilted at about the same angle as the earth, and hence it has seasons. Astronomers believe that its poles are even covered with ice caps which would presuppose the presence of water on this planet. Great arguments have raged among scientists whether certain markings were canals, dug by some intelligent inhabitants of this planet. But today astronomers no longer seriously regard this as a possibility and the "man from Mars" has become a mere figure of speech.

The distance between Mars and the sun is 142,000,000 miles, and its size is only about one half that of the earth. Mars has colored rocks that constitute its surface. Because of the great distance from the sun, the temperature on Mars must be such that life on it would be impossible.

Jupiter

The largest planet among the nine is Jupiter. In size it is large enough to contain all the other planets of the solar system with some room to spare. Jupiter measures 88,640 miles through its diameter—that is, it is about 11 times greater than that of the earth, and its distance from the sun is 483,000,000 miles.

It takes Jupiter nearly 12 years to complete one orbit around the sun, but its rotation around its own axis is much faster than that of the earth, despite its enormous size. It makes one complete rotation every 10 hours, which means that a day on Jupiter has only 10 hours. The temperature on Jupiter is very low, believed to be about 220 degrees Fahrenheit below zero.

Jupiter has 12 satellites, 4 of which are larger than the moon and two larger than Mars. All its satellites orbit around it on an accurate, fixed time schedule. One remarkable feature about Jupiter, which has puzzled astronomers, is that 2 of its outmost satellites revolve in counter-direction to all the other planets and other heavenly bodies. This feature has caused a serious problem to the astronomers, because according to the theory that they have accepted, the heavenly bodies originated by some portion having been hurled off from a parent body; if this were so, it would mean that the part hurled from the parent body would have to orbit in the same direction as the parent body; the fact that these do not has caused much unhappiness among the astronomers. But they forget that the divine Creator can wind His cosmic clock by turning the key in either direction.

Saturn

Far beyond Jupiter, at about 900,000,000 miles from the sun, orbits the planet Saturn.

In size, Saturn is next to Jupiter, measuring 74,000 miles at its equatorial diameter. Because of its great distance from the sun, its temperature is extremely low, again making all life on it impossible. A remarkable feature about Saturn is the peculiar ring that surrounds it at its equator. This ring measures about 170,000 miles through its diameter but is comparatively thin, measuring only about 10 miles in thickness. The origin and character of this ring have been a puzzle to astronomers. Saturn has 9, possibly even 10 or more, satellites.

Only one of them is about the size of the moon; the others are smaller. And as in the case of two of the satellites of Jupiter, those of Saturn also revolve in the opposite direction of the other heavenly bodies, adding to the perplexity of the astronomers.

To the early astronomers, the orbit of Saturn represented the outer rim of the solar system. But with the discovery of Uranus in 1781, followed by Neptune in 1846 and of Pluto in 1930, these spacial boundaries have been pushed to infinite distances. Uranus is about 2 billion miles from the sun, and Neptune nearly 3 billion miles, while the orbit of Pluto varies between 3,800,000,000 and 4,600,000,000. The planet earth revolves around the sun once a year, but it requires 248 1/2 years for Pluto to complete its orbit. Because of the great distance from the sun, the temperature on Pluto is estimated at 380 degrees Fahrenheit below zero.

All the planets with their satellites receive their light from the sun, and their reflected light appears as stars to us on earth.

The other heavenly bodies within the solar system, besides these planets, are the asteroids, meteorites, and comets.

The Asteroids

The asteroids seem to be minor planets, varying in size from a few miles to 480 miles through their diameter, all moving in orbits parallel to some of the major planets.

The Meteorites

A meteorite seems to be a fragment of some other celestial body which in some way became detached from its parent body and by some unknown force was caused to travel towards the earth. Its glowing fiery streak, while plunging through the sky, is caused by friction as it passes through the atmosphere of the earth. Most of the meteorites burn up before they reach the earth, but occasionally one strikes our planet. That happened in 1908 when an enormous meteorite crashed down in an uninhabited region of Siberia, in Central Asia, completely devastating an area of about 1,000 square miles.

The most spectacular falling of meteorites occurred on November 13, 1833, over the greater part of North America, when for hours the sky was lit up by a magnificent display of cosmic fireworks of shooting stars. A witness of this great celestial show described it "as a Niagara of the firmament, descending in fiery torrents over the dark and roaring cataract. No spectacle so terribly grand and sublime was ever beheld by man before."[2]

Comets

The solar system includes among its members the 9 planets described above, 26 or more known satellites, 1500 or more asteroids and several hundred thousand comets, of which only about 10 percent are visible to the unaided eye on earth.

A comet is a most remarkable celestial body in every way, quite distinct from all the other heavenly bodies. It consists of an enormous nuclear head with an immense shining tail attached to it. Its head may vary in size from 10,000 miles to 1,000,000 miles through its diameter, and its tail from many thousands to 100,000,000 miles in length.

We can imagine that even the angels in heaven were startled when suddenly, and unexpectedly, out of nothing, roared the first great comet like a monster celestial dragon, with its gigantic shining tail, winding its way through the empty spaces between the stars, only to disappear again into nothingness.

The great comet of 1858 traveled at the speed of 350 miles per second. It was visible to the naked eye for 112 days and through the telescope for 9 months. Its tail was 54,000,000 miles long; it traveled in retrograde order through an orbit of 15,000,000,000 miles and required 2,000 years to make its circuit.

Many great comets have been observed since historic times and their appearances have always caused great consternation among men. One of the most noted of the great comets appeared suddenly in 1843. It had an indescribable brilliancy; in fact, it was so bright that it could be seen even in the daytime. Its greatest length visible was 108,000,000 miles, and its heat was estimated at 47,000 times greater than that received on earth from the sun. Many people at that time believed that its appearance marked the beginning of the end of the world.

Halley's Comet

Probably the best known of all the great comets is Halley's Comet, named after the British astronomer Edmund Halley, who had predicted its appearance.

Halley's Comet was last seen in the spring and summer of 1910 and is slated to reappear in 1986. During the 76 years

---

[2] R.M.Devans, *The Great Events*, p. 229.

in which it will be out of sight on earth it will travel a total of 3,000,000,000 miles, which will take it far beyond the most distant planets of Uranus, Neptune, and Pluto. And yet, by their mathematical calculations, astronomers are absolutely sure of its reappearance on accurate schedule in 1986, as it has always appeared on schedule in previous intervals of 76 years.

Consider what this means! During that period of 76 years, this comet is now traveling without stopping for refueling or repairs, a distance of 3,000,000,000 miles—that is about 100,000 miles a day. Its tail alone is 37,000,000 miles in length. Yet we can be sure it will arrive exactly on schedule according to its fixed timetable. And this fantastic race has been going on since creation. For any normal, rational human being this is a most overwhelming and sublime demonstration of the infinite and incomprehensible power of our God. And yet, there are those who remain positively blind, dull, and unmoved by these wonders who even try to persuade us that all this happened again and again in the same accurate pattern by sheer accident and chance, and regard Christians as naive and credulous when they believe and confess with the Psalmist, "The heavens declare the glory of *God*; and the firmament sheweth his handywork."

In former years, the appearance of comets was always a cause for superstitious fears among people who did not know what they were. Today astronomers know a great deal about comets and are able to predict their appearance with accuracy, but even now comets are still a source of "distress and perplexities among men on earth" (Luke 21:26) and are regarded by many as portents of some great calamity such as war, famine, or pestilence.

I remember distinctly the time a minor comet appeared. That was in 1919. Some people in Edmonton, Alberta, where I lived at the time, awaited the time of its appearance with fear and trepidation. Many stayed up all night, believing that the end of the world was at hand, and even some suicides were reported as a result.

The Galaxies

All the heavenly bodies we have discussed thus far are a part of our solar system and receive their heat and light from the sun. But there are countless other worlds in the heavens which are not dependent upon the sun, but like the sun, have their own light. These are the real stars. In fact, our sun is such a star. And every one of the twinkling stars in our sky is like our sun, a burning furnace of incredible heat and energy, moving at an inconceivable speed through space. Our sun, with all its heat and energy, is not even the greatest among them. Some are of a much greater size, and at least one among them is large enough not only to contain our sun but our entire solar system.

The number of stars visible to the naked eye on a dark night varies between 3,000 and 5,000, but the telescope has increased that number to many millions. It is estimated that the number of stars in the heavens may exceed 30,000,000,000, and that does not include the galaxies, all of them moving in their specific orbits and in a fixed relation to other stars as can be observed in such constellations as the Great Dipper or the Southern Cross in the Southern Hemisphere. Astronomers have cataloged a total of 88 constellations. The distance to the stars from earth and the infinite space in which they travel in each case are so inconceivable that though expressed in mathematical terms by the astronomers, no human mind can really grasp what they mean.

For example, the star Sirius, the brightest star in the sky, is nine light-years removed from the earth. The astronomers use light-years as a unit for their astronomical measurements in order to assist our imagination somewhat in grasping the inconceivable figures involved. Just as we may say to a person, "Such and such a place is about one hour's drive from here," or "a 20 minute walk" in another case, so the astronomers speak in terms of time to indicate the distances that are involved. The unit of a light-year is obtained by multiplying the distance that light travels within a unit of time with the number of these units in a year. Light travels at the rate of 186,000 miles a second; this figure is then multiplied by the number of seconds in a year which gives us the figure of 6,000,000,000,000. On this scale Sirius would be about 54,000,000,000 miles from the earth, and yet its light is still visible. The light and heat of Sirus are so great that if it were to come as close to the earth as the sun is, the entire earth would melt and vanish in a puff of smoke. And yet, there are those who scoff at the idea that Peter expressed when he says of the last day, "The heavens shall pass away with a great noise, and the elements shall melt with fervent heat, the earth also and the works that are therein shall be burned up" (2 Pet. 3:10).

The farthest light in the sky visible on earth is the great Andromeda galaxy, 1,500,000 light-years away. Multiplying that number by 6,000,000,000,000, we get the fantastic figure of 9,000,000,000,000,000,000 miles from the earth, where this cluster of stars orbits in outer space.

But even these distant stars are not yet the rim of the universe. Beyond them are millions and billions of other stars, but because of their great distance from the earth they are no longer distinguishable as individual stars, but their light is merged into great white clouds or shining white paths in the sky, which because of their appearance have been given the names of Milky Way, or Milchstrasse in German, or Galaxies in Greek.

The modern, high-powered telescope has revealed that these shining clouds and white paths consist of countless numbers of brilliant stars, clustered together and merging their light in these great galaxies. The number of stars in all these galaxies has been estimated at 200,000,000,000 with incredible dimensions. A single galaxy has been estimated at somewhere between 100,000 and 200,000 light-years across, and from 10,000 to 20,000 light-years in thickness. Some 10,000 of such whirling galaxies have been discovered, moving in great spirals in infinite space of the heavens above us, and only God and the angels know what is beyond.

This has been a brief review of some of the wonders that happened on the fourth day of creation.

What an overwhelmingly sublime spectacle this must have been for the angels when they witnessed these indescribable manifestations of the power and the majesty of their God on this fourth day of creation.

All of us have experienced the exciting thrills at a Fourth of July celebration, when we witnessed the great skyrockets screaming into the sky and exploding high above us in a thousand shining colorful stars.

What the angels saw on this day must have been something like that, only on a cosmic scale far beyond the grasp of human imagination. And we can well imagine that that was the moment "when the morning stars sang together, and all the sons of God shouted for joy" (Job 38:7).

We can be sure that at this very moment all the heavenly hosts—angels and archangels, cherubim and seraphim—bowed in humble adoration before the throne of their almighty King and Creator and shouted their "Holy, holy, holy, is the Lord of hosts: the whole earth is full of his glory" (Isa. 6:3).

A spectacle like this could happen only once in all eternity. And yet, another great and mighty spectacle is awaiting the world, a spectacle that will also be cosmic in scope and involve the entire universe; but it will be a magnificently frightful spectacle for all the sons of men who have refused to acknowledge and worship the only true and living God, and who have failed to give honor and glory to Him who made heaven and earth. This will happen, as St. Peter writes, when "the heavens shall pass away with a great noise, and the elements shall melt with fervent heat, the earth also and the works therein shall be burned up" (2 Pet. 3:10).

But that will not be the final tragic curtain-fall with everything again reverting to nothingness. Peter assures us that new heavens and a new earth shall rise from the ruins of the old. And when that happens the heavenly hosts will shout for joy as they did once before. This time they will be joined by all of God's saints that have ever lived on this earth, and they will sing their triumphant Hallelujahs in praise and adoration of their Lord and Redeemer who has created and redeemed them and has given them power to become the sons of God and heirs of the new heavens and the new earth which shall abide forever.

If men everywhere would honestly and reverently thus contemplate the great works of God's creation which are so far beyond human understanding, the arrogant confidence in their own superior intelligence and wisdom would soon wither and their ego would shrink to its real size; each would see himself as a very little, insignificant, ephemeral creature before the great majesty, wisdom, and power of the Creator, and each would be constrained to pray with David, "O Lord our Lord, how excellent is thy name in all the earth! who hast set thy glory above the heavens . . . When I consider thy heavens, the work of thy fingers, the moon and the stars, which thou hast ordained; what is man that thou art mindful of him? and the son of man, that thou visitest him?" (Ps. 8:1, 3, 4)

And God's children, or Christians everywhere, will speak with the other angels seen in a vision by St. John, flying "in the midst of heaven, having the everlsating gospel to preach unto them that dwell on the earth, and to every nation, and kindred, and tongue, and people. Saying with a loud voice, Fear God, and give glory to him; for the hour of his judgment is come: and worship him that made heaven, and earth, and the sea, and the fountains of waters" (Rev. 14:6, 7).

And so, in conclusion to this meditation on God's works on the fourth day of the creation week, let all Christians join the hymn writer, Isaac Watts, and sing:

> Give to our God immortal praise;
> Mercy and truth are all His ways,

Wonders of grace to God belong;
Repeat His mercies in your song.

He built the earth, He spread the sky
And fixed the starry lights on high.
Wonders of grace to God belong;
Repeat His mercies in your song.

He fills the sun with morning light;
He bids the moon direct the night;
His mercies ever shall endure
When sun and moon shall shine no more.

12.

The Works of God on the Fifth Day of Creation

The fifth day of creation included the creation of fish and birds, and the beginning of animal life on earth.

The events of the fifth day of creation are described in Genesis 1:20-23, where we read: "And God said, Let the waters bring forth abundantly the moving creature that hath life, and fowl that may fly above the earth in the open firmament of heaven. And God created great whales, and every living creature that moveth, which the waters brought forth abundantly, after their kind, and every winged fowl after his kind: and God saw that it was good. And God blessed them saying, Be fruitful, and multiply, and fill the waters in the seas, and let fowl multiply in the earth. And the evening and the morning were the fifth day."

With the fifth day in the creation week we move another step upward in the progressive wonders of God's creation. We now enter the mystery of animal life.

On the third day God had created the plants. That was the beginning of life on earth. Life in every form is an incomprehensible mystery, which no man can understand, and the origin of which defies all scientific investigation or explanation. And now, on the fifth day, we witness another unfolding of this mystery, the creation of conscious life.

The plant has life, is a living thing, but is not a conscious living thing. The plant is not conscious of its own environment; it has no sense organs; it does not feel, does not consciously choose its environment, is fixed to one place, does not recognize its offspring. But now, with the creation of the animals, life becomes conscious life. The animal is conscious of its existence, is aware of its environment, is endowed with sense organs; it feels, sees, hears, is aware of heat and cold, feels hunger and thirst, selects its food, and recognizes its offspring.

But as in the world of plants, so animal life appears in a systematic gradation, from the lowest forms, hardly distinguishable from the plant, to the highest species of land animals where it reaches a stage of development resembling a degree of human intelligence and a human mode of existence.

God in His wisdom saw fit to begin animal life on earth with the creation of fish and birds. These are two very distinct categories in animal life, each radically different from the other, and yet they have a number of striking similarities.

1. Both were created on the same day and in the same way. God said, "Let the waters bring forth abundantly the moving creature that hath life, and fowl that may fly above the earth in the open firmament of heaven."

Both the fish and the birds had the sea as their common origin. When God on the following day created the land animals, He said, "Let the earth bring forth."

And God said, "Let the waters bring forth *abundantly*." This abundantly applies, in the first place, to the varieties and kinds in which these new forms of life were to appear; but in the second place, it also refers to the numbers in which each kind were to appear and their ability to multiply their kind. As a result, the capacity of both birds and fish to increase is truly phenomenal. For example, it is claimed that a single herring can produce as high as 68,000 eggs; a carp, 200,000; and the cod fish even as high as from 4 to 9 million. Millions of tons of fish and other forms of marine life are annually taken from the sea, lakes and rivers, and millions and billions of tons more are devoured by other fish and forms of sea life. And yet, the gap is always replenished by a new generation, and the supply has never been exhausted.

And then when we consider the enormous resources of petroleum found in the bowels of the earth in all parts of the earth, even under the sea, which have been recognized as the fossil remains of an inconceivable abundance of fish and other sea life that perished in some great universal world catastrophe, and then consider the billions upon billions of barrels of oil that have been pumped out of the earth since the first well was drilled in Pennsylvania in 1859, this word "bring forth abundantly" takes on a staggering meaning. (The catastrophe in which all this happened was, without a question, the great Biblical Flood, described in Genesis 6 to 9. (See my book on *The Flood*, Concordia Publishing House, St. Louis, Missouri.)

This command, to increase abundantly, also included the birds; and so the capacity to multiply at a fantastic rate is also one of their characteristics. For example, it has been estimated that one pair of robins would be capable of producing more than 19,500,000 offspring in ten years if there were no natural enemies to reduce this number. A similar or even greater rate is possible with other species. A single flock of thunderbirds on Bass Island, off the southern coast of Australia, was estimated to have consisted of 150,000,000 birds.

Millions of wild geese and ducks gather every year on the wildlife reserve of Horicon Marsh in Wisconsin. Other millions congregate in Tule Lake National Wildlife Reserve in northern California. Jack Miner's bird sanctuary in southern Ontario is another place where countless migratory birds gather every season. Lake Myvatn on Iceland is a sort of international bird sanctuary, where birds by the millions from Europe, Africa, and America gather every year to hatch their young. And one of the greatest rookeries, especially of Australian birds, is found in the Coral Islands off the eastern coast of Australia. Ornithologists have found that some of these islands are literally covered with nests of Australian migratory birds in the nesting season.

Birds are exposed to many dangers. They become the victims of the natural enemies of their own kind and of other predatory animals. But the greatest threat to bird life has been man. In early years, man often destroyed birds for purely selfish reasons. He was ignorant about the important services birds render him in his struggle against all kinds of insects in all their forms. But in recent years, the use of pesticides, insecticides and chemical fertilizers have become the greatest threat. These destroy the source of the natural food supply of the birds and in that way starve them out of existence. Some species of birds have already become extinct and others are rapidly becoming so.

And yet, because of God's creative command to increase abundantly, birds have survived all these hazards through the centuries of their existence, and their number here in America alone is placed at the fabulous estimate of 5,000,000,000.

When God said, "Let the waters bring forth abundantly,"

both birds and fish appeared in about the same number of separate species. Biologists have found that in each case they number about 9,000. But both sets of these 9,000 species are again subdivided into countless subspecies, each distinct from the other so that the number of the varieties and forms becomes almost infinite. A few examples from the bird kingdom alone will illustrate this.

For instance, there are 145 subdivisions among the water fowls; 205 different birds of prey; 153 species of owls; 309 species of hummingbirds; 690 different sparrows; 200 species of woodpeckers; 43 kinds of gulls; 80 species of wading birds; and so on through all the 9,000 major species.

The same would apply to the fish and all forms of marine life.

We are impressed by the imagination and the creative genius of such great artists as Michelangelo, Leonardo Da Vinci, Raphael, Thorvaldsen, Phidias and others like them because of the variations of wonderful forms they were able to create in their respective fields of art. But even when all of these are taken together and then compared with the infinite varieties and wonderful forms created by the divine Artist, all the creative achievements of man fade into utter insignificance. And the wonder of each of God's masterpieces is that each is able to reproduce itself in kind with all the peculiar characteristics of the original.

For uncounted generations, these different varieties have existed side by side in the same environment, but there has been no confusion, no crossing over from one to the other. The salmon is still a salmon and the herring a herring; the crow is still as black as it ever was, and the chirp of the sparrow has remained the same. No species has dominated the world for the annihilation or the destruction of others, but a perfect balance has been preserved in nature. Only man, endowed with reason, has tried throughout the ages to destroy his own kind.

2. The bodily structure of birds and fish.

A second remarkable similarity between birds and fish is the structure of their respective bodies, each provided with the shape of a body wonderfully adapted for the respective sphere of its existence: the birds for the earth and air and the fish for the water.

The body of the fish has a perfectly shaped form to glide with ease and alacrity through the waters. Its body is covered with smoothly fitting scales, lubricated with a slimy substance to facilitate its movement in the water.

The body of the bird is equally well adapted for its sphere. Its general structure is spindle-shaped and perfectly formed for maneuvering in the air. It is covered with feathers, the lightest substance known for body covering and the most efficient insulation for temperature changes which enables birds to live in the Arctic region where other animal life would become impossible or to ascend to heights where other life could not exist. But in every other way, the body of the bird with its organs is wonderfully adapted for the kind of life for which it was intended.

It is no wonder, therefore, that engineers have copied the one as a pattern for the construction of the submarine and the other for the jet plane.

The birds are equipped with wings (another most amazing mechanism, from an engineering point of view), which man has not been able to copy. The fish have fins and flappers as a counterpart, which function equally well in their elements. And both birds and fish are provided with a tail which serves them as an efficient rudder to steer the birds' flight in the air and the course of fish in the water.

3. The propagation of the birds and fish.

Both birds and fish propagate their kind by means of eggs.

The birds build nests to hatch their young; the fish do not, but merely select special areas of waters for depositing their eggs, sometimes traveling hundreds or even thousands of miles in response to that mysterious instinct. And every generation follows the same pattern.

The female fish deposits her eggs in certain waters where they are then fertilized by the male and left for the energy of the sun to hatch them. The parent fish do not remain to protect or guide their young but leave them to the resourcefulness of their own instincts.

All eggs, whether of fish or birds, are a mysterious wonder, but because they are so common, one seldom thinks of them as that. The greatest mystery of the egg is that it contains the germ of life for the perpetuation of the species. This germ of life cannot be seen or tasted nor chemically analyzed. It remains completely dormant and unchanged when the egg is stored or left by itself. But this undiscernable something in the fertilized egg promptly becomes very active when the egg is exposed to a change of temperature by a carefully regulated degree beyond the normal, in each case extending over an accurately fixed period of time. The required degree of heat for the fish is provided by the sun; but for the birds it is provided by the body of the parent itself. During this process, called the incubation period, something begins to happen within the hard shell of the egg. Both the white and the yellow substance within the egg gradually disappear by being converted into a miniature replica of the parent, with bones and flesh and feathers and all the necessary organs for the independent existence of the young; and at a given moment the hard shell breaks as the young bird pecks its way out, and out hops a hungry, chirping bird.

This process is common to all birds, though the period of incubation may differ widely. But each species is governed by the same specific laws which never change. Hens' eggs always produce chickens and require the same period for incubation; duck eggs always produce ducklings within their own fixed period of time. There is no mix-up no matter how many hens and ducks and other fowl may be living in the same barnyard or how many different species may be hatching their eggs in the closest proximity in the same rookery.

In shape, size, and color the eggs of the birds differ as widely as the birds themselves. In shape they differ from the nearly round egg of the screech owl to the pear-shaped egg of the hen or the plover; and in size, from the two-pound egg of the African ostrich to the one-hundreth of an ounce egg of the hummingbird. In color, nearly all the shades of the rainbow are found among them, but each species always retains its own color.

Another mystery of the egg is the shell. This seems so unimportant and is rarely given any serious thought. But only a moment's consideration will reveal that even the shell is another great wonder of creation. Few people ever think of that when they nonchalantly break open an egg for their breakfast and throw the shell away.

Every female bird has in its body a miraculous chemical laboratory in which part of the mineral content of its food is converted into a substance of the calcareous shell and at the same time molded into an egg the same size, shape, and color common to that species. The male eats the same food, but strangely enough, in its body no shells are produced.

The time required for incubating the eggs also varies from species to species, but always remains the same for the same species. For the small birds, the time may vary from 10 to 15 days; for birds of the hen and the pheasant size, from 3 to 4 weeks; for the ostrich, the great giant among birds, 7 weeks are required. And while birds have no system for reckoning time, they have within themselves a mysterious and accurate calendar or self-winding clock which tells them the exact time for hatching their young. When that time is up they know that the young must appear. If nothing happens, they also know that something has happened to their eggs, and they will abandon their nest; and if the season is early enough, they will start the same process all over again.

Before feeling the urge to lay her eggs, the female starts to build a nest; in some species, the male may assist the female. Each species builds its own peculiar kind of nest; none imitates the other. Some build a very simple nest, using twigs, grass, or leaves or any other building material that happens to be available in the vicinity. Others are more fastidious in the choice of their materials and are most ingenious in weaving or glueing these materials together into an intricately constructed and marvelously artistic masterpiece. Some birds reoccupy the same nest year after year.

Mr. Herman W. Shaars, a famous teacher and dedicated naturalist, includes a description of the bald eagle's nest in his book, *Nature and Nature's God*; on page 108 he writes: "The eagle is mated for life. The nest, called eyrie, is built near the top of the highest tree around. That nest is used year after year, a new top of sticks being added each year.

"One such large eyrie was located near Vermillion, Ohio, along the shores of Lake Erie. It was 80 feet up in a shagbark hickory. It was used for consecutive years. It was built of sticks, some being 10 feet long, cornstalks, weed and grass clumps with dirt clinging to the roots. It had a depth of 12 feet and was wide enough for a man to spread across without the head or feet touching the edge. It weighed about 2 tons.

"The mother eagle usually lays two eggs which take 35 days to hatch. The young grow up fast. Both parents are tenderly devoted to their offspring. The male hunts the food and lets the female feed the young. For three months the young remain in the nest; by that time, with the good food and little exercise, they are larger than the parent."

Every species knows the most suitable place for its nest, where neither the weather nor the natural enemies may interfere with it. Some glue the nest to the eaves of a barn or building or on a cliff and provide the necessary adhesives for this purpose from their own saliva. Some birds expect their young to survive in a very primitive nest, offering very little protection. Others provide artistic little cradles for their little ones, beautifully constructed, comfortable and protective, lined with fluffy, soft materials from plants or animals. The eider duck of Iceland even plucks the soft and silky feathers from its own breast for this purpose.

The most beautiful nest I ever saw was that of a little wagtail, a bird common in South Australia. Often on my early morning walk, I had occasion to watch this interesting little bird, flitting about with great agility and speed, catching flying insects for its breakfast. But my admiration grew into wonderment when I saw the nest of this little fellow in the National History Museum of Adelaide. It was truly a masterpiece of artistic beauty and construction. As I stood there in admiration, wondering how evolution would explain this miracle, I could not help but exclaim with the Psalmist, "O Lord, how wonderful are all thy works," even in this insignificant, humble little Australian wagtail.

But there are other mysteries in the process of bird propagation. The eggs must be hatched—that is, exposed to a certain degree of temperature for a definite period of time, varying in length for the different species.

For the fish, the sun performs this service. But the birds must do this hatching themselves. Here is another unexplainable wonder of nature.

When the female has produced a specific number of eggs, and that may vary from 1, 2 or 3 to a dozen or more, according to the different species, then suddenly the mother bird, normally a very active creature, mysteriously becomes quiet and sedentary in its habit, remaining on her nest day after day, carefully covering all the eggs with her feathers, while at the same time her body temperature begins to rise and remains at this new level of warmth for a specific period of time. When the eggs have been hatched and the young have appeared, she again returns to her former normal life habit and now begins to gather food, not only for herself but for her little ones who have taken the place of the eggs which had required no food. And she always gathers the kind of food her young offspring require to survive.

And so we ask all those who reject the Genesis account of creation: How could all this happen? How could these little creatures, not endowed with reason or human intelligence or creative imagination, do all these things? Who taught them the art of building their nests, selecting the proper diet for their young, and turning on and off the temperature of their body, as needed, to hatch their young? Who regulated the timetable for the hatching period? How did the mother bird know that the brood that had taken the place of the eggs now required food to survive? How did they acquire the mystery of transmitting the spark of life? And if the answer commonly given is that all this happened in the process of evolution over a period of millions of years, then we ask, and how did they survive before all these skills and essential requirements for survival had come into existence, or before the foods necessary for their survival were available? And when speaking about food habits of the birds, we might continue asking more questions for the evolutionists to solve for us.

How did it happen that the different species confine themselves to a specific kind of food, and why have the species continued these limitations? Why have some birds chosen a food which is so unattractive or so difficult to secure when other types of food were available for them as it had been for other birds? Why, for example, did some birds choose carrion, the most loathsome and repulsive of all substances, and even poisonous for some, when plenty of clean food was available for them as it was for other birds? Some birds feed on fish, others on rodents, snakes, worms, and other creeping things, though they seem to be so remote from the taste and food habits of other birds. How did they acquire the knowledge of where to find this food and the skills to secure it? How did they survive before they had these skills or before their specific kind of food such as worms and insects and creeping things was available?

The food habits of birds are as different as the species and subspecies themselves. But in each case they are provided with the proper equipment to secure and eat this particular food. And here, among other things, we must consider the variety of bills by which the different species are equipped and are distinguished one from the other.

The bills of the birds are the knives, forks, and spoons on the birds' table, and what a variety of shapes and sizes and forms we find here. Compare, for example, the bill of a hawk with that of a pigeon, or the bill of an owl with that of a hen, or the bill of a stork with that of a crow, and so on through all the varieties of bird species. And then notice that in each case, the bill of the species is exactly right for the kind of food required. The question arises, was the food habit first or the shape of the bill first? If the food habit was first, why did it change, or what caused it to change and take on the present form when apparently there was no need for such a change? How, for instance, to mention only a few striking examples, would the pelican or the grosbeak or the duck and other extreme forms like them, acquire their peculiar bills if there was no need for them? How could the woodpecker come by that chisel-like beak to peck his way into the interior of a hardwood tree to secure food for himself? And before that, how did he know that there was food within that tree and in that inaccessible place?

How did the owl develop its uncanny vision in the dark, and its noiseless flight to enable it to catch its nocturnal prey? Did it change from daylight eyes to its present nighttime vision? And if so, why? Other birds did not do their hunting at night, why did the owl acquire that strange habit? And when in the alleged long evolutionary history did that change take place?

How did the falcon and the related species develop their telescopic eye which enables them to detect the smallest prey on the ground from a great height in the air?

How did the crane, the snipe, and other wading birds acquire their long and spindly legs and their spear-like bills for gathering their food in lakes and streams? Why did they choose the water for the source of their food? And why have they continued this habit generation after generation?

Then, what about the beautiful, feathery dress patterns of the different birds? How did this happen? And why the infinite varieties of patterns for the different birds?

To appreciate this wonder of creation one must examine the coat of the birds at close range or with the aid of a powerful field glass or telescope. Let us begin with the common barnyard Plymouth Rock rooster as he struts proudly about in his harem of hens in his gorgeous coat. Every feather in his coat is a marvel in itself in the quality of the material and in the shape of each individual feather, and in the colors and artistic design in which they are laid together and securely fastened to form a beautiful coat of a smooth and silky sheen, suitable for all kinds of weather, never fading and never wearing out.

Look at the beautiful blend of colors in the dress of the robin as he hops about on your front lawn, or at the bluejay in his unique garb of an entirely different pattern and color, or at the nervous cardinal in his gorgeous red coat with the cocky crown on his head, or at the beautiful blue of the Rocky Mountain bluebird, or even at the humble sparrow. All of them are dressed in their own style and each is arrayed in a garment of such delicate fabric and exquisite beauty that man in all his vanity cannot equal it. And then, on top of this, consider such creations of artistic beauty as the Australian lyre bird and the bird of paradise of New Guinea. Each is clad in such dazzling beauty that even Solomon in all his glory and the

Queen of Sheba with her glittering jewelry were not arrayed like any one of them.

And we ask, how could all of this have happened without an omnipotent, divine Artist with inconceivable resourcefulness?

And then, what about the songs of the birds? What did these contribute in their alleged upward evolutionary struggle? Why the difference in their songs? Why didn't the crow improve her voice while your little pet canary learned to warble his beautiful melodies? Why does the rooster crow and the hen cackle? Who taught the meadow lark its cheerful song of thanksgiving at the close of the day and the robin his happy chirp so early in the morning? And what caused the European lark to rise so high into the sky to sing her jubilant songs of praise to the Creator?

And then we must also remember that these vocal abilities have been passed on unaltered from parent to offspring through all the countless generations of birds since the day of creation. They still sing the same songs and entertain us with the beautiful melodies that first delighted Adam and Eve in the Garden of Eden.

So we could continue to ask a thousand more questions about the wonders of our feathery friends, the birds, for which there are no rational answers without a supreme and an all-wise Designer and Creator who made them as they are, preserved them each in his kind through all these generations, and planned them to fit into a magnificent interdependent system of the universe.

4. The mystery of the migratory instinct found in both fish and birds.

Another very remarkable similarity found in both fish and birds is the migratory instinct. This peculiar phenomenon has mystified biologists ever since the days of Charles Darwin and before. But no satisfactory explanation has yet been found. For some unexplainable reason, some species of marine life and of birds are prompted periodically to leave their natural habitat for a season and travel great distances to another locality, only to return again to the same place they had occupied before. Sometimes this migration takes place during the mating season and for the propagation of their kind, but not always.

For obvious reasons, our knowledge about the migratory habits of birds is more extensive than that of fish. But today we have also learned enough about marine life to have discovered a remarkable similarity between the life habits of birds and fish in this respect. A few examples will suffice to demonstrate this point:

The salmon of the Pacific coast is a salt water fish, but for some mysterious reason this fish in the spawning season leaves its natural habitat and migrates far up one of the rivers that empty into the ocean, even overcoming cataracts and other obstacles, often arriving in a battered condition, and there again, for unknown reasons, selects a specific place to deposit its eggs. The male, enduring the same hardships, follows the female to fertilize the eggs. They then both return to their natural habitat in the sea, where they soon die. The eggs are hatched by the warmth of the sun, and when the young are mature enough they return to the sea without aid or guidance from their parents. In the next season the young will repeat the same cycle; and so this process continues generation after generation and nobody knows just why.

Fishermen are familiar with the migratory habits of such species as the herring, the tuna, the eel, the smelt, and others like them. These migrations usually take place in certain seasons of the year, and sometimes in enormous numbers, which then provide the harvest season for the fishermen.

There are other forms of marine life which are known to be migratory in their habits. Among them is the tiny organism called "plankton." The plankton is an important source of food for some species of whales and also for myriads of smaller creatures of the sea. Plankta migrate in two directions: up and down and also horizontally. Every night they rise to the surface but sink again when the morning sun appears. But they also migrate horizontally, traveling over great distances, and in so doing carry themselves as food to other forms of sea life in distant parts of the sea.

Another most peculiar denizen of the sea is the turtle, a creature quite distinct from all other forms of marine life—neither fish nor fowl. The natural habitat of the turtle is the sea, but to propagate its kind the turtle leaves the sea, migrates to the land to lay its eggs, and then returns again to the sea.

But turtles are also known to migrate great distances over the sea. An interesting example of this occurred a few years ago when a sea captain had caught a large specimen of the green turtle, off the coast of Nicaragua. He marked this turtle and then shipped it to Florida, about 800 miles away. There it was set free and returned to the ocean. Eight months later, the same turtle was caught again at exactly the same place where it had been captured in the first place. Without compass or radar, this awkward creature had traveled 800 miles across an uncharted sea and had found its way back to the very spot where it had been hatched in the first place.

In his book *The Great Barrier Reef*, W. J. Dakian, for many years a professor of zoology at the University of Sidney, Australia, describes the mystifying habits of some species of the turtles as he had observed them on a number of islands of the Capricorn group. He reports (p. 48 ff.) that the female of the green turtles visits these islands at regular intervals from October to February, up to seven times a season, to lay her eggs. With slow and awkward efforts she manages to crawl out of the sea and up to the shore, far enough inland to reach an elevation beyond the water level. There she excavates a pit with her clumsy flappers and lays her eggs, as high as 120 in one laying; she covers them up carefully, smoothing the surface to match the surrounding area, and then returns to the sea.

The eggs are hatched in the sand, warmed by the heat of the tropical sun. The period of incubation is between nine and ten weeks. When the young are hatched, they find themselves entombed in a sandy grave, without light or ventilation. But instinctively they know how to burrow their way upward, through the sandy cover, and once they reach daylight they promptly start for the sea. They have never been in the sea before, and yet they know that this is their natural and normal habitat where alone they would be able to survive.

And so we ask again, How could they know this, and how could their ancestors have survived during the millions of years of their alleged evolutionary development without the kind of an environment necessary for their survival, and without the proper degree of temperature to hatch their offspring in a world which was supposedly still in the process of emerging from chaos?

Among the most interesting migratory creatures of the sea are the whales. There are many species of whales, large and small, each having its own migratory route. A species of the smaller type of the whale is found in the waters of the North Atlantic, off the coast of North America, and from there it migrates annually into the Hudson Bay in northern Canada. The whales arrive suddenly, in great numbers, about the middle of June in the region of Fort Churchill. They remain there for about ten weeks and then disappear as mysteriously as they came. No one knows where they came from or where they have gone. But everybody at Fort Churchill knows that they will be back at exactly the same time the following June. They are so sure of this that the local whaling plant was getting ready for operation when I was there early in June of 1969. The plant had been closed when the whales had left in the previous season. These whales return as regularly and as punctually as the swallow of Capistrano.

The great blue whale is found in the Arctic waters of the northern Atlantic, beyond Iceland. This species has the peculiar habit of practicing absolute segregation between male and female for the greater part of the year. The male seeks the icy waters of the North while the female apparently prefers the warmer climate of the South. But in the mating season, the males migrate southward, join the colony of the females, and after mating, return to their icy habitats in the North, only to repeat the same southward journey in the following season.

Whales of the Pacific have been observed to have similar migratory habits.

The Migration of Birds

More interesting than the migration of fish, turtles, and whales, is the migration of birds. Birds are closer to us and their life habits affect us more directly, and anyone with normal interest in the world around him can observe them without special training or effort.

About one-third of all birds are migratory in their habits. Some of their migrations are more spectacular than others. Some migrate only a short distance from their natural habitat to a warmer region during the coldest period of the winter months. Others travel from the northern part of Canada to as far south as the Gulf States. And still others fly almost from pole to pole.

The regular flight of the wild geese and ducks in the spring and the fall of the year is always an interesting spectacle. And nature lovers everywhere always welcome with enthusiasm the return of their beloved swallows as the first harbinger of spring; and of course, the return of the saucy little wren from its winter sojourn in the south to reoccupy its little wren house in the backyard always is a happy occasion for the whole family.

But few people have an idea as to how far many of their friends have traveled during their absence. The swallow, for example, traveled all that way from the northern part of our continent to Argentina, some 9,000 miles away, requiring 18,000 miles for its round trip.

A pair of ruby throated hummingbirds were branded before they left their parental nest. When the migratory urge came upon them they flew south and arrived at the self-same spot where their parents had wintered the year before and there established themselves only 30 feet away from the spot where they had been hatched, and that, after traveling about 5,000 miles.

The bobolink of the Great Lakes region travels all the way to the pampas of Argentina for his winter vacation, requiring about 18,000 miles of flying for the round trip.

A bird lover writes, "It was on April 15, a few years ago, that I banded a robin. The next year, as it would happen, on April 15, a robin was in my trap. When I removed him I found that it was the same robin I had banded just a year before." This robin had been away for the entire winter in the far south and now had come back to the exact place where he had nested the year before.

The golden plover nests along the shores of the Arctic Ocean, the most forbidding region in North America. There he hatches and raises his young, and when they have reached maturity he leaves this world and flies southward to spend the winter somewhere in central Brazil. But when spring appears in the northern hemisphere, his innate wanderlust again reasserts itself; and he returns to the same region where he had been hatched, and all his ancestors before him, requiring about 16,000 miles of travel to conform to this instinct.

But the greatest globe-trotter of them all is the arctic tern. The arctic tern nests in the extreme northern edge of the North American continent, all the way from Alaska to Greenland. But when the short Arctic summer has come to an end, the parent birds with their young start their journey southward and do not stop until they reach the southern tip of South America, which means a flight of about 22,000 miles for one season. That is almost equal to the distance around the world at the Equator, and these birds make that trip every year.

This remarkable and powerful migratory instinct in some of the birds is a mystery indeed for which most certainly the evolutionists' theory can give no cause or offer any solution. What is it that gives rise to this irresistible compulsion and causes them to start on their hazardous journey, generation after generation, every species having its own timetable, its own route to travel, and its own destination? How did they acquire their remarkable knowledge of climatic conditions and of world geography? By what calendar were they informed when to leave and when to return? How did the tern at the southern point of South America know when the spring had come in the region of the northern Arctic?

Biologists have found that this instinct is so strong that it overshadows even the normal parental urge of the birds to care for their young. It was found, for example, that some birds would forsake their fledgelings that had been hatched late in the season and start on their journey, leaving their young behind to starve. And it was also observed that when migratory birds were confined in a cage, they would become very restless. When the migratory urge was upon them, they tried to gain their freedom, even beating their breasts against the enclosing bars.

Then there is the mystery of how they find their way over an uncharted route in all kinds of weather and even in the darkness of the night. There is also the question concerning the enormous output of energy and muscular endurance required for their long nonstop flight over seas and mountaintops with no opportunity for rest or a break for food. Man-made jet planes, propelled by motors capable of generating energy that can only be measured by hundreds of units of horsepower and requiring thousands of gallons of fuel for a flight equal to or less than the flight of these migratory birds, are compelled to stop at regular intervals to refuel and to recheck the mechanism for safety's sake. But these living jets, large and small, designed by the divine Creator, require no refueling and no mechanical check-up; they continue their flight without interruption from continent to continent, over distances of thousands of miles; and they always arrive at their intended destination on scheduled time. There is no rational or evolutionary explanation for this mystery. Every unbiased observer and honest scientist must humbly confess here with the Egyptian magicians who were opposing Moses before Pharaoh when they said, "This is the finger of God."

But not only these long-distance flights are a mystery; the very ability to fly and the mechanism required for this performance are so wonderful and so great that only a fool could assume that this could have happened by chance and of itself.

The flight of the birds has been photographed and then carefully studied with the aid of a slow-moving projector. And these studies have revealed an intricate mechanism so amazing in technical detail and mechanical refinement that all man-made attempts to fly appear crude and clumsy in comparison.

And to make these wonders even more wonderful is the

fact that there are some 9,000 species of birds and countless subvarieties, and no two are completely alike. Each has its own peculiar type of flying. There is really a variety of different models here.

Observe, for example, the slow and dignified flight of the Canadian geese, as they follow their leader in rigid formation as if on a military parade.

Or note the graceful gliding of the sea gulls in their playful girations when following an outgoing ocean steamer.

Watch the bullet-like speed of a falcon as he pounces on his flying prey, or the noiseless wings of the night owl as it seeks its food in the darkness of the night.

Or who has not been fascinated by the exciting flutter of the hummingbird, hovering over the flower from which he gets his nourishment, or the cruising of the giant condor over the snow-covered peaks of the Andes where I had the thrilling experience of observing him? And so we could continue through all the ranks of the birds, each rank having its own pattern of flight and rate of speed as needed for its specific place in the universe.

The Speed of the Birds

Another interesting aspect of bird life is the varying degree of speed.

Birds are the fastest creatures on earth. Their speed had not been surpassed until man invented the airplane. Most birds fly at an average rate of about 30 to 40 miles an hour. The mallard duck is able to travel at the rate of 60 miles an hour. The homing pigeon can make 94 miles an hour; the African eagle swoops down on its prey at 100 miles an hour, and the falcon dives at 180 miles an hour. Even the little hummingbird is able to travel 60 miles an hour and is able to fly backwards, sideways, and hover helicopter-like in midair.

The hummingbird is the smallest of all birds but is unsurpassed in flying skills by any of them. When he hovers over a flower, the movement of his wings is so fast that they become a mere blur to the human eye. The beat of his wings at that time is 55 times per second and can rise to 75 times. The energy output required for that performance is so great that a man of average weight would have to produce the equivalent of 40 horsepower to equal it. This little creature is able to fly nonstop the 500 miles across the Gulf of Mexico to South America.

It took man nearly 6,000 years to learn to travel in the air. But God's airplanes have been flying all these thousands of years, ever since the fifth day of creation. They require no elaborate factory to produce them, no skilled engineer to build them. The old reproduce themselves by merely laying a few eggs and hatching them, and in a few weeks the new model is ready to take to the air. Each has his own built-in pilot and needs no compass or radar to guide him on his way. They require no runway to take off, and can stop at an instant wherever they happen to be. They can land on a spot so small as a swaying twig on a tree. They can rise like a helicopter, change their speed fast enough to catch a flying insect or slow enough to maneuver in playful gyrations around their nesting place.

And so we can see that even a limited survey of the wonders of God's creation in the bird kingdom alone supplies overwhelming evidence to prove that there is a divine, omnipotent and allwise Creator as the Bible teaches. No one of normal intelligence is left with an excuse for his unbelief, as is explained so well by St. Paul in the first chapter of Romans, and even affirmed by the pagan philosopher Cicero.

And yet, the great masses of people in the western, so-called-Christianized world today are willfully blind to all these wonders. They have been so thoroughly brainwashed by their educational system and by their super-wise, unbelieving intellectual leaders that they prefer to believe an absurd, mythological theory rather than the truth. But that is what happens to men who willfully refuse to accept the truth. Then they are condemned to believe the lie rather than the truth and thus become fools, as St. Paul describes them.

Since the days of Charles Darwin, it has become fashionable to reject the Genesis account of creation, and instead to accept the evolutionary theory, which rejects the accepted scientific principle of "no effect without a cause," as an explanation for the origin of the universe and all the wonders in it.

For example, the author of an otherwise excellent book titled *The Birds of the World* (published by Golden Press, New York) on page 12 makes this dogmatic assertion, "Birds evolved from reptiles at least 150,000,000 years ago and possibly even earlier." He offers no proof for this assumption, nor does he offer any explanation why he places the origin of the birds back 150,000,000 years. Why not 200,000,000 or 500,000,000? How does he get this precise period of time? His assertion is merely a guess and a bluff. And remember, this is supposed to be science, which has proved the Genesis account of creation to be a myth. And, of course, the 150,000,000 years makes the whole assumption so nebulous that no human mind can possibly penetrate into that hazy mythology and even imagine what 150,000,000 years really mean or what could have happened that far back if time really existed then. The average person finds it difficult to turn his imagination back only a few hundred or at most a few thousand years, and then to try to think of 150,000,000 years! But to speak so glibly of such astronomical periods of time impresses the naive and those whose mentalities are still in the fairytale stage of development. It causes them to stand in awe of the super-intelligence of those who make those claims, and like the people in the days of Elijah, they fall down and worship the new Baal of science. And so, here again, we find Hitler's famous dictum verified when he said, "If you must lie, lie boldly, and make your lies big enough if you want people to believe them."

But the claims made by the author quoted are by no means an isolated occurrence. The same assumptions are repeated over and over again in most of the high school and college textbooks which introduce our youth to the study of zoology and other sciences. It is an indictment on the Christian world today that very few voices are raised in protest.

It sounds so profound to the young, inmature, and inexperienced minds to hear their teachers with advanced degrees in science attached to their names tell them just how the birds around them got to be birds and how long they have inhabited this planet. As science teachers they ought to produce the demonstrated evidence for such claims, either from bird and reptile life as it is known in the world today or from fossil remains of these creatures in the past. The Pterodactyl fossil, to which they like to refer, proves nothing more than that such a creature once existed, together with other bizarre reptiles of the antediluvial period of our world's existence.

Then consider what this reptile-bird theory really involves. It means, among other things, that somewhere in the nebulous past, some ambitious offspring of a reptile-like creature got tired of dragging its ugly body through the slimy waters of some tropical river and suddenly, for reasons unknown, decided to change its environment, leave its cozy watery habitat where it had an abundance of food all about it, and take to the air. But, of course, that required some radical changes in its body structure and habits of life.

How this came about is not explained—it just happened

by itself without any guidance or direction from without—and you are expected to accept this monstrous metamorphosis by faith. But among the changes required were such "simple" things as converting its tough panzar-like scales that covered its body into delicate, silky, and light feathers; its heavy and clumsy bones into light and hollow tubes; and its awkward front legs into wings enabling it to fly; and its snarling grunts into the beautiful melodies of your canary. And again for some unknown reason, its powerful tail just conveniently dropped off. It is all as simple as that.

If you do not understand this or still hesitate to be convinced by this as scientific truth, it is because you have not yet learned to think scientifically, or it is because you have prejudices which you acquired in your early childhood religious training. And so, forget all your misgivings and know that the great-great-great-grandfather of some 150,000,000 years ago of this beautiful little pet canary in your cage, so cheerfully warbling his golden melodies for your present delight, was once an ugly, voracious crocodile or some monster like him, with a snout full of horrible teeth that could crush a dog with one bite, and a tail so powerful that could fell an ox with a single blow, but then for some mysterious reason decided to metamorphose some of its offspring into beautiful canaries and other birds like them, large and small, fully equipped with songs, and feathers, and the skill that enabled them to fly.

And then, for more unexplainable reasons, some of the descendants of this illustrious crocodile ancestor decided to go it alone and follow their own independent course. One chose to become a wabbling duck with webbed feet, and with this choice was able to fix these same characteristics on all of its offspring. Another decided to become a strutting peacock who was able to design for himself and all of his descendants that beautiful, feathery garment of gorgeous color and design. A third, very modestly, was satisfied to be a tiny little hummingbird, but was equipped with wing-power surpassing that of all the other birds. A fourth proudly arrogated the royal prerogative of becoming a bald-headed eagle, the king of birds. And the great-great-grandmother of the crows humbly chose herself for all her children to be forever dressed in the drab and somber black of human mourners. And so, with all the thousands of other bird species.

But even that is not yet all these early offspring of the crocodile ancestors were able to do. By some mysterious vision, they were able to design and fix for themselves and all of their present and remote offspring, specific laws governing each individual species, laws governing their size and general structure, and color of their eggs, the food and propagating habits, their nesting place and migration routes, and even their potential lifespan. And probably the most wonderful of their achievements was that they succeeded in organizing themselves into an integrated, unified, interdependent system of natural laws, completely integrated into the complexities of the universe which has functioned faultlessly ever since.

And then remember, all that happened by chance, of itself, without an overall plan, designer or master builder! And don't ask whether that is a reasonable explanation for the origin of the universe and all the things that are in it. If you are modern in your thinking and really intelligent and no longer bound by the outmoded religious scruples you might have had, you will accept this as scientific truth because you have been told that most modern scientists who have a Ph.D. degree say that that is the way it happened.

And remember, you are expected to accept these nonsensical beliefs in place of your faith in an eternal, omnipotent Creator, of infinite power and wisdom, revealed in our Bible, confirmed by your own conscience, witnessed to by the Lord Jesus, the greatest personality that ever lived on earth, and confessed by all of Christendom throughout the ages in the words of the Nicene Creed:

> I believe in God the Father Almighty, maker of heaven and earth and of all things visible and invisible.

In one of his dramas, Shakespeare has a character cry out in utter disgust over the folly of men as he has observed it, saying, "Oh what fools these mortals be!"

That is the normal emotional reaction of every unsophisticated human being endowed with reason and common sense, and not yet brainwashed by such nonsensical fiction, when confronted with such impossible absurdities.

The Humble Sparrow

Dear Lord, I've been thinking
about the sparrows of this world: we are so many,
gray, brown, in the way, around at all times,
but never good for very much.
Pests really, and when you consider all
the beauteous birds of this world, nothing;
we are nothing.

Everyone waits for the first robin of spring
and tells everyone else; the blue jay has a pretty color
even if he isn't so good-natured.
Everyone is happy with all other birds
of varied colors and sizes and shapes—
flickers that hang on the side of the post,
wookpeckers that eat bugs from the trees,
bluebirds that live in nests hung on fencerows.

Every bird
I can think of is something special:
flamingos of Florida, swans of Traverse Bay,
wild geese aflying, and the tiny hummingbird
traveling thousands of miles to get here to suck
out the trumpet vine. There are the swallows of Capistrano. . .
So many are so notable.
Even the wrens sing a glorious song—
and then there are the rest of us, the sparrows.
Some of us are molting, and our songs are hoarse
even for a sparrow. We are busy at very little,
and in the way; everybody knows our song
never will be sweet. And yet. . . .

The Lord said He would mark each one of us that falls,
and I don't remember that He said anything that specific
about the rest of the feathered creatures—
those beauteous ones that are kept in zoos
for people to come to see, those of jungle
or arctic or middle plains. Did You say,
Lord, they are worth more than we?

Lord, You said You'd mark every one of us,
and, Lord, we believe You.

—Hazel Krumwiede

Lutheran Witness
August 1969

Mighty God! While angels bless Thee,
May a mortal lisp Thy name?
Lord of men, as well as angels,
Thou art every creature's theme:
Lord of every land and nation,
Ancient of eternal days!
Sounded through the wide creation
Be Thy just and awful praise.

For the grandeur of Thy nature,
Grand beyond a seraph's thought;
For the wonders of creation,
Works with skill and kindness wrought;

For the providence, that governs
Through Thine empire's wide domain,
Wings an angel, guides a sparrow;
Blessed be Thy gentle reign!

—Methodist Hymnbook 1877, No. 148

13.

The Fish and Other Creatures of the Sea

So far, in our consideration of the works of God on the fifth day, we have confined ourselves almost exclusively to the wonders of the bird kingdom; but God also created the fish and the other living things of the sea on the same day. And so we must return once more to the works of God on the fifth day, and we shall see that God also filled the seas with creatures as diversified, manifold, and wonderful as the birds and other land animals of the world.

Only about one-fourth of the earth's surface is dry land, while three-fourths are seas. In the course of time, man has succeeded in exploring the greater part of the earth and has been able to exploit its riches for his sustenance and comfort. But the sea is still, to a very large extent, a terra incognita, and our knowledge of it is still quite fragmentary. Much of it perhaps will never be known; its great depth with the resulting weight and pressure of the water will probably make the exploration of the deep places forever impossible. But despite these difficulties we have learned many things about the wonders of the sea, some of which are larger and more perplexing than those found on the land.

When God created our planet, He divided it into three distinct spheres: the dry land, the sea, and the air. He provided them all with living creatures, each designed for and adapted to its specific element: the birds for the air, the land animals for the land, and the fish for the sea. In each case God created them in great numbers and distinct varieties, all of them forming an interrelated system, from the lowest to the highest, and each governed by specific laws for their individual existence and survival.

Since the water segment of our planet is so much greater than the dry land, the number and varieties of sea creatures are correspondingly greater. Biologists place the ratio of living organisms at one-sixth for the land and five-sixths for the sea.

I have already referred to the migratory habits of the lowest form of marine life, a microscopic organism called "plankton." The name "plankton" is a collective term, including myriads of microscopic forms of plant and animal life. Plankton does for life in the sea what plants do for human and animal life on land. Plankton is the link between the organic and the inorganic in the sea. It absorbs the inorganic chemicals of the sea water and converts them into organic food for the living things in the sea. This means that ultimately all life in the sea is dependent upon plankton. To provide a permanent supply for life in the sea, these microscopic organisms multiply at a truly prodigious rate—in fact, so rapidly that they would eventually have filled all the seas if a balance had not been provided by other creatures that feed on them. Hence, it is evident that the lowest and the highest forms of sea life were created simultaneously at the very beginning because neither could have existed or survived without the other.

Any attempt to enumerate or describe even a limited number of the known forms of marine life would obviously be futile and utterly impossible in a treatise like this. And so I shall limit myself to a more detailed discussion of just a few species. And my choice is determined, partly, by the unique characteristics of the subject and partly because of my own personal experience in that area. The examples I have chosen are the corals of the South Sea and the whales of the icy waters of the Arctic.

The Corals

I was very fortunate to observe this unique phenomenon of nature in two areas of the world: first, on Cocos Island, a small island in the Indian Ocean, midway between South Africa and Australia, and then again in greater detail on Green

Island, a small island in the chain of islands forming the Barrier Reef off the eastern coast of Australia.

The Barrier Reef is one of the great wonders of nature; it is the longest chain of coral islands in the world, stretching 1,250 miles along the eastern coast of Australia, from the Tropic of Capricorn to Cape York.

This chain of coral islands is created by a tiny organism about the size of a pinhead called a "polyp." The reef is composed of massive corals, a white limestone, up to five miles wide and running nearly parallel with the eastern coast of Australia, varying from 100 miles off the mainland in the south to about 5 miles in the north, and thus forming the so-called Coral Sea, which has been the watery graveyard of many early explorers.

The Reef is a mass of corals, built up from the bottom of the sea, forming what looks like a chain of low, chalky hills. Sometimes the coral islands appear in a ring-shaped structure, forming what is then called an "atoll." When the corals are exposed to the weather and action of tide and waves, they disintegrate into a dazzling white sand, causing the beaches of the islands to appear as though they had been covered with a heavy layer of white sugar.

Green Island is at the northern end of the Barrier Reef, about 18 miles from Cairns on the mainland. The Australian government has developed this island into a beautiful tourist resort. One of its interesting features is a submarine observatory, a round, steel chamber resembling a giant silo lowered into the sea, with winding stairs leading down to the bottom of the sea, and provided with port-hole windows, making it possible to observe the varied and colorful wonders of the sea at close range. And the scenery that unfolds itself on such a trip to the bottom of the tropical sea is truly breathtaking. It cannot be described in words, but it may be compared with the exotic beauty of a tropical flower garden.

Here I saw some of the strange and wonderful creatures that God made on the fifth day. Here were the large and the small, the beautiful and the grotesque, the lovely and the frightful, all living together in the same water, each supplied with its own specific type of food, each preserving his own kind among the apparent confusion. Here was a whole menagerie of the sea, performing before me as if on a circus parade. Among them were great numbers of goldfish of every size, some not more than an inch or even less in length, others measuring three to four feet, all of them playfully flitting about like animated little stars or—the larger ones in groups—like sheets of polished gold.

There were countless other strange and bizarre-looking creatures, some difficult to describe. There was the giant lobster with sheers large enough to sever a man's leg or arm, a monster clam, as large as a full-grown pig, with enormous prongs continually opening and closing in an effort to gather in its food. There were starfish of every conceivable color and size; sea urchins and sea anemones; the odd little sea horse; sponges; the horrible octopus with its frightful tentacles lashing out in all directions to gather in its food. Then there was a gruesome-looking monster before me that seemed to be half-plant and half-animal, opening and closing its flabby lips and waving in some of the living things around it for its food.

But among them all was one little fish called "butterfly-fish" of such superb beauty that it surpasses anything I have ever seen in the animal world. In size this little creature measured about 8-10 inches in length and approximately 4-5 inches in width and had a shape of body similar to that of bass. Its tails and fins were like gently vibrating strips of silvery lace; its body was draped with appendages of dazzling colors resembling in delicacy the silky feathers of the Australian lyre bird. Words cannot describe it; it must be seen; only by means of our eyes can we experience and appreciate the unsurpassed beauty of this fish. And then, think of it, this creature with all its beauty spends all its life in the depth of the sea and is rarely seen by human eyes.

* * * * *

And so again we will ask all those who refuse to acknowledge a divine, omnipotent, and all-wise Creator of heaven and earth, how will you explain the origin and the development of all these wonders of the sea? How will you account for the first coral polyp, and whence came the spark of its life, so peculiar, and the ability to perpetuate that life? How did it acquire its marvelous chemical laboratory which can convert ocean water into a skeleton of coral rock?

How will you account for the countless species, forms, and colors among these creatures of the sea? And how did the butterfly-fish learn to dress himself in such a gorgeous array of dazzling colors and style? And then, finally, why aren't some modern crocodiles growing feathers and wings and getting ready to take to the air? Why did they stop this practice?

To say that all this just happened by itself, but required millions of years to develop, is no answer. It is a cheap and dishonest evasion of the real issue. And to wrap that kind of an answer in bombastic scientific verbage is merely resorting to the tricks of the magician to deceive the naive and the credulous who delight in being deceived. This is not science, though proclaimed so by an ever-increasing crescendo in all the modern textbooks on this subject. This is not science. It is nothing less than the world's greatest hoax and fraud—sheer scientific quackery.

Every normal, intellectually honest person knows that every effect must have a corresponding cause; that is science and is also common sense.

And hence, for every person of normal mentality, these mysteries and wonders of the sea and all of creation are a wonderful manifestation of the power, the infinite wisdom, and the resourcefulness of our omnipotent God, who called them into existence as they are, just as the Bible says.

The Whales

The second category selected for special consideration includes the whales of the icy regions of the Arctic. Whales have the distinction of being the largest living creatures in the world.

I had a wonderful opportunity to learn firsthand a great deal about these mysterious monsters of the sea during my travels in Iceland and Greenland in the summer of 1968. While spending some time in these northern regions, I visited a whaling station about 65 miles from Reykjavik, the capital of Iceland, and there had the good fortune of meeting a biologist from London University, whose specialty was marine life, and who happened to be there in Iceland at that time for the special study of whales in these waters. And so, with his generous and gracious help, a new and exciting world of God's creation opened up for me.

And as another good fortune for me, it so happened that the very morning of my arrival there, two monster whales had been brought into the station, each of them measuring about 50 feet in length and weighing approximately 50 tons apiece. I was told that the blue whale in the waters farther north attains a length from 90 to 100 feet and a possible weight of 150 tons, which would be the equivalent of 40 elephants. These are undoubtedly the leviathans which had made such a profound impression upon Job and the Psalmist (Job 41:1, Psalm 104:26).

Imagine a living creature measuring 50 to 100 feet in length and attaining a possible weight of 150 tons! That is like a great submarine suddenly coming to life and beginning to operate on its own power. One must have seen such a creature to believe that it is real.

Apparently the number of these monsters in these waters is very large; at least I was told that the annual catch of whales in these northern waters around Iceland and Greenland alone is about 400 a season, and for all the seas of the world, approximately 60,000.

Then consider the enormous quantities of food these monsters require to gain such a leviathan size. According to the information I received there, a whale requires about a ton of special food for his daily diet. Multiply that by hundreds of thousands or even millions and then ask yourself, "Where does all that food come from and where do they find it?" But that is another question the evolutionist conveniently ignores. Because of his willful unbelief, he fails to recognize a wonderful, unifying plan in all of God's creation, a plan by which all of the parts are intimately linked together to form a magnificent, unified, cosmic cathedral in which every part is at the right place and in perfect harmony with the whole.

But despite these evident facts, these men that will not believe ignore all of this and try to explain the origin of all things by an uncaused process of evolution. They insist that each individual part evolved independently of any other, all of them without plan or guiding purpose, and then miraculously came together by sheer accident to form the complex and wonderful world as it is. Hence, it is not surprising that they will speak of the universe like the four blind men who tried to describe an elephant which they had never seen. Each had only touched a part of its anatomy: one had felt its legs, a second had grabbed its tail, a third had touched its trunk, and a fourth its tusks, and then each tried to explain what the elephant was like. There is no such creature as they described, and so it is with the scientists who try to create the world with the speculation of their own imagination.

Our universe is not a conglomeration of countless isolated objects such as sun and moon, stars and planets, land and sea, plants and animals, birds and fish, but a magnificent unified system with all its parts interlocking like the wheels in the works of a great clock, one depending upon the other for the proper functioning and continuation of the whole.

God did not only create the birds of the air and the fish

of the sea and the multitudes of the whales and other monsters of the sea, but also provided for each and every one a specific kind of food for their continued survival. He fixed a wonderful law in nature by which the millions and billions of marine organisms, living side by side in the seas of the world, supply food for each other, each multiplying at a carefully regulated rate so that the supply never gives out and the balance of nature is always preserved.

Life here follows the strictly regulated rhythm of:

"Big fish eat little fish
And everything that's like them,
And little fish eat lesser fish
And so ad infinitum."

Whales are the most unique creatures in the animal world, not only because of their enormous size, but also because they are not fish at all, though they originate in the sea and spend their entire life there. They are warm-blooded mammals like land animals. They have no gills, but breathe by means of lungs, and therefore must come to the surface for breathing at regular intervals; these intervals vary between one half to one hour at a time.

Whales do not propagate by means of eggs, like fish, but like other mammals they give birth to their young, and the infant whale is fed by the milk of its mother like the calf of a cow. The period of gestation is 16 months. The young are born under water, measuring about 14 feet in length and weighing approximately a ton at birth. What a baby! As soon as the baby whale has left his mother's womb, he rises to the surface to take his first breath of air, and then, like the calf of a cow, seeks the nipple of his mother to take his first meal—and all of that under water.

For every thoughtful observer, all these procedures raise a host of questions for which the evolutionists cannot offer a rational answer. For instance, how did the nonfish-mammal originate in the sea, and how did it manage to survive there before it had reached its present stage of development?

How did the baby whale learn to rise for air immediately after its birth, and how did it know that there was air up there?

How did this monster baby find its mother's nipple in the darkness of the sea, and how did it know that food was there?

How did the mother acquire that wonderful chemical laboratory to convert its own seafood into the nourishing milk for the young? Why does that laboratory cease to function after about two years, when the young are able to take care of themselves?

What caused the whale to grow to such an enormous size when other creatures of the sea did not? And what caused even the whale family to divide into different sizes?

Why did the whale choose the unattractive icy waters of the Arctic? Why do some whales have teeth, and others sheets of whalebone in their mouths?

And so we might continue asking question upon question about the mystery of the whale and other creatures of the sea, and of course also about the wonderful laws of nature by which all are governed and a perfect balance of nature is preserved.

No person in his right mind would attempt to tell another that a complex, modern computer just evolved by itself, and out of nothing, without the aid of an inventive genius to conceive and design it and a skillful technician to build it; and yet, what is even the most complex computer compared with the wonders and complexities of God's creation on the fifth day?

And so I would say again and again, not we, who would accept the Biblical account of creation as the only rational answer to the mysteries and wonders of the world, are on the defensive, but they, who deny this and claim that all of it evolved by itself. Even the pagan Romans of ancient times knew better and would not have accepted this. They expressed their conviction in a terse maxim, "De nihilo nihil" ("out of nothing comes nothing").

And St. Paul, writing to a later sophisticated generation of Romans, who had become blind to the wonders of creation and failed to see in them the revelation of the only true and living God, said, "For the wrath of God is revealed from heaven against all ungodliness and unrighteousness of men, who hold the truth in unrighteousness; because that which may be known of God is manifest in them; for God hath shewed it unto them. For the invisible things of him from the creation of the world are clearly seen, being understood by the things that are made, even his eternal power and Godhead; so that they are without excuse: because that, when they knew God, they glorified him not as God, neither were thankful; but became vain in their imaginations, and their foolish heart was darkened. Professing themselves to be wise, they became fools" (Rom. 1:18-22).

And we, who believe in the Father Almighty, Maker of heaven and earth, as revealed in our Bible and in the works of God's creation, when reverently reviewing the wondrous works of our God's creation, are compelled to join the Psalmist, glorifying our God and saying: "Bless the Lord, O my soul."

> O Lord my God, thou art very great;
> Thou are clothed with honour and majesty.
> Who coverest thyself with light as with a garment:
> Who stretchest out the heavens like a curtain:
> Who layeth the beams of his chambers in the waters:
> Who maketh the clouds his chariot:
> Who walketh upon the wings of the wind: . . .
> Who laid the foundations of the earth,
> That it should not be removed forever. . . .
> Oh Lord, how manifold are thy works!
> In wisdom hast thou made them all:
> The earth is full of thy riches.
> So is this great and the wide sea,
> Wherein are things creeping innumerable,
> Both small and great beasts.
> There go the ships: there is that leviathan,
> Whom thou hast made to play therein.
> These wait all upon thee;
> That thou mayest give them their meat in due season. . . .
> Thou openest thine hand, they are filled with good.
> Thou hidest thy face, they are troubled:
> Thou takest away their breath, they die,
> And return to their dust.
> Thou sendest forth thy spirit,
> They are created:
> And thou renewest the face of the earth.
> The glory of the Lord shall endure forever:
> The Lord shall rejoice in his works.

—Psalm 104

14.

The Works of God on the Sixth Day of Creation

On the sixth day God created the land animals and man.

The events of the sixth day of creation are recorded in Genesis 1:24-31, where we read:

"And God said, Let the earth bring forth the living creature after his kind, cattle, and creeping things, and beast of the earth after his kind: and it was so.

"And God made the beast of the earth after his kind, and cattle after their kind, and every thing that creepeth upon the earth after its kind: and God saw that it was good.

"And God said, Let us make man in our own image, after our likeness: and let them have dominion over the fish of the sea, and over the fowl of the air, and over the cattle, and over all the earth, and over every creeping thing that creepeth upon the earth.

"So God created man in his own image, in the image of God created he him; male and female created he them.

"And God blessed them, and God said unto them, Be fruitful, and multiply, and replenish the earth, and subdue it: and have dominion over the fish of the sea, and over the fowl of the air, and over every living thing that moveth upon the earth.

"And God said, Behold, I have given you every herb bearing seed, which is upon the face of all the earth, and every tree, in the which is the fruit of a tree yielding seed; to you it shall be for meat.

"And to every beast of the earth, and to every fowl of the air, and to every thing that creepeth upon the earth, wherein there is life, I have given every green herb for meat: and it was so.

"And God saw every thing that he had made, and behold, it was very good. And the evening and the morning were the sixth day."

The composer Joseph Haydn paraphrased the events of the sixth day in the following poetic form:

> Strait opening her fertile womb
> The earth brought brought forth at God's command
> Creature of every kind,
> All fully grown in countless numbers.
> Contented, roaring, stands the lion there;
> Here, supple and light, the tiger appears;
> Raising his antlered head, speeds swift the stag:
> All vigor and fire with flying mane,
> Impatient neighs the noble steed;
> The pasture green the cattle seek
> Their food, divided into herds;
> And o'er the meadows, see scattered far and wide
> The fleecy, quiet sheep;
> Like sandclouds whirling, in myriads swarming,
> Rise hosts of insects. In long processions creep . . .
>
> —Aria 22, "The Creation"

The sixth day, like the third, was distinguished by a twofold creative act: first, the creation of land animals; second, the creation of man.

In the creation of land animals, God said, "Let the earth bring forth." And as He spoke, so it was. When God created the first animal life, the birds and the fish, He said, "Let the waters bring forth," and we noted the many similarities between the two. The land animals, however, are quite distinct from both.

In the second place, we note the broad classification of the animals into three distinct divisions:

1. The cattle—that is, the large grass-eating quadrupeds.
2. The creeping things, which move either with or without feet, such as the reptiles, insects and worms, etc.
3. The beast of the field—that is, the wild carnivora of field and forest.

In the third place, we note that for each division God added the significant words "after his kind." And we read, "And it was so, and God saw that it was good."

Every form of animal life created by God was good and perfect in its kind and equipped for the purpose for which God had intended it.

The broad classification of animal life, from the lowest to the most highly developed mammals, is not the result of gradual evolution extending over millions or possibly billions of years, but God made all of these classes and species at the very beginning and established a basic law by which each form and species were to have their being and fulfill their specific place in the total creation order as God had designed it. All the living creatures were fully developed as they came from the Creator's hand (Gen. 2:19, 20) and were ready to increase and multiply, each his kind.

The so-called biological tree of the evolutionist, showing a gradual upward development of life from the amoeba to the mammals and man, is a pure creation of the imagination and has no shred of scientific proof for it.

But we must remember that a great world revolution occurred between creation and the present age in the universal Flood of Noah (Gen. 6-9). In this universal catastrophe, the first world perished with all its land animals, excepting those that were in the ark with Noah, and the new world that emerged was not only stripped of its original glory but also experienced radical changes in climate, fertility, living space, plant and animal life, and in many other respects.

The great Flood was a turning point in the history of our world, and everything in it was changed as a result.

We know this from the fossil remains of the antediluvial world that have been found in all parts of the world. Hence the animals that survived the Flood with Noah in the ark found a completely changed world as they emerged from it and had to adapt themselves to these changed conditions. This was made possible by the creative blessing which God pronounced upon them, just such a blessing as He had given the original world. And so we now find variations in species and their living habits in accordance with the climatic conditions and other environmental changes in which they now live. But these changes and adaptations occur only within the classification described as "of his kind." There is no crossing over from one kind to another and no demonstrated evidence of any upward evolution. In fact, the contrary is the case now. The law "each after its kind" had operated without change throughout all the ages, and there is no demonstrated proof for the contrary.

And as we now turn our attention to the creation of the land animals, we note again as we did with the plants, birds, and fish, a systematic gradation from the simple to the complex and from the lower to the higher forms. But we are also again impressed with the infinite variety of species and forms.

Biologists are not agreed on the number of species found among the land animals. One recognized encyclopedia mentions 500,000 species, another places the number at over 1,000,000 and still another at over 3,000,000.

But whatever the exact number might be, the fact is that the varieties and forms among them are almost infinite, each subject to and limited by definite laws which govern them.

On the basis of certain traits and characteristics common to larger groups, biologists have divided the land animals into the following six categories: amphibians, reptiles, insects, spiders, worms, mammals.

Amphibians

The amphibians are unique in that they form a sort of bridge between marine life and the land animals. The name "amphibian" means double life. This group has its existence partly in water and partly on the land. They begin life in the water like the fish and are cold-blooded creatures, but after reaching a certain stage of development they leave the water and replace their gills with lungs and continue their life on land.

Frogs, toads, and salamanders belong to this class, and each is again divided into a great number of sub-varieties.

If these amphibians just happened, as the evolutionists claim, why did this change just happen to them and not to other forms of marine life? How was the original selection made, and why was it made? Why would creatures of the water shed their gills when there was no need for such a change? And how did they manage to survive during the period of change? The lungs are a very complicated organ in the body of a living creature; how did that happen?

And if this just happened somewhere in the distant past, why are not other creatures of the sea converting themselves into amphibians today? And how was it possible for them to develop the complex law that governs their life and the lives of all their offspring? How could they have existed before these laws were in existence?

Reptiles

Next to the amphibians are the reptiles. The reptiles appear in four major divisions. These are: snakes, lizards, turtles, crocodiles.

1. *Snakes*

Snakes are found in all parts of the world, except in the extremely cold regions and on some isolated islands. They are most frequent in the tropics. About 2,300 different kinds of snakes have been identified.

In size they vary from the giant boa constrictor of the South American jungles to the harmless green garter snake in our fields and gardens.

Some snakes are beneficial to man and helpful to him in his battle against harmful rodents, bugs, worms, etc. Others are poisonous and a serious menace to the life of men and animals. The best known of these poisonous reptiles are the cobra of India and the rattlesnake of America.

And here is another mystery for the evolutionist to solve for us. If snakes just happened, how did the original progenitor of the snakes get the idea of defending itself against possible attack with the deadly weapon of poison? How did it know that poison would kill? How did it acquire the skill of manufacturing such poison in its own body? How is it possible for it to immunize itself against its own poison? How did the cobra develop that highly specialized but terrible fang by which, hypodermic-like, it injects its poison into the body of its victim? Just happened? Did the doctor's hypodermic just happen? And why are only some snakes equipped with this poisonous weapon while others are not?

And how did the American rattlesnake develop its peculiar rattle? And why does the rattlesnake curl up and warn its possible victim with its rattler before it strikes? Why does it add a new rattler to its equipment every year?

Could any rational person be persuaded that all of this could just have happened by itself?

2. *Lizards*

Somewhat similar and yet different from the snakes are the lizards. About 2,500 different species among lizards have been identified. Among them, one interesting species is the little chameleon. It has the ability of changing its color almost instantly to harmonize with its immediate surroundings. This is a protective device, and it is so effective that it literally disappears before one's eyes.

3. *Turtles*

The third group of reptiles are the turtles. There are 225 different species among the turtles, varying greatly in shape, size, and habitat, as well as in other respects. The giant among the turtles is the Atlantic Leatherback, which is known to have attained a size of three-quarters of a ton in weight and in length, 12 feet from the tip of one flipper to the end of the other.

A most unique characteristic of the turtle is its longevity. Turtles are known to have lived to an age of 200 or more years. Another equally remarkable characteristic is its ability to survive without food longer than any other living creature. A case has been reported where a turtle lived without food for six years.

4. *Crocodiles*

The crocodiles and related alligators complete the group of reptiles. There are 24 different kinds of crocodiles. Their normal habitat is in a warm climate; they are most numerous in the tropical waters of Africa. The crocodile is the most dangerous and ferocious of the reptiles—the dragon of the modern animal world. In Africa, crocodiles are known to have reached the length of 33 feet.

The large class of prehistoric animals known as the saurians belonged to this class. Their fossils have been found in every continent, sometimes in great numbers. The dinosaurs of the Red River Valley in Alberta must have lived and died there by the thousands, so thickly are their skeletons scattered over the adjoining region known as the Badlands. Some writers on the subject hold that they must have been as numerous as the buffalo on our western prairie two generations ago, but with much greater variety and number of species. In point of size they ranged from the size of a small dog to monsters of over 80 feet in length. In point of diversity they represent almost a world by themselves. In Alberta alone, 26 different species have been identified. There were those that lived on land, others in water, and still others in the air.

From the fact that the fossils of these strange creatures have been discovered in all parts of the world and are found buried under similar conditions, pointing to water as the active agent, it is reasonable to conclude that they perished and were buried under the universal Flood reported in the Bible. And either they were not able to adapt themselves to the changed conditions after the Flood or no representative of this kind was taken into the ark.

Insects, spiders, and worms constitute the next three categories of land animals.

Again, space and purpose do not permit a thorough discussion, and so I shall select only a few examples to show that even these strange, lowly, and little understood creatures reveal the greatness and incomprehensible resourcefulness of our God who created them for the world as He had designed it.

Insects

Possibly the most important of these three groups is the insects, partly because of their great number, and partly because of the role they play for good and for ill in man's own life and in his struggle for existence.

In number, the insects constitute the largest single group of living creatures. The United States National Museum estimates the number of insect species at the fantastic figure of 10,000,000. Other estimates are more conservative, but still place them at about 6,000,000. But whether the number is placed at 6 or 10 million, either of these figures is incomprehensible, especially when considering that these figures represent that many separate creatures, each different from the other, each endowed with the mystery of life, each capable of propagating its kind, and each requiring a specific kind of nourishment for its survival.

Some insects are man's friend and servant for good. Others are enemies that annoy and torment him, destroy his fields and orchards, and compete with him for his very survival. The beneficial insects are in the minority, numbering only a few hundred, while the harmful ones are numbered by the millions.

But this raises some interesting questions about the place and function of the insects in the original world of Adam. Surely Adam and Eve did not require screen doors or insect-repelling chemicals to protect themselves against flies and mosquitoes, fleas and ants, and other annoying insects that now make life miserable for man. But if not, what then was the nature and the function of these insects in the world of

Adam? The answer to that question must be: We know not, because we cannot even imagine what a perfect world could be like without the curse of sin upon it. Besides that, we must also remember that there are many other mysteries in our present world for which we have no satisfactory answer.

As to the question of how they became what they are today, when all of God's original creation was very good, the answer can be found in the curse that God pronounced upon the earth and upon Adam and Eve when they disobeyed His commandment and fell into sin. Then God said to Adam, "Cursed is the ground for thy sake; in sorrow shalt thou eat of it all the days of thy life; thorns also and thistles shall it bring forth to thee" (Gen. 3:17, 18). As a direct result of this curse of God, original nature was radically changed; good plants became thorns and thistles and a hindrance and a burden in Adam's life and in the lives of all of his descendants.

At the same time millions of insects originally intended to contribute in some way to man's comfort and benefit now became a curse to him. They were changed into annoying flies and mosquitoes, lice and bedbugs, cockroaches and termites, grasshoppers and locusts, fleas and chiggers, and all the other annoying and harmful insects that now make life miserable for both man and beast. All this is the result of man's disobedience and sin.

But though the great bulk of insects are a curse to man today, yet, when considering them as individual creatures, each after its own kind, and then thinking of the great number and varieties in which they are found, we are again overawed by the greatness and the resourcefulness of the Creator.

1. *The honey bee*

Possibly the most interesting member of the insect family is our beloved little honey bee.

There are many interesting features found in the honey bee which arouse our attention; one of them is the social instinct.

The honey bee is a social insect and only lives in colonies. A single colony may consist of from 20 to 60,000 individual bees. Each colony is a highly organized and a strictly stratified society. The soul and center of the colony is the queen. In size, the queen is much larger than any other member of the colony, and in many other ways quite distinctly separated from all of the rest. All the others are servants of the queen and care for her.

The queen has but one function: to produce the eggs by which the colony perpetuates itself. A single queen may produce as high as 50,000 eggs in one season, which means that she is able to lay as high as 1,500 eggs per day. She deposits each egg in a separate cell, prepared by the workers for that purpose; and with that act, her responsiblities are ended. The eggs are hatched in about three days, and from that moment on the worker bee takes over the care for the young until they are able to take their own place in the colony.

The second group are the drones, or the male bees. They are in the minority. At the end of the season, they are driven out or killed by the workers and removed. The society of bees adheres strictly to the principle that "he who will not work neither shall he eat," and so they get rid of the drones.

The third group are the worker bees. They are the under-developed females that do all the work. They feed the young, gather the honey, and build the cells to store what they have gathered.

In its structure and anatomy, the bee is a most wonderful little creature. Its head is equipped with two multiple eyes, like those of the fly. Besides the eye, it has two rod-like projections on the head which serve as a sense organ for touch and for smell. Each rod is again supplied with countless microscopic sense receptors by which the bee receives the sensory stimuli. Its feet are shod with sharp claws, which enable it to walk over rough surfaces; and in between the claws are attached suction pads which make it possible for it to walk on glass or any smooth surface, or even to hold itself in an upside down position on the ceiling. On its hind legs are attached little basket-like devices in which it carries the pollen gathered from the flowers for food to share with the rest of the colony. But while the bee gathers the pollen for food, it also carries it from flower to flower, and thereby performs a most important service by fertilizing the flower, thus making full development possible.

The wings of the bees are amazingly efficient and powerful, moving at an incredible speed of 75 beats a second, and they are so constructed that the bee can move either up or down or sideways or even hover motionless over a flower or any other object.

Perhaps the most remarkable feature about this little insect is the chemical laboratory in its little body, in which it converts into honey the nectar it has gathered from the flowers.

This honey is the sweetest substance in the world. And when we add to this its skill as a builder of the wax cells to store honey and its unique ability to manufacture its own building materials, the wax from which the cells are made, and its uncanny sense of direction which enables it to go far afield to gather nectar, and yet always find its way back in the shortest and straightest line possible, we again are overawed by the wisdom and the goodness of the Creator who designed this little insect and assigned to it its task of producing honey for man's enjoyment.

And all men, when seeing these wonders of our Creator, ought to burst into a song of praise at their sight and sing with the composer Joseph Haydn:

> Sing the Lord, oh all ye voices!
> Give Him thanks,
> All ye His works so wondrous!
> Sing His honor, sing His glory,
> Bless and magnify His Name!
> Jehovah's praise endures forevermore,
> Amen, Amen!
> —33rd Chorus, "The Creation"

2. *The ant*

Another remarkable member of the insect family is the ant. Even Solomon was already impressed by this little creature: "Go to the ant, thou sluggard; consider her ways, and be wise: which having no guide, overseer, or ruler, provideth her meat in the summer, and gathereth her food in the harvest" (Prov. 6:6-8).

And again he writes, "The ants are a people, not strong, but they prepare their meat in the summer" (Prov. 30:25).

The ants are found in all parts of the world: in fields and forests, in deserts and jungles, in cities and on the farm. About 2,500 species have been identified. Some ants are winged, but most of them are wingless. In color they vary from red and black to brown and yellow, and in size they may differ from the near microscopic to the large black ants, one half inch long.

Like the bee, the ant is a social insect and always lives in colonies. A colony of ants may consist of 200,000 or more individuals; some even number as high as many millions. Their habitation, or the so-called ant hill, is of an ingenious construction consisting of countless tunnels, cells, and large assembly rooms.

The mound-builder ants of Africa build large, dome-shaped dwellings, four and 5 feet or even more in height and up to 10 feet in diameter. These dwellings are built of dirt and sand carried together from the surrounding territory, and cemented together by a substance the ants produce from their own bodies. The resulting building material is almost as hard as brick, and is able to withstand the ravages of weather for many decades. In some regions of Africa I found a large number of such dwellings in the same area, forming a sort of ant city similar to the early prairie dog towns of Wyoming. It is estimated that some colonies of the mound-builder ants consist of over 100,000,000 individuals. All ants recognize all the other ants of the same colony but will promptly destroy any intruder who may venture into the colony from the outside. Every ant colony consists of three strata or castes, each caste having its own specific duties to perform.

There are several queens in the colony of ants. Their sole function is to produce eggs for the perpetuation of the colony. When the queens have produced their eggs, the worker ants carry the eggs into the hatching places, and there often move them from gallery to gallery and even out into the sun. In due time, a tiny larva will emerge from the eggs, completely helpless, requiring the care of the worker ants, even to the extent of feeding them. The food provided is a semi-predigested substance produced by the workers themselves. This care continues until the young creature has reached the chrysalis stage; then it is buried by the workers; and now it begins to spin a silken cocoon around itself. The silk flows from its mouth and not from the abdomen, as in the case of the spider. In some mysterious way, the workers know when the chrysalis has finished its cocoon and will then bring the cocoon back into the open of the colony. From the cocoon will emerge a fully developed adult ant, ready to take its place in the colony.

Many other wonders about the ants are equally incomprehensible, especially certain food habits that some have. Some ants live on green vegetation, others on seed; some on insects, and some on other living things. Some enslave another kind of an insect which then oozes a honey-like substance from its body, and this becomes food for the ant.

Some ants store honey in the bodies of fellow ants. These storage ants are selected early in their development and are fed great quantities of honey dew, which causes their skin to stretch into round balls about the size of peas. They are completely helpless in this stage and serve only as living food storage tanks for the rest of the colony.

The driver ants of Africa are ferocious insects. They travel in great armies and destroy every living thing that comes in their way while on the march. It is said of them they are able to kill a wounded elephant and pick his body clean in one night. A case to illustrate this ravenous characteristic in these ants came to my attention while traveling in Africa. A family of my acquaintance there had a pet family dog which they left outside during the night. One night an army of the driver ants passed by. The next morning their pet dog had disappeared, and all they found were the bones of its skeleton, all picked clean.

The ant is a very humble little creature, but it proclaims, together with its cousin the bee and millions of other insects, each in its own way, the majesty, wisdom, power, and incomprehensible resourcefulness of the Creator.

And so I suggest that the unbelieving scientist and all those like him should follow the advice of wise old King Solomon and go to the ant and learn from it to recognize the folly of their unbelief, and then humble themselves with the man in the Gospel and say, "Lord, I believe; help thou mine unbelief" (Mark 9:24).

The Spider

The fourth category listed in the lineup of land animals created on the sixth day includes the spiders.

Spiders, like the insects, belong to the smallest creatures God created for the land, but they must not be confused with insects. There is a distinct difference between the two in body structure, habits of life, and in many other respects.

Spiders appear in all sizes, from the smallest, nearly microscopic, to the frightening tarantula. About 2,500 species of spiders have been classified, each having its own design, size and purpose. A few spiders are poisonous in their bite; chief among them are the tarantula and black widow.

A distinguishing characteristic of the spiders is their ability to spin nets of exceedingly fine silken threads. These nets serve the same purpose for the spider which the fisherman's nets do for him. They are an ingenius device to trap insects and other victims for their food.

Each species of spider has its own distinct pattern of webs, and each is perfect in its own class of designs. Some webs are wheel-shaped with spoke-like strands radiating out from the center den of the spider to the periphery, with a number of crossbars connecting all the strands into a familiar geometric design. Some nets are of a hammock shape, others are more like a sack, and still others are mere blanket-like nets spread over the grass or some other surface to catch whatever may cross them.

The silk of the spider is produced in a specialized gland in its body. Minute ducts called "spinnerets" lead from the gland to the rear part of the spider, to carry its secretion to the surface where, exposed to the air, it becomes a silken thread. These threads are so fine that *no man-made instrument could make them so fine.* But at the same time they are strong, elastic and can stretch like rubber bands. In an experiment it was found that a rope, one inch thick, woven of spider webs was stronger than a rope of the same thickness made of steel wire!

Spiders are not particularly attractive to man. There is something about them which seems to repulse man and arouses a secret feeling of fear or horror; but spiders, nevertheless, are most unique and complex creatures which cannot be accounted for by saying, "It just happened that way." Things as complex and as varied as spiders don't just happen. For the thoughtful observer, the spider, therefore, raises many questions which even the most unbelieving scientist cannot answer. How, for instance, did it happen in the first place that a spider became a spider with all its peculiar characteristics?

How could it develop the unique gland for producing those incomparable silken threads? How did it know that it could trap insects for food by means of these nets? And how did it survive before it acquired all these skills if it just gradually developed in the long process of evolution? And so we see that also the humble spider joins the chorus of all creation, glorifying the wisdom and the wonders of our God.

Worms

Worms are the lowliest of all creatures. If there were a hierarchy among animals, the worm would be at the very bottom, and even there below the first rung. To be called a worm is the ultimate in superlatives of contempt and loathing.

According to the Psalmist, the suffering Messiah, in the lowest depth of His humiliation, cried out, "I am a worm, and no man; a reproach to men, and despised of the people"

(Ps. 22:6). And Isaiah compares the torments of hell with the ravenous gnawing of devouring worms (Isa. 66:24).

The explanation for the loathsome character of worms must also be sought in the curse that God pronounced upon the earth after man had fallen into sin. But even the despised worm is a mystery beyond comprehension. The scientists and engineers have been able to create the complex computer. Doctors have transplanted the human heart from one body into another, and the President of the United States has spoken by telephone from his office on earth to the astronauts on the face of the moon. But no scientist or engineer or even a president can produce the mystery of life, even as it is found in the despised worm.

Man, with his finite limitations, can see and investigate only comparatively small fragments of the universe. Even the most advanced scientist is limited in his knowledge of nature and its laws to a very small area of the whole. If he could rise above the universe and see the whole from a vantage point beyond the outer limits of space and see it as God sees it and as He designed it in the first place, he would then be able to understand that the world is not merely a collection of individual disconnected objects that developed each by itself, but that all, from the cosmic galaxies on the rim of outer space to the humble insects and worms, constitute an intricate, unified system, all working together in a unit and each contributing its part to fulfill the purpose and the plans of the Designer and the Creator.

Even the worm has its place in this system and is an evidence of the infinite wisdom of the Creator.

15.

The Mammals

The last of the animals to be created on the sixth day were the mammals. With the creation of the mammals, animal life reaches its highest form of development.

The name mammals is derived from the Latin word *mamma*, which means mother's breast. The mammals are creatures whose young are nourished with the milk of their mothers.

Evolutionary biologists trace the origin of mammals back to "an extinct mammal-like reptile of the Triassic Age" (*Encyclopaedia Britannica*, Vol. XIV, p. 748).

We recall that another biologist traced the origin of birds to the same reptilian ancestry.

The versatility of these early reptiles apparently must have been most phenomenal, when considering their ability to direct their offspring into so many divergent channels which, in turn, gave rise to the countless species and forms of animal life in the world today. But this popular evolutionary assumption gives rise to a number of important and very basic questions for which it offers no logical or reasonable answer:

A natural question would be, how did it happen in the first place that some of the offspring of these reptiles grew feathers and others hair, while the original ancestor had neither?

How could an offspring originate from a parent so completely different in body structure, habits of life, food requirements, etc., from the parent?

How did that change come about? Nothing just happens; as the Romans would say, "De nihilo, nihil." What were the causes for these effects, and what produced the causes before that?

Great masses of fossils of animals long extinct have been found in all parts of the world. Why have not some convincing links been found in the long chain of this alleged evolutionary development between the original reptile ancestor and the mammal of today?

And if the evolutionary process is an automatic, ongoing system, why are not some new creatures appearing somewhere between the original great-great-great-reptilian grandfather and the modern cow, dog, elephant, or goat?

No reasonable answer is offered for any such and many other questions; and yet, because it is the established style of today, everybody blindly accepts it as science and truth. Unbelief makes fools of people and even beclouds the mentality of otherwise intelligent and highly trained men.

There are a number of distinguishing characteristics which separate the mammals from all other animals. Chief among these are:

1. Mammals give birth to their young.

2. The newly born young is nourished with his mother's milk.

3. Mammals have a highly developed brain and nervous system.

4. Mammals breathe by means of lungs.

5. Nearly all mammals have their bodies covered with hair, some more, others less.

6. Most mammals have four limbs.

7. The vital organs of mammals, such as heart, lungs, liver, kidney, digestive organs, circulatory and reproductive systems are very similar to those of man and quite distinct from that of other animals.

About 5,000 species of mammals have been identified. These are again subdivided into a number of major groups, and each of these into countless further subdivisions and subspecies. Mammals are found in all parts of the world, from the tropics to the Arctic.

In size, they vary from the tiny little flying bat, the only flying mammal, to the giant African elephant on land and the monstrous whale in the sea.

In food habits they are divided into herbivora (vegetarians), carnivora (meat eaters), and omnivora (both vegetable and meat eaters).

According to their relationship with man, we speak of them as domesticated and wild animals: the one serving man, the other fleeing from him and sometimes confronting him as an enemy.

Mammals have been closely associated with the life of man from the very beginning. Some have always been his most faithful and unselfish servants. They gave their bodies to him for food, their skins for shoes, and their hair for clothing. They have patiently borne his burdens, carried him on his journeys, provided him with sports and entertainment, and have even given their own lives to assist man in his battle against his fellowmen. They have served as watchmen and bodyguards and have helped him to protect his home and his community against criminals. And in all ages mammals have been the beloved pets and friends of children and of the whole family.

Of the domesticated animals, sheep, cattle, camels, donkeys, and dogs seem to have been man's closest associates from the very beginning. Abel, the son of Adam, brought of the firstlings of his flock as a sacrifice to the Lord. Abraham and Lot had great herds of cattle and sheep, and of Job we read that he was exceedingly rich in cattle, sheep, and camels.

We first encounter the dog in Scripture in Ex. 11:7, and thereafter it is often mentioned. We meet it in literature in Homer's Odyssey (about 900 B.C.) where we are told that while Ulysses, king of Ithaca, was involved in the Trojan War and his adventures in the Mediterranean Sea, his faithful dog patiently waited for his return. And when finally, after ten years of waiting, his master came home, the faithful dog recognized him and in loving dog fashion expressed his joy by licking his master's hand and then lay down to die.

In the Apocryphal book of Tobit (about 250 B.C.) it is recorded that Tobias, the son of Tobit, is sent by his father to a relative in a distant city of Media. On this long journey he is accompanied by the Angel Raphael and his faithful dog.

Perhaps the most eloquent tribute ever paid to a dog was made by Senator Vest, of Missouri, before the jury in a trial to recover damage for the killing of a dog belonging to a neighbor. He pleaded as follows:

"The best friend a man has in this world may turn against him and become his enemy. Those who are nearest and dearest to us may become traitors to their faith. The people who are prone to fall on their knees when success is with us may be the first to throw the stone of malice when failure settles its cloud upon our heads.

"The one absolutely unselfish friend that a man can have in this selfish world is his dog. A man's dog stands by him in prosperity and in poverty, in health and sickness. He will sleep on the cold ground when the wintry winds blow and the snow drives fiercely, if only he may be near his master's side. He will kiss the hand that has no food to offer; he will lick the wounds that come in encounters with the world.

"He guards the sleep of his pauper master as if he were a prince. When all other friends desert he remains. And when death takes the master in its embrace and his body is laid away in the cold ground, no matter if all other friends pursue their way, there by his graveside will the noble dog often be found, his head between his paws, his eyes sad but open in alert watchfulness, faithful and true even to death."

The wild animals are slowly disappearing in the world as human population increases and an industrial society gradually takes over the last wide open spaces left on our planet, crowding the wild beasts out of their existence.

Africa is the only continent where the large wild animals still survive in great numbers and enjoy their original freedom. I saw them there in the great wildlife reserves set aside by wise and thoughtful governments for their protection and survival. What an unforgettable and inspiring sight that was indeed! Here were large herds of the giant African elephants, carefully surrounding the baby and juvenile elephants for their protection; a group of giraffes reaching high up into the trees for their food; a family of lions with their playful little cubs cavorting under the trees in the grass; the monster hippopotamus cooling himself in the river; the ferocious rhinoceros suspiciously watching us; the cheetah, the leopard, the dangerous African buffalo, the ugly and arrogant baboon, and all the other colorful and fascinating creatures of God's wilderness—all living together as they did when Adam first saw them.

But even here in Africa the future of these magnificent creatures is threatened by the expeditions of glamorous safaris of wealthy playboy hunters who come here from all parts of the world, armed with high-powered rifles to slaughter them for the sheer joy of killing, then carry away their heads, horns, and pelts as proud trophies of their own great prowess, to adorn their villas and homes. And in the last years native ivory hunters have created still greater havoc. Yes, here, too, it is true that "every prospect pleases and only man is vile."

We noted above that the first basic distinguishing characteristic of mammals is that they give birth to their young. Birds and fish propagate their kind by means of eggs, but mammals produce living offspring which were conceived and developed within the body of the mother. We are here again confronted with the mystery of life and the origin of life in the individual living creature.

Life in the mammal begins with conception. Conception means that a living female cell, called ovum, has been fertilized or penetrated by a male cell, called sperm. When these two cells meet they coalesce and form one cell. This new cell is the beginning of a new, individual life, which contains all the distinguishing characteristics of the adult in that species. This new life is nourished with the blood of the mother by an intricate network of blood vessels lining the womb of the mother.

The period of development within the mother is called gestation. This period differs in length with different species. For the possum, for example, it is 13 days; for the rabbit, one month; for the dog, 4 months; for a cow, 9 months; for a horse, 11 months; for a lion, 3 1/2 months; for a giraffe, 14 months, and for an African elephant, 22 months, and so with varying differences in all the other species. The law of nature that regulates this process is constant, and the calendar for each species never changes.

The birth of mammals may be a single or a multiple birth. A multiple birth may vary from 2 to 10 or even more.

The period from conception to birth is accompanied by another most remarkable procedure in the body of the mother called lactation. The word lactation is derived from the Latin *lac*, meaning milk. Lactation is the process of secreting milk as food for the young. This process takes place in specialized glands called mammary glands and is always accurately synchronized with the progression of the pregnancy. When the young is born, its table is set and its food is ready for it. And this food is not only geared to fit the digestive organs of the young, but it also contains all the food elements essential for its normal development. When the young no longer requires this food, the function of the glands ceases automatically.

All these mysterious processes in the animal life are commonplace experiences in nature; everybody is at least vaguely familiar with them, and they are, therefore, generally taken for granted as a natural phenomenon. Very few ever stop to think of the mysterious wonders that occur at the birth of every mammal in the world, or of this wonderful law by which these processes have continued unaltered throughout the ages and through the millions of mammal generations that have lived on the earth.

Part of this apparent indifference, no doubt, comes because most people today are so far removed from actual animal life in our industrial society of machines and things that they know little about it; and whatever knowledge they have, they have acquired from reading in natural history magazines or biological textbooks.

But to become vividly aware that an animal is not merely another machine or thing, but a most wonderful living creature which only God could have designed and made, a person must come in close contact with animal life, observe it at close range and find out for himself how an animal actually lives. Only then will he get a faint glimpse of the supernatural wisdom that created the animal world.

I am thankful for the wonderful opportunities I have had for such observation of both wild and tame life at close range. What I learned on these occasions filled me with reverent wonderment for the Creator, and gave me a feeling approaching a sort of reverence for the animals themselves, of whatever kind they might be.

One of these experiences I had in South Africa, in the famous Krueger National Wildlife Preserve. Here I spent some time surrounded by almost every species of wildlife found on that fascinating, but little-known, continent. This was one of the most exciting experiences I have ever had in all my life, and at the time I would have liked to have stayed there permanently.

Another profitable experience was a visit to a ranch in northern California, a ranch specializing in raising thoroughbred Hereford breeding cattle. Here I learned much about the science of breeding so-called thoroughbreds. Thoroughbreds are produced by an artificial selective process, directed by a trained breeder. There is no selective breeding in nature; hence, there is no upward evolutionary development of individual or species; rather, the reverse is more apt to happen through a process called "inbreeding." Deterioration and death are the rule in nature; the fossil remains of the entire world prove that nature has deteriorated rather than developed upwardly. But here, on this interesting ranch, I learned from the manager that even man-directed selective breeding has its built-in limitation, fixed there by nature itself. The upward selective process is effective only to about the fourth generation. After that it stops. The female will either become sterile or the young die either before or immediately after birth, and if they survive they revert completely back to the original kind. And so I found that this professional cattle breeder unconsciously or unintentionally gave me a most devastating argument against the theory of an upward evolutionary development of both individual and species. There is no such development possible; nature itself blocks it.

A third interesting experience I had on another farm, this time in southern Minnesota. The operator of this farm specialized in hog raising. He was a prosperous and a progressive modern farmer, and also a very intelligent, humble, Christian gentleman who thoroughly understood every phase of his hog-raising business. But to him, his hogs were not only an interesting means for gaining a livelihood, but he saw in every one of them a wonderful creation of God, each disproving in its own way the absurdity of the evolutionary theory. He knew from experience, not from books, that every one of his pigs was a bundle of unexplainable mysteries that could never have happened by accident.

He first spoke to me about the special breed of hogs he had selected for his business and explained the merits of the various breeds known to the farmer. Then he talked about the food hogs require for their most rapid development, the cost of raising a pig for the market, and other related matters dealing with the hog business.

But then he pointed to a large brood sow immediately in front of us, surrounded by her brood of squealing little ones, and said: "This sow is able to produce 2 litters a year, the period of gestation for hogs being 114 days. A litter," he continued, "may consist of 2, 4 or even 10, 14, and sometimes even more than that, the average being about 10." He went on to explain that this litter of 10 little pigs developed simultaneously in the womb of the mother, and while the sow was a rather large-sized animal, yet, the womb in her body would nevertheless be a comparatively small compartment and must have been a very crowded place to contain 10 young pigs at the same time, each weighing about 3 pounds at birth. And yet each of the 10 had its own individual life. And when they were born, each one of them was a perfect individual, a miniature replica of its parents. Each had two ears, two eyes, a pointed nose with the familiar round, flat tip, and all of these parts were in the right place. Each had its body covered with the same kind of short, bristly hair. Each was equipped with a complete set of vital organs ready to go into high gear as soon as it came off the assembly line. Each had four legs perfectly coordinated, and even the miniature tail, with its cute little curl, and the familiar squeal were not missing. And no sooner had this brood of little pigs seen daylight for the first time than they at once began to cry for something to eat, and by another miraculous instinct with which they had been endowed, they were able to find the source of that food without any special help or guidance.

And then I learned about another strange trait in these little fellows. The food they were seeking and required was their mother's milk. This milk is available for them in the nipples or teats of the mother. The mother has 10-14 teats arranged in two parallel rows on the lower part of her belly. As soon as the little ones are born, they begin to scramble towards the source of their food, and they seem to follow the principle: first come, first served. But once they have chosen one of the teats for themselves, they remain with that one throughout their nursing period and will not permit a change. If in a rush one of their little brothers or sisters would seem to encroach on their private domain, there follows an immediate noisy, squealing row in that pig family. The mother then tries to pacify her brood with her soothing motherly grunts that only a little pig can understand.

And then it occurred to me that this humble brood sow, surrounded by her brood of squealing little ones, could make a modern, sophisticated evolutionist Ph.D. professor look foolish and silly with his theory of evolution, trying to convince people that all these wonders just happened by accident, without any design or Creator, and that the Bible is all wrong. How ridiculous can you be!

This process of lactation is by itself one of the most mysterious processes and wonders in the mammals' lives which deserves some further and special attention. I acquired some further interesting information on this phase of animal life on a dairy farm in northern Kansas. The farm I visited was operated by an intelligent, progressive young farmer, a former student of mine, who had chosen farming as his life's vocation. He proudly introduced me to his herd of beautiful Holstein cattle, numbering about 50 head. He explained the merits of the Holstein cow for the dairy business and discussed other matters pertaining to dairy farming. And then he pointed with justifiable pride to a cow in the herd which in size and general behavior seemed to be the recognized queen of the herd. "This cow produces an average of 100 pounds of milk a day in her best productive period," he said. I was not sure whether I had heard him correctly and asked him to repeat that statement. He did, saying, "Yes, 100 pounds of milk a day." I tried to visualize the quantity of that amount of milk in a concrete form and concluded that 100 pounds of milk would be about the equivalent of four large buckets. And then I began to think some more about the wonders of milk produced by this Holstein cow.

When I had this interesting conversation with my young farmer friend, his herd had just come in from the pasture. There these cows had been feeding on green grass. When they came into their stalls for milking, their diet was supplemented by a portion of ensilage and some ground-up corn and some other grains. The grass which the cows had eaten was a bright green color; the ensilage had been green but now had wilted into a grayish green and brown color, and the grains varied from yellow to brown and other colors. The cow had taken these substances as food into her body and then by a miraculous process the green and the brown and the yellow were converted into red blood, white bones, reddish flesh, and these four buckets of mysterious white liquid we call milk.

Milk not only provides the proper food for the young of the cow, but it is also a well-balanced nourishment for human babies, and is a delicious and refreshing drink for adults everywhere in the world, among all races and people. Its flavor is unique. It is neither sweet, sour, salty nor bitter, but a perfect blend of all four of these basic tastes. And when analyzed, milk is found to consist of butterfat, casine, albumen, sugar, salt, and infinitesimal bits of various acids and water. And all of that is produced in the body by this Holstein cow at the rate of four bucketfuls a day.

And then it occurred to me that if this cow could think and speak like a human being, I am sure she would have said to me: "You men of the human race are very proud of your great inventors who have given you the telephone, the electric light, the Harvester machinery, the sewing machine, the automobile, and all the other countless machines, instruments, and gadgets that have contributed so much to the comfort and enjoyment of life. In recognition of what they have done, you write their biographies for posterity to remember, you erect memorial tablets in their honor in your halls of fame, and you teach your children to honor their memory. And now I would like to ask you, Why do you not recognize, honor, and glorify the great Master inventor, who invented me and all of my kind, and all the other wonderful creatures about you in this world? Why are you so concerned about the limited inventions of your fellowmen and so indifferent towards the one truly great Inventor? And why are you so blind to the greatest of all inventions?"

"Yes," I thought, "why are men that way?" How can a human being endowed with normal intelligence be so blind to, and so ungrateful for, all the wonderful creatures God has given us in the world around us, inventions a thousand times more wonderful than the finest and greatest achievements of men? And not only are men so blind, but even contrary to all common sense and reason, they ascribe these wonders to a process of self-development without cause or intelligent direction. Unbelief is an incomprehensible mystery. It dehumanizes man and makes him a fool despite his vaunted wisdom and scientific knowledge.

"Oh Lord," I sighed, "have mercy upon us. Have mercy upon us and cast not all of us away because of the stupid unbelief of the wise ones in this world."

There are many other wonderful aspects of animal life which should receive at least a passing consideration, such as the peculiar and different devices for self-defense found in the different species of animals.

The ox and buffalo and their kin have powerful, pointed horns; the deer, elk, and moose have antlers with sharp and dangerous prongs; the rhinoceros has a fearful spear-like weapon on his nose; the lion and his relatives are equipped with deadly teeth, a powerful jaw, and dangerous claws; the elephant, hippo, and boar are armed with terrible tusks; the horse has hammer-like hoofs and the skill to use them effectively; some animals resort to poison, others to mimicry; some depend on their speed, or their truly fantastic sense of smell, vision or hearing; and not to be forgotten is the skunk, the first to resort to chemical warfare in which it has proved itself most efficient. And again we ask, how did all these strange and diverse devices come about? Just happened?

And then there is the great diversity of food habits in the animal world:

The ox thrives in a field of clover, while the lion would starve there. The reindeer are able to survive on the meager diet of lichens and mosses in the barren regions of the subarctic, while other animals would perish there in a very short time.

Some animals are limited to a vegetarian diet; others live exclusively on the flesh of other animals, and some feed on anything. How did they happen to choose their particular food? Why doesn't the goat feed on mice and a rat on hay? Why? Just got that way by chance? How naive can one be!

However, there is one more important question that must be considered before we leave this subject: "Was man, and were the animals in the world of Adam and Eve complete vegetarians and was there no animal food in that first world?"

When we read Genesis 1:29, 30, it would seem to indicate that this was the case:

> And God said, Behold I have given you every herb bearing seed, which is upon the face of all the earth, and every tree, in the which is the fruit of a tree yielding seed; to you it shall be for meat. And to every beast of the earth and to every fowl of the air, and to every thing that creepeth upon the earth, wherein there is life, I have given every green herb for meat: and it was so.

This impression is confirmed by a statement which God made to Noah after the Flood, which is found in Genesis 9:3 where we read:

> Every moving thing that liveth shall be meat for you; even as the green herb have I given you all things.

This passage seems to indicate that animal food was first permitted by God after the Flood. This has been the common interpretation of these passages.

This question evidently poses a very difficult problem, which is accentuated by the brevity of the words that God spoke to Adam.

However, there are many reasons compelling one to question the interpretation that man, and originally all animals, were completely confined to a vegetable diet.

1. In the creation account of the land animals, there is mentioned a threefold division of kinds—namely, cattle, creeping things, and beasts of the earth.

The beasts of the earth mentioned are the wild animals of the field and of the forest, and among them many are the carnivora, as we know.

2. After creation of the birds and the fish, God blessed them and said, "Be fruitful, and multiply, and fill the waters in the seas, and let the fowl multiply in the earth." We have

earlier discussed the almost unlimited potential for propagation of both birds and fish. If God would not have provided a balance in nature—that is, provided that one class of animals depended for its food upon another, the seas and the air would literally have been filled within a very short time to the extent that would have made life altogether impossible.

The same applies to the land animals: Land animals do not increase at the same rapid rate as the fish and the birds. But what would have happened, for example, if rabbits, rats, mice, cats, dogs, and of course other animals would have increased without any limitation or some natural check on their number? In matters of a few years, or at most a few decades, even the rabbits alone would have completely filled the earth, and there would not have been any vegetation left for any other creature. This was demonstrated very dramatically by the rabbit plague in Australia some years ago. And even now, at the present time, the increase of kangaroos in some areas has been so great and unchecked that they have become a menace to other creatures who also depend upon the vegetation of their environment.

3. The discovery of antediluvian fossils shows that there were carnivora in the world which perished in the Flood.

4. Some animals, evidently, were created as flesh-eating animals. The law fixed in their nature made it possible for them to prey upon other animals. They were provided with the necessary skill and equipment to catch their prey and were given the kind of teeth and the digestive organs necessary to convert the flesh of other animals into food for themselves. If these were not created at the beginning, it would have required another creation after the Fall, or at least after the Flood, to bring about these radical changes. But we have no Biblical or any other evidence for such a new creation.

To meet the objection that in Genesis 1:30 God gave to man and to animals the plant as food, it must be remembered that even the carnivora are ultimately dependent upon animals that derive their food from plants. And so, in the last analysis, all animals and also man are dependent upon the plant, as God says. As we have heard before, the plant is the only bridge between the organic and the inorganic.

5. All carrion-eating birds and animals, which are commonly called the scavengers among the animals, presuppose the death of other animals; otherwise they would have had no purpose and would have been without food. There had to be food for them, or they would have had to be basically different creatures to have existed at all. But again, we have

no evidence that after the Flood such a radical change was made by God.

6. God gave man dominion over the fish of the sea and over the fowl of the air. But what would this mean to man if he could not use the fish for food? What possible use would the fish have been to him if he could not have eaten them? And the same applies to birds. Even the eggs of the bird are animal food and thus are, in fact, potential animals.

7. Death came to man as a curse for his sin. That does not necessarily mean that death was not there in the world for animals before the Fall. But now, after man's sin came into the world and death came to man as a curse, death has also become a curse for the animals, and the fear of death is upon them, as we learn from Romans 8:19, 22.

And so we might well conclude that even from the very beginning there were vegetable-eating and also flesh-eating animals in the world, and God made them so in order to preserve a balance in nature. God said of all of His creation that it was very good, and that also applies to the carnivora.

God moves in a mysterious way
His wonders to perform;
He plants His footsteps in the sea,
And rides upon the storm.

Deep in unfathomable mines
Of never-failing skill
He treasures up His bright designs,
And works His sovereign will.

Ye fearful saints, fresh courage take,
The clouds ye so much dread
Are big with mercy, and shall break
In blessings on your head.

Judge not the Lord by feeble sense,
But trust Him for His grace:
Behind a frowning providence
He hides a smiling face.

His purposes will ripen fast,
Unfolding every hour;
The bud may have a bitter taste
But sweet will be the flower.

Blind unbelief is sure to err,
And scan His work in vain;
God is His own interpreter
And He will make it plain.

—William Cowper

16.

The Creation of Man

We now come to the climax of the creation drama, as recorded in the first two chapters of Genesis:

The Creation of Man

God designed man as the crown and masterpiece of all His creation on this planet. He exalted him to an unparalleled dignity by creating him in His own image and likeness, thereby raising him above every other creature in the universe and fixing an unbridgeable gulf between him and all other creatures on earth.

When contemplating the glory of the last of God's creation, the composer Joseph Haydn burst into an excited song of exultation and sang:

> Now in full splendor shine the heavens;
> Now robed in beauty smiles the earth.
> The air is filled with fluttering creatures
> And shoals of fish the waters are taming.
> The earth abounds in living things
> And still not all was yet achieved.
> The whole was lacking still that being
> That should the works of God behold,
> With thankful heart His glories praise.
>
> —Aria 22, "The Creation"

There are two accounts of the creation of man. The first is in Genesis 1:26, giving a general account of this act of God, which reads as follows:

> And God said, Let us make man in our image, after our likeness: and let them have dominion over the fish of the sea, and over the fowl of the air, and over the cattle, and over all the earth, and over every creeping thing that creepeth upon the earth. So God created man in his own image, in the image of God created he him; male and female created he them. And blessed them, and God said unto them, Be fruitful, and multiply, and replenish the earth, and subdue it: and have dominion over the fish of the sea, and over the fowl of the air, and over every living thing that moveth upon the earth.

A more detailed account is found in Genesis 2:7.

> And the Lord God formed man of the dust of the ground, and breathed into his nostrils the breath of life; and man became a living soul.

According to the two accounts of man's creation, God formed man's body from the dust of the earth, which means that the substance of his body was the same matter of which the physical universe around him was created. Then God breathed into his nostrils the breath of life, and so man became a living being. In his body man is related to the physical world about him, and in his soul he is related to the spirit world, and even to God himself.

Man is a microcosm in contrast to the macrocosm of the universe, not only because the Creator endowed him with a mind which enables him to encompass the entire universe and relate himself to it, but also because in his body he incorporates elements that are found in the universe, and so he becomes a part of it. He is the epitome of God's whole creation. Man is the bridge between the material and the immaterial, between the visible and the invisible, between earth and heaven. Man was created for both.

And God said, "Let us make man in our own image, after our likeness."

Man was created in the image of God. Man was a replica of God himself. Just as a child now is created in the likeness of his parents and resembles them, so, originally, man was made in the likeness of God and therefore resembled his Creator. In his genealogical table of chapter 3, St. Luke directly calls Adam a son of God. Man was the flesh and blood mirror and the reflection of God himself.

Man is not the product of blind evolution, nor is he a descendant of the lower animals as the evolutionist would have us believe. Man was a very special creation, designed and formed with forethought and infinite wisdom by an omnipotent Creator. He was given a dignity which was only a little lower than that of the angels. The image of God distinguishes him from every other creature; it constitutes the unbridgeable gulf between man and the lower animals. Man is the most exalted and the most precious and the most wonderful creature in the entire universe. Only man was created after the pattern of God himself, and only man will survive forever. Heaven and earth and all things will pass away, but man will continue to be. Once the spark of human life has been kindled, it cannot be blotted out. Although physical death separates soul and body for a while, they will be reunited again on the great day of resurrection.

The Method of Man's Creation

When God made man we notice a distinct change in the procedure in the method of creation.

First of all, God began to take counsel with himself, saying, "Let us make man." He was now about to create the crown of all His works, and so He took counsel with himself in the mystery of the Trinity to plan, as it were, the greatest of all His works.

He formed the body of man from the dust of the earth. The material side of man is of the same substance out of which heaven and earth are made, but the method by which God created man was different. In the creation of the other living creatures, God merely spoke: "Let the earth bring forth" or "Let the waters bring forth." But in the creation of man we read that He formed his body, as it were, with His own hands, giving him His shape, size and appearance. This is spoken in a language comprehensible to man.

And then He breathed into his nostrils the breath of life, and man became a living soul. This is, again, anthropomorphic speech.

The soul is the essence of life, and it includes all those qualities which distinguish man from every other creature in the world. In his soul, man is related to God, and with it he is endowed with powers similar to those of the Creator himself. Body and soul are united in man. Therefore both the material and spiritual work together to form the human personality.

Adam received his soul directly from God. It was created, and it is not a part of the divine spirit of God himself. Now the soul is propagated from parent to child in the natural process of generation. The technical term for that process is Traducianism, in contrast to Creationism, the view which holds that even now the soul of every child conceived and brought into the world is a special and an independent creation of God.

The mystery of man's soul, and, for that matter, of his whole being, is beyond comprehension. Man with his finite mind cannot comprehend the infinite God. And finite man is not even able to comprehend himself, created in the image of the infinite God. Poets and philosophers and psychologists throughout the ages have tried to unravel this mystery and have tried to find the key that would unlock this secret of man's being. But all that probing has not been able to go beyond the surface. Only Scripture, that is God's own revelation, can give us a glimpse into the mystery of the great unknown of man.

Shakespeare caught some of the majesty and the mystery of man and found, as always, fitting words to express his wonderment when he says, in Hamlet,

> What a piece of work is man! how noble in reason! how infinite in faculty! In form and moving, how express and admirable! in action how like an angel! in apprehension how like a god!

And David, contemplating his own being, exclaimed, "Thou hast made him [man] a little lower than the angels, and hast crowned him with glory and honour. Thou madest him to have dominion over the works of thy hands; thou hast put all things under his feet" (Ps. 8:5, 6).

And Joseph Haydn, in "The Creation," Aria 2, sings:

> Sublime, in noble dignity
> With beauty, courage, strength endowed,
> Erect with gaze towards heavenward
> He stands, a man.
> A man, the king of nature's realm,
> The lofty broad and noble brow
> Proclaims that wisdom dwells within;
> From eyes serene and steadfast shines
> The soul. His Creator's breath and image he,
> And on his breast there fondly leans,
> For him and from him formed,
> A woman, spouse, a helpmeet fair,
> Her smile so soft and innocent

Of lovely spring the mirror
Betokens him love and joy and bliss.

God Made Them Male and Female

"And the Lord God said, It is not good that man should be alone; I will make him a help meet for him. And the Lord God caused a deep sleep to fall upon Adam, and he slept: and he took one of his ribs, and closed up the flesh instead thereof; and the rib, which the Lord God had taken from man, made he a woman, and brought her unto the man. And Adam said, This is now bone of my bones, and flesh of my flesh: she shall be called Woman, because she was taken out of Man. Therefore shall a man leave his father and mother, and shall cleave unto his wife: and they shall be one flesh." (Gen. 2:18, 21-24). (See also Matt. 19:4, 1 Cor. 6:16, and Eph. 5:31).

And God said, "It is not good that man should be alone." This pronouncement of God was a creative word: It implanted into man's nature the social instinct and man thereby became a social being. It was now a fixed law of human nature for man to seek the fellowship of others of his kind. Man in isolation is in an unnatural state. The hermit is abnormal; he does not live a life according to God's plan. The highest potential of man's existence can be achieved only in his association with fellowmen. Human progress, organized society, government, and all that which we include in the term "civilization" would be impossible without this social drive.

No man can be an island unto himself. Regardless of the degree of one's self-sufficiency, no man can long live to himself in isolation and remain either happy or normal.

Human beings were created social and gregarious beings. God made us that way. We congregate for fellowship, joint protection, government, and our highest achievements.

We need to learn that we need each other, that we are interdependent, and that we would be impoverished unless group relates to group in a manner that will make each conscious of his dependence on the other.

Again we read, "Male and female created he them."

God made a man and a woman, two very distinct and different forms of human beings; yet, though different, they were created for each other, one to complete the other. How wonderful! What a royal gift of the Creator to the lord of His creation, that He gave him this female part of himself as a companion. It is the most precious jewel in his crown and the source of his greatest happiness in this world. And what a masterpiece of design and formation are men and women in their bodies and in their respective functions! The two are so different and yet, so much alike. Adam recognized Eve at once as being "bone of [his] bones, and flesh of [his] flesh." And though different, the two are created for each other, the one complementing and completing the other. Only when the two are united is a whole and perfect human existence possible. Or as Henry Wadsworth Longfellow has so beautifully described it:

> As unto the bow the cord is,
> So unto man is woman.
> Though she bends him, she obeys him,
> Though she draws him, yet she follows,
> Useless each without the other.
>
> —Hiawatha, *Canto X*

In the beginning God created *one* man and *one* woman. There was a perfect balance between the sexes; neither one outnumbered the other.

By a strange, mysterious law, this balance in the human race has been preserved throughout the ages. The number of men and women have remained essentially equal, though the human race has increased to number millions and billions of individuals, and though it is scattered over the entire face of the earth and divided into countless races, cultures, and different standards of living. There is no national or international agency to control this balance but an unseen, mysterious law, fixed by the Creator, which regulates it on a worldwide scale in the most wonderful manner. When a major imbalance occurs, as it has at times, and in certain periods and countries, its cause can be traced to wars or to the result of the more hazardous occupations of men, but also to the greater survival potential of women.

Let the evolutionist or all those who refuse to believe in a Creator of infinite power and wisdom explain this phenomenon of male and female and the perpetual balance between the two!

In the beginning God created only one pair, one man and one woman. Birds, fish, and other animals were created in great numbers to populate the earth and the sea with their kind. But in the case of man, God again changed His procedure. According to His own infinite wisdom, He saw fit to create only one human pair and decreed that the whole human race was to spring from them—in fact, from only one original man created in His own image. Even Eve, the first woman, was taken from Adam.

By creating a male and a female God divided the human race into two distinct sexes with distinct and separate functions. By adding the blessing "Be fruitful and multiply," He implanted in them the sex drive and the power to propagate the human race.

Sex and all its functions, including the mating instinct, conjugal love, the desire for offspring, the sexual urge and pleasure are the creation of God, and are included in the works upon which He pronounced His "very good" at the end of the creation week. The sex drive is, therefore, good in itself and is one of the most wonderful, mysterious powers with which the Creator has endowed man. It is through this power that man becomes a co-creator together with God for the perpetuation of the human race. God wanted the race to increase abundantly to take possession of the earth that He had created for man, and so He planted in him this drive, and made it strong and urging, and enriched it with pleasure in order that man would carry out His will. God did not leave it to man's own reason or judgment whether or not the human race was to be perpetuated. God endowed man with a drive so insistent and so strong that he would at all times carry out His plan in this regard.

But the function of sex is not limited to the perpetuation of the race. It has other implications, which affect every phase of human existence. The sex drive is basic for the establishment of the home and the family, which are fundamental for the progress and well-being of human society.

Sex accounts for the masculinity in men and the femininity in women with their respective physical, mental, and emotional characteristics. It accounts for the peculiar attraction that men and women have for each other. It is a source of the paternal and maternal instinct in men and women. In fact, most of the virtues which we associate with the ideal home have their roots in this mysterious drive.

Sin has affected the sex instinct as it has influenced every other power in man. It is because of this moral corruption of man's nature that sex also becomes an instrument of evil and has become a major source of crime, moral degeneration, and the decay of nations, and the source of much misery, much sickness, much suffering, and unhappiness in the world today. But sex and the sex drive in itself are not bad. Even after sin has polluted human nature and has marred all of his innate drives, the sex instinct is still a wonderful gift of God to mankind.

The Physical Appearance of the First Man

Here the question might well be raised, What did Adam and Eve look like as they came forth from the hands of their Creator? Was their appearance like that of men and women today, and their mental capacity and speech already completely human, or were they subhuman, animal-like creatures, grotesque in their appearance and with an intelligence not unlike that of other animals around them?

This very question is raised by the editor of *Time-Life Books*, and then for an answer to this question, the editor suggests that the reader consult a richly illustrated volume titled "Early Man" in the *Nature Library* series.

In this volume are shown 15 progressive drawings or paintings, graphically demonstrating the imaginary upward development of man's early ancestors, from the lower animals and apelike creatures to the modern Homo sapiens.

Similar pictures are frequently found in other publications presenting the history of man from the evolutionary point of view. And in many natural history museums one can see lifesize models or at least the heads and shoulders of brutish-like creatures, demonstrating to the viewer, in concrete form, his own ancestral background.

And to impress the public still more, high-sounding Latin names are given each state in this development, and even the dates of their existence are affixed, ranging all the way from 2 million to 25 million years. But that these assumed dates differ by millions of years does not seem to disturb these learned archeologists at all. What would we think of a historian who would differ from other historians by 50 or 100 years in recording the important events of our history?

And then to give additional dignity and credence to these assumptions, the names of some noted archeologists from one of the great universities are added, and that is regarded as sufficient proof for the truth of the claims that are made.

But what are the actual known facts about this alleged history of early man?

The answer to that question is that there is not a shred of evidence or actual factual proof for any of these fantastic claims! No such creature has ever been seen as the alleged process of man's evolution claims there should be in the world today if the evolutionary process is or ever was operative. No fossil of such a creature, nor any complete, or even partial, skeleton has ever been found. All the archeologist had upon which he built his spectacular theory were a few isolated bones, a part of a jaw bone, some teeth, part of a skull, and the like;

and from these fragments (found in different parts of the world) he then proceeded to develop their likenesses to fit into his preconceived theory of evolution. To make his imaginative theory sound authentic to the uninformed, he gives these fossil fragments mysterious names, such as the Neanderthal Man, the Java Man, the Piltdown Man, etc. But it might be added here that this famous Piltdown Man, about whom so much was formerly made, has been exposed as a ridiculous hoax.

All of these supposed ancestors of the human race are brutish-looking creatures with animal bodies covered with hair, long forearms like the front legs of an ape, and an ugly orangutan-like face and forehead, and a mouthful of savage teeth.

But now what does the Bible really say about the appearance of the first man? What was he like?

The answer to that question is "very little!" The only direct reference to man's physical appearance in the Garden of Eden are the few words, "and they were both naked, the man and his wife" (Gen. 2: 25). They were naked, says the text. But that remark is quite significant. It indicates that the bodies of Adam and Eve were covered with a smooth, velvety skin and not with a hairy pelt like that of the animals. No one would say that an ape or a bear, or for that matter any animal or bird is "naked." Nature supplies them with a dress of furs and feathers from the very beginning, but this is not so in the case of man. Man can choose his clothes and pattern them according to his needs and desires. It is, therefore, a contemptible hoax and a shameful distortion of the nature of man to present his ancestors as mere brutish animals. And while the creation account does not give us any further details about the first man's physical appearance, we are able to construct for ourselves a fairly reliable picture of what Adam and Eve were like when they were in their first home from other evidence concerning them and from creation in general.

In the first place, the Genesis account says that man was created in the image of God. And while it is true that the divine image in man is in his soul, yet body and soul are so intimately united in the human personality that both body and soul partake of the characteristics of the other. And so, the godlike qualities of man's soul must also have shown through the physical appearance of his body and glorified it. It would be sheer blasphemy to assume that the divine image of God was in the body of an ape or some other brutish animal-like creature.

In the second place, man was created to have dominion over

all things that God had made on the earth. He was to rule over all creation as God's own vice-regent here on earth. Even that presupposes a supreme, royal personality expressing itself in his appearance, intelligence, and general bearing. It is absurd to think that an ape-like creature would have been appointed as lord over all creation.

And finally, we know that God is a God of beauty. This is manifest everywhere in His whole creation, and so it would follow inescapably that man, the ultimate crown of His creation, would reflect these characteristics of God in the fullest measure possible. Therefore, we are safe to assume that Adam and Eve, our ancestors, were a man and woman of surpassing beauty, intelligence and dignity, never equaled or surpassed to this day, and that the most perfect physical specimens of our race today are but faded copies of the original masterpiece of the divine artist.

And as to the first man's mentality, that, too, was in harmony with his appearance and his intended purpose in the world. Adam was not a grunting, snarling, brutish beast, but a highly intelligent, godlike being with a mind not yet beclouded by sin. Adam proved this at the first moment he opened his eyes and saw his lovely Eve beside him. Without explanation or introduction, he immediately recognized her as being flesh of his flesh and bone of his bones and promptly accepted her as his wife and helpmeet. He also proved his superior mentality by recognizing the nature of the animals around him and giving them appropriate names in harmony with their nature and purpose.

Man begins not as a savage but as a superior, highly intelligent royal creature—truly the crown of all creation. When history raises its curtain on the beginning of the human race, we find men in an advanced stage of civilization with great cultural achievements to which the magnificent monuments of Egypt, the ruins of Babylon, and the excavations in Ur so eloquently testify.

The existence of savage races in the world in all ages is certainly no proof that all of mankind developed from that stage. It is instead a proof, not of evolution but of devolution; that is, they demonstrate that man, despite his great and noble origin, deteriorates into savagery when he separates himself from his Creator and ignores the moral standards that God established for all men at all times. Man was created a moral being; when he violates that moral law, he eventually ceases to be truly human and sinks to the level of a savage.

Man's First Home

Continuing with verses 8-15 of Genesis 2, we read: "And the Lord God planted a garden eastward in Eden; and there he put the man whom he had formed. And out of the ground made the Lord God to grow every tree that is pleasant to the sight, and good for food; the tree of life also in the midst of the garden, and the tree of knowledge of good and evil. And a river went out of Eden to water the garden; and from thence it was parted, and became into four heads. The name of the first is Pison: that is it which compasseth the whole land of Havilah, where there is gold; and the gold of that land is good: there is bdellium and the onyx stone. And the name of the second river is Gihon: the same is it that compasseth the whole land of Ethiopia. And the name of the third river is Hiddekel: that is it which goeth toward the east of Assyria. And the fourth river is Euphrates. And the Lord God took the man, and put him into the garden of Eden to dress it and to keep it."

The beautiful home which God had prepared for man is called a garden. This must not be understood in its narrow, restrictive sense, but the Garden of Eden must have comprised a large territory lying between or being traversed by four rivers—namely, the Euphrates, the Hiddekel or Tigris, the Pison, and the Gihon. Of these four rivers mentioned, the Euphrates and the Tigris can still be identified to their sources in the Armenian highlands. The other two have disappeared. No doubt they were wiped out through the great world Flood by which this whole territory was completely changed. However, there are still a number of fossil riverbeds discernable in the lower course of the two river valleys.

Of the Pison it is said that it compasses the whole land of Havilah where there is gold, and the gold is characterized as especially good. Precious stones are also mentioned. It is not known definitely where the land of Havilah was, but it is commonly placed somewhere in Arabia. The Flood must have caused radical changes in the whole region west of the Babylonian valley, a territory as large as that portion of the United States which lies east of the Mississippi. It does not have a single river and it is one of the most forbidding desert regions in our world; but it could not have been that way in the first world which God called "very good."

Of the Gihon it is said that it compasses the whole land of Ethiopia. This raises a difficult problem. The land of Ethiopia is in Eastern Africa, separated from this territory by Arabia and the Red Sea. However, the Hebrew text has this wording: "It encompasseth the whole land of Cush." Cush can properly be translated Ethiopia, but Cush was also the name of one of the sons of Ham. In Genesis 10:6, we read that one of the sons of Ham was Cush, and Cush was the father of Nimrod. Of Nimrod we know that he established the kingdoms of Babel, Erech, Accad, Calneh in the land of Shinar. But all these places were city-states in the two river valleys. If the Gihon encompasses the whole land of Cush, it must have been another river in this valley, possibly a tributary of the Tigris, having its source in the mountain regions to the east. The Pison might have been a tributary of the Euphrates with its source somewhere in the present Arabia.

The whole region of the Garden of Eden was completely changed through the Flood. Today it is a bleak and barren desert without any vegetation or animal life and as level as a prairie in North Dakota. The Garden of Eden was completely wiped out by the Flood. No traces of its location have remained, except the two rivers mentioned.

17.

The Image of God in Man

Man is the most precious, the most complex, and the most mysterious creature in the universe. And the reason for this is that he was created in the image and likeness of God.

If therefore psychologists, anthropologists, and others would try to understand the distinctive peculiarities of man and his behavior, they must begin at the beginning and start with his creation and there note especially the words, "God created man in his own image after his own likeness" (Gen. 1:26).

Because of this unique distinction in man which separates him basically and fundamentally from every other creature, even from the highest forms of animal life, the study of comparative animal psychology can never lead to an understanding of the real mysteries of man's being. No other creature was created in the image of God or has godlike characteristics. And so it is of the greatest importance for a proper understanding of man that we inquire into the meaning and significance of this exalted dignity bestowed upon man alone.

What Is Meant by the Image of God in Man?

The image of God in man includes all those faculties of his soul which distinguish him from every other creature.

There are two aspects to this image of God in man. To distinguish the one from the other, and to make its meaning more intelligible, two terms have been invented: the one we call the "material" and the other the "formal" side of the image of God.

By "material side" are meant the moral and spiritual qualities of man's being, or the moral and spiritual perfection in which Adam and Eve were created. Adam and Eve were holy and sinless as they came forth from the hands of the Creator, and in that sense they bore the image of God in themselves.

They were also created free moral agents. That is, they were able and free to choose by themselves the good and the evil. But they were persuaded by Satan to choose the evil and become disobedient; thereby they lost the consecrated holiness and righteousness and became sinful in their nature. And this sinfulness and corruption were passed down from father to son by natural generation to all the offspring of Adam. Jesus said to Nicodemus, "Whatsoever is born of flesh is flesh" (John 3:6). And now all men must confess with David, "I was shapen in iniquity; and in sin did my mother conceive me" (Ps. 51:5). This sinful condition in human nature is the cause of death and the source of all evil in the world. And as long as man remains, evil will not be eradicated from human society.

This material aspect of the image of God in man was lost in the fall of Adam, but is restored, at least in part, in the Christian in this life; and it will be completely restored in the state of blessedness in the world to come.

The Formal Side of the Image of God

By the formal side of the image of God is meant the "form," or we may also call it "the general structure in which the image of God manifests itself in man." This phase of the image of God in man still survives, though not in its original perfection. It has also suffered as a result of man's fall but has not been wiped out completely (Gen. 9:6 and James 3:9).

The formal side of the image of God in man is that which marks him as distinctly set apart as a human being and distinguishes him from all other creatures. The formal image of God in man includes such characteristics as his personality, self-determination, rationality, emotionality, morality, and his sovereignty over all other creatures in this world.

1. *Personality*

Man was created a person. God is a person. Man is a finite replica of the infinite personality of God. By person is meant the ego in man, the "I am" in man. A person is a self-conscious and self-determining being. Man is self-conscious—that is, he is aware of himself as an independent being. Man alone can contemplate himself: he can know that he is, that he was, and that he will be. He knows that he is a distinct individual, that he has a history, that he is responsible for what he does or has done. He alone is able to consciously relate himself to the universe and to God.

2. *Self-determination*

Man is a free, moral agent. That means he is endowed with a will and the freedom to exercise that will. Man can determine his own conduct and shape his own destiny. He is free to choose what he will do or will not do and what he will be or will not be, limited only by his physical and mental capability. Man is not governed by the law of necessity or by instinct. He is free to make his own decision for good or ill. Freedom, however, always includes a corresponding responsibility. Man is a free and responsible person, responsible to God and to society, and that puts him into a category all by himself.

By means of his will man is free to make himself master of his environment. He is free to change that environment, to let himself be enslaved by it, or to remove himself from it.

The animal is limited by its environment. It is not able to change its environment but must adapt itself to its surroundings or perish. But man can re-create that environment, change it as he chooses. Man is free. He has the power to subdue nature, to harness the forces of nature to serve him, or he is also free to submit to nature and be controlled by it. He is free to learn, to benefit by past experiences and the experiences of others, and to raise himself to the highest level of existence, but he is also free to remain ignorant and inactive. Man is free to create his own civilization in keeping with the highest potential with which the Creator has endowed him, but he is also free to be satisfied with less. Man creates his environment and then is affected by what he has created. He may decide to remain in the African jungle and limit his ambition to merely satisfying his biological drives; or he may choose to vegetate indolently in the decaying slum of a modern, industrial city. It is the will of man that has prompted him to search out what is beyond the distant hills, to build a modern city, to invent the automobile and a thousand other devices for his comfort and enjoyment. But man is also free to create for himself a slum, to live in filth, to remain on a near-animal level, or to destroy himself in devastating wars.

Man's will is always in harmony with his whole being. Man always wills as he is. Every act of man, except his reflex action, is always a response to his will. Even his habits result from an original act of the will. And the sum total of such habits ultimately constitutes his character.

When man forfeits his freedom and refuses to assume his responsibility as a human person, he loses the very essence of humanity. God created man a free, responsible being, and therefore holds the individual responsible for his actions. Today men constantly stress their freedom and rights but never their responsibility. The structure of our industrial society today, the machine, the theory of evolution, and militarism—all tend to reduce man to a mere statistic, a number and impersonal cog in a wheel, thus destroying human personality. Current moral and social philosophy place the emphasis on society. God places it on the individual. Society was not created in the image of God, but the individual was. God directs His moral precepts to the individual and holds the individual responsible. The Ten Commandments say, "Thou shalt, or, thou shalt not." By the mouth of the prophet Ezekiel, God says to the individual: "The soul that sinneth, it shall die" (18:20). And Paul, writing to the Corinthians, says, "For we must all appear before the judgment seat of Christ; that every one may receive the things done in his body, according to that he hath done, whether it be good or bad" (2 Cor. 5:10).

3. *Rationality and intelligence*

Man was created a rational being, endowed with intelligence. This means that man was endowed with the faculty of reason and the ability to learn. Man is not like the animal, limited by instinct to a fixed pattern of life; he can benefit by past experience and direct his course of action accordingly. He is free to select a course of action, weigh the consequences of his choice, and act accordingly. But this implies other aspects of the mind, such as the faculties of perception, understanding, judgment, and above all, the faculty of memory.

Memory is a mystery and a wonder beyond all understanding. Memory implies the ability to retain a past experience within the nervous system, recall it, and recognize it as an experience that we have had perhaps many years before. The vocabulary we use to communicate with one another, the ability to recognize those whom we have seen or met before, the ability to recognize a specific odor, sound, or touch, and even our habits of life are all dependent upon this mysterious faculty of memory. Memory is basic for all mental life. Without it, life could not be a unit. We could live only in the light of each moment, and the past would be as though it had never been. There would be no learning, no knowledge of anything, no possibility of thought or speech, no meaning of any kind. Everything that happens would be as new and strange to us as if it had never happened before. Personality, morality and character would be impossible. Man could know neither God nor man.

It has been said that all other abilities of the mind borrow from memory their beauty and perfection. In a very real sense, it is true that all other faculties of the soul are useless without memory. Of what profit are all our wisdom, our reading, our studying if we are unable to preserve what knowledge we have acquired? Memory makes rich the mind by preserving all that results from our studying and learning. Without memory the soul of man would be a poor, destitute, naked being, with an everlasting blank spread over it except for the fleeting ideas of the present moment.

It may be safely said that memory is the basis of all knowledge, that without it neither science nor art is possible. This being true, the more a man remembers, the greater is his amount of knowledge, and the greater his foundation for further study and research. Our memory makes it possible for us to comtemplate the goodness and the blessings of our God, thus prompting us to sing with the poet:

"All the hosts of earth and heaven
Wheresoe'r I turn mine eye,
For my benefit are given,
That they may my needs supply.
All that's living, all that's growing,
On the heights or in the woods,
In the vales or in the floods,
God is for my good bestowing.
All things have their little day
God's great love abides for aye."

4. *Emotionality*

The image of God includes emotionality—that is, capacity for feeling.

God has revealed himself as a God of emotion and feeling:

He is a God of love; He is a God of anger who hates sin; He has compassion; He is merciful and long-suffering.

Man's emotional faculty is another phase of the likeness of God in man.

Emotion is a wonderful gift of the Creator to man. It gives him color and richness, feeling, and the capacity of joy, happiness, and laughter. Man's existence would be bleak and barren without feeling. The sense of worth of possession and of personal self-respect is in the realm of the emotions. What is worthwhile to man depends upon the feeling he has towards a certain object. The bond between mother and child, between husband and wife, between friend and friend is an emotional bond. The value we place upon treasures or heirlooms, upon the enjoyment we receive from music or the other arts, or from the beauty of nature grows out of our emotions. Emotions provide man with the dynamo for action and with the motives that move his will. Man's noblest actions, but alas, since sin has polluted his nature, also his basest actions, grow out of his emotions. The emotions, like all of man's being, are a mystery. They cannot be defined or explained, and that is so because the emotions, too, are a part of the divine image of God in man.

Intimately connected with the emotion is the *esthetic* sense in man.

By the esthetic sense we mean man's innate capacity to perceive and appreciate beauty and the ability to respond intellectually and emotionally to that which is beautiful, in whatever form it may appear.

Only man, of all creatures, is endowed with a sense of beauty. The animal has no appreciation nor understanding for the beautiful. The most intelligent dog is unmoved by the beauty of a rose. The statues of Venus and Apollo mean nothing to an ox or a mule. The purest whiteness of a lily is, at best, only food for the goat; and the most precious necklace of pearls and diamonds does not appeal to a herd of swine.

God is a God of beauty. He created a beautiful world. The heavens declare the glory of God, and the earth is resplendent with the wonders of its beauty—beauty of form, beauty of color, beauty of sound, beauty of taste, and beauty of smell. What radiant beauty is revealed in the golden glow of the setting sun or the mellow light of the harvest moon! What charming beauty of form, color, and smell is found in the myriads of plants and flowers everywhere in our wide world! Who can adequately describe the beauty of the rose, the lily, the orchid, or the delicate tissue that covers the peach? What a gorgeous feast for the eye is the exquisite beauty of the trees of the forest and of the mountainside, especially in the fall of the year when the oak and the maple, the chestnut and the birch, interspersed with the spruce and the pine, vie with one another in the display of their resplendent robes of many colors, from the palest gold to the brilliant pumpkin-yellow and in all nuances of red, from the most delicate pink to the most brilliant scarlet. Every one of the billions and trillions of leaves thus painted is a masterpiece of the divine Artist. And there is beauty everywhere in nature, even where the human eye never penetrates. "Full many a flower is born to blush unseen and waste its sweetness on the desert air."

What wonderful artistry, for example, is found in the design of the wing of a butterfly, in the crystal of a snowflake, in the microscopic diatom of the sea, or in the feathery covering of the bird of paradise of New Guinea, the peacock of India, the pheasant of America, the lyrebird of Australia, or the other wonders of the bird kingdom, especially in the tropics. What grandeur and awe-inspiring scenes are provided in the rugged, snowcapped mountains of all the continents, in the roaring billows of the restless sea, in the mystic solitude of the sun-scorched desert, or in the star-spangled canopy of the heavenly dome above us. Everywhere God has surrounded us with the majesty of His glory and the beauty of His creation! And because of the implanted esthetic sense in man's soul, he is able to recognize and appreciate that beauty and is able even to imitate the Creator by himself creating beauty in his works of art, such as his statues, his paintings, his cathedrals and temples, his carvings and tapestries, and his songs and symphonies.

5. *Morality*

The image of God in man includes his morality. Man was created a moral being. He alone, of all creatures on earth, has the capacity for moral experience; he alone is able to distinguish between the morally right and the morally wrong, to form moral judgments and to follow moral ideals. He alone is endowed with the freedom of will and the corresponding responsibility. The law of nature places a creature under compulsion. The moral law places man under obligation. He may accept that obligation or reject it, and therein lies the real distinction between right and wrong, between man and animal.

The animal is amoral. It is not governed by a moral law,

is incapable of moral or immoral acts, and is outside of the moral law.

The goal of morality is to establish the right relation between man and God and between man and his fellowman. No other creature has that ability.

The moral sense in man also includes his *conscience.*

Conscience is that faculty in man by which he distinguishes between the morally right and the morally wrong, which urges him to do that which he recognizes to be right and restrains him from that which he knows to be wrong, which passes judgment on his acts and executes that judgment in his own soul.

Conscience is another inexplicable mystery in man's being.

Even Kant was so impressed by the awesomeness of the fact of conscience that he said, "I know of nothing more awe-inspiring than the starry heaven above and the conscience within us." No process of evolution can account for its origin or explain its function and its power, or even how the concept of morality could have originated within him if original man was the descendant of an animal and, therefore, altogether amoral. The difference between moral and amoral is not merely a matter of degree and therefore within the possibility of development, but it is distinctly a difference in kind. Morality implies a personality endowed with a will and freedom of action, freedom of choice. But how could man emerge a free, moral personality out of an unfree condition through a process of evolution which, in its very nature, is unfree and solely governed by the law of necessity? This would mean that, contrary to all reason and logic, the effect would be the very opposite of the cause.

The only explanation to account for morality in man is the fact revealed in the Scriptures: namely, that man was created in the image of God and, therefore, made like God, a moral being.

6. *Immortality*

God is immortal. God is without beginning and without end. He is eternal. Therefore the image of God in man also implies immortality.

Man has a beginning, but once he comes into being he is like God himself, immortal. Originally, man was immortal in both body and soul. God said to Adam in the Garden of Eden, "In the day that thou eatest thereof, thou shalt surely die." Had Adam not taken of the forbidden fruit, he would not have died. Death came into the world of man through sin. Now his body is subject to death because of sin, but his soul, even now, lives on forever; and in the resurrection of the last day, body and soul will be reunited, and there will be again an immortal body and an immortal soul.

7. *Sovereignty*

And finally, the image of God in man also includes his *dominion* over all creatures which God has made. For we read, "And God said, Let us make man in our image, after our likeness: and let them have dominion over the fish of the sea, and over the fowl of the air, and over the cattle, and over all the earth, and over every creeping thing that creepeth upon the earth" (Gen. 1:26). But note, this dominion does not include the moon and the other planets. It is limited to the creatures here on earth.

The history of human civilization is the history of man's gaining dominion over all creation and compelling the forces of nature to be his servants. No other creature on earth has been able to gain supremacy over other creatures.

It is the image of God in man that raises him to the lordship over all things, which exalts him above every other creature and gives him a place of honor only "a little lower than the angels" (Ps. 8:5). And even after sin has polluted his nature, it still survives in him as a faint and blurred reflection of the majesty and glory of God himself.

To this last mentioned aspect of the divine image in man, a few additional remarks are called for, and they concern man's responsibility as lord of all creation around him.

God said to Adam and Eve: "Be fruitful, and multiply, and replenish the earth and subdue it: and have dominion over the fish of the sea, and over the fowl of the air, and over every living thing that moveth upon the face of the earth" (Gen. 1:28).

God gave this commission to Adam, and Adam represented the whole human race which was to come from him. Therefore the commandment with its blessing applied to all generations that were to follow. But no generation, and, of course, no race or nation has a monopoly on this dominion or lordship over all the world, All are under God who remains the supreme Ruler of the universe and who holds man accountable for the exercise of his lordship. But every generation is also responsible to those generations that come after it. We are entitled to use the riches of the earth for our existence and comforts while we are here, but we have no right to waste or to destroy them.

We are not absolute owners, but rather stewards of these wonderful gifts of the Creator, and we are accountable for our stewardship to Him. People who are selfishly reckless with this trust will eventually lose what they have and will bring upon themselves the curse from those who have been deprived of their rightful share by the irresponsible recklessness of their predecessors.

The nations of our generation, and especially we here in America, seem to have forgotten this.

God has given us a beautiful world, and has enriched it with an abundance of good things for our benefit, enjoyment, and pleasure. And that is especially true of our own beloved America. But men in their selfish greed and blindness have marred this beauty with their grimy cities; they have mutilated the landscape by converting it into unsightly wasteland with ugly heaps of litter, garbage and waste; they have poisoned our beautiful rivers and are converting our magnificent Great Lakes into gigantic cesspools; and even now they are in the process of polluting the great oceans of the world with the poisonous drainage of our industrialized, scientific civilization and are contaminating the very air we breathe.

And closely related to this gross irresponsibility are the unscrupulous exploitation and wasteful destruction of irreplaceable resources of our earth, such as productive land, iron ore, oil, coal, forest reserves, parklands, wildlife, and many important minerals of which the earth has only a limited supply. Our own national waste has become scandalous. It is estimated that we throw away, year after year, about 48 billion tin cans, 26 billion bottles, 30 million tons of paper, 100 million discarded tires and mountains of worn out automobiles, farm machinery, and other objects made of materials that are irreplaceable.

All of these wasted materials should be collected and converted into usable resources to be recycled for new machinery and other useful articles of daily life.

And why is this not done? The answer given is, "It does not pay." It is cheaper for the industries. That means that it is immediately more profitable to abandon the used products and let them rust and rot away, and get new materials directly from the original sources. Immediate profit is the criterion that governs our actions in this respect.

Think of the millions of discarded automobiles, piled high, that mar the approach of nearly every city or village in our country.

Who can estimate the waste of the billions of tons of precious steel, blasted into atoms in the bombs dropped on the cities of living human beings in the four destructive wars we have waged in my own lifetime?

Consider the billions upon billions of gallons of precious, irreplaceable oil burned up in the horrible bombing raids in these same wars.

Steel that is blasted into atoms and oil that has been burned up are gone forever, and the mines eventually become exhausted and oil wells dry up.

God gave us a wonderful world for our habitation, but He gave it to the human race, not only to the present generation, be that generation ever so smart and advanced. Every generation possesses it for a season and has the right to use it, but only as its accountable tenants.

We have become irresponsible, wasteful stewards. We as a nation are following the philosophy of Louis XIV, that wicked king of France, who recklessly wasted the resources of his country in ambitious wars abroad and in unrestrained luxury at his court, and then glibly defended his way of life by saying, "After us, the flood," meaning in a genuine Epicurean spirit, "We live now as we like it and are not concerned about those who may come after us."

But the flood about which he spoke so flippantly came in the generation that followed him, in the frightful horrors of the revolution with its terrible, bloody guillotine and mad destruction.

Be not deceived; God still controls the destiny of the earth He has created. If men arrogantly ignore Him and His unalterable laws, they are headed for their own destruction.

The people after the Flood became puffed up about their great achievements and in their pride would storm even the very heavens itself with their tower. But God cut them down with a single stroke by confusing them.

God's judgment of confusion upon our own generation is evident to anyone who would open his eyes to see.

The population explosion is real and a most frightening phenomenon of our times, and together with our unscrupulous waste, it is an ominous foreboding of a worldwide famine such as mankind has never seen. But like the people before the Flood, we continue as always, eating and drinking, marrying and giving in marriage, completely unconcerned about what may follow; and in our national conceit, we waste even the talents of our greatest minds to find ways and means of invading the uninhabitable worlds in outer space. Oh the blindness of sinful man!

In our arrogance we are rushing headlong towards our destruction. And yet we continue to boast of ourselves as being the greatest and the most advanced guardian of the history of the world. We ought to learn from those who followed that philosophy before us.

18.

The Wonders of Man's Body

In keeping with the exalted position of man in the universe is the wonder of his body with all its members, faculties and powers. And so, when we begin to contemplate the creation of man, we must begin with the study of his body.

The body of man is only the material and mortal side of his being, and yet, what a bundle of incomprehensible wonders it is! It is the most wonderful and the most complicated machine in the universe and has no parallel in the whole world of wonders. The most refined creations of man are crude compared to the human body.

The first thing to note is that the body of man is not made. It becomes. The human body is composed of the same materials found in the rest of the world all about us, but these materials are not put together by an outside agent, mechanic or builder, as men would construct a machine, make a watch, or build a house. It grows from within. We say "it grows" and then think we have solved this mystery. But what does it mean to grow? What is growth? What directs the course of its development? Why does one become a male and the other a female? Or one white and the other black, brown, or yellow? Why is one tall and the other short?

So many of these wonders in the human body are taken for granted because everybody has them, and whatever has become common no longer arouses excitement. Take, for example, the beauty and graceful form of the human body. Consider the perfect harmony of all its parts: the lordly dignity of its upright stature, the marvelous mechanism of its bony framework, the miracle of its vital organs. The body grows—that is, the body itself collects the heterogeneous materials of which it is composed from outside of itself and manufactures them into itself. It follows a definite pattern in this process and always develops harmoniously in all its numerous parts. It has the ability to improve its own capacity and potentialities. It repairs itself when damaged anywhere in its members and reproduces by itself new models like itself, and yet sufficiently different to make each a distinct new model, a new and a different individual personality. Among the billions of human beings that have lived on the face of the earth or are living today, there have never been two people exactly alike.

The human body consists of thousands of individual parts, large, small, and microscopic; but all are so joined together that they function as a perfect, synchronized organism. The human body consists of billions and trillions of individual cells, and every cell is a distinct unit that functions in perfect harmony with every other cell.

Hence, the study of the human body reveals, more than all the other wonders of creation put together, the infinite wisdom, power, and goodness of the omnipotent Creator, who designed this masterpiece of His hand to be His vice-regent here upon earth.

Of all creatures, man alone stands upright with his face turned from the earth upwards toward heaven. In his very appearance, man reveals his lordship over all other creatures.

What a magnificent piece of art is a beautiful woman or the body of a well-coordinated athlete, or the angelic face of an infant! The great artists of all times have tried to copy these models and reproduce their beauty in marble, granite, bronze, or some other material for the delight of man.

"The world is full of wonders," sang Sophocles, "but nothing is more wonderful than man." And the Roman philosopher Cicero was profoundly impressed with the physical beauty of man. He wrote as follows:[1]

> Many further illustrations could be given of this wise and careful providence of nature, to illustrate the lav-

[1] Cicero. Marcus Tullius, Loeb Classics LVI, 257.

ishness and splendour of the gifts bestowed by the gods on men. First, she has raised them from the ground to stand tall and upright, so that they might be able to behold the sky and so gain a knowledge of the gods. For men are sprung from the earth not as its inhabitants and denizens, but to be as it were the spectators of things supernal and heavenly, in the contemplation whereof no other species of animals participates.

A prayer by Michel Quoist expresses in beautiful language the sentiments of a Christian when contemplating the wonders and beauty of the human body. It reads as follows:

And yet, Lord, man's body is beautiful.
From the beginning You, the Supreme Artist,
held the model before You, knowing that one day
You would dwell in a human body when taking on
the nature of man. Slowly you shaped it with
Your powerful hands; and into its inert matter
You breathed a living soul. From then on, Lord,
You asked us to respect the body, for the whole
with those of our brothers.

Words in a long procession lead us towards other
souls.

A smile on our lips, the expression in our eyes,
reveal the soul.

The clasp of the hand carries our soul to a friend;
A kiss yields it to the loved ones;
The embrace of the couple unites two souls in
Quest of a new child of God.
But it was not enough for You, Lord, to make of
Our flesh the visible sign of the spirit.
Through your grace the Christian's body becomes sacred,
The temple of the Trinity, a member of the Lord
And bearer of His God,
Supreme dignity of this splendid body!

Man's skeleton consists of about 200 individual bones, all of a different size and shape and composed of crystals of calcium phosphate in a complex array, which the body itself absorbs from the different foods it takes in. By unseen forces from within, it forms them, without supervision from without, into their respective forms and puts them each in its specific place. The bones provide the leverage by which the muscles can do their work and also, as with the skull and pelvis, protect the vital parts of the body. The bones are hollow to give them greater strength and are joined together in an ingenious ball and socket device which is lined with a smooth, cartilaginous substance to eliminate all possible friction. The joints are supplied with an automatic lubrication system which functions throughout life. The body itself manufactures this lubricant.

All the bones are wonderful in their structure and function. This is especially true of the bones of the spine, the feet, and the hands.

The spinal column is a system of 24 highly specialized bones called vertebra, ingeniously constructed and joined together to protect the spinal cord running through its center and to give flexibility to the back so that the body can turn and bend and yet to provide at the same time the rigidity necessary for the upright position of man. Every human being has exactly the same number of bones in this column and all are exactly of the same general structure and function. Who counted these bones? How is it that they are always placed in exactly the same order? If this could have happened once, it would have been a spectacular miracle, but it happened billions and billions of times over and over again. Only one who has ceased to be rational would assume that this might have happened by chance.

The Bones of the Human Foot

The foot is the humblest member of man's anatomy.

The human foot with its five toes is a miracle of construction. It consists of 26 separate bones of various sizes and shapes bound together by a system of ligaments. It is supported by a complex array of muscles and supplied with a network of fibers and blood vessels. The different bones articulate in gliding joints, giving the foot a degree of elasticity and a limited amount of motion. The arrangement of the bones is such as to form several arches, the most important of these being the long arch from the heel to the ball of the foot.

These arches are held in place and supported by a complex of strong muscles to carry the weight of the body just as the steel cables carry the load of a suspension bridge; the construction also gives elasticity to the foot, making walking and running and other movements possible. The ability to walk and to move from place to place and to balance the tall upright body on a comparatively small pedestal is itself a most remarkable feature of the human body. If the foot were flat and rigid, fixed at right angles to the bone of the leg, walking would be difficult or impossible. The elastic arches also serve as shock absorbers to soften the jar resulting from walking on a hard surface. The human foot is a masterpiece of engineering. It is a miniature suspension bridge but more complicated than an ordinary bridge.

Also to be noted is the fact that the foot always appears in proper proportion to the rest of the body; tall people have large feet and short people have small feet. And how would the evolutionist analyze this mystery and explain how the human foot has remained exactly the same throughout all generations and with all races of people whether savage or civilized? Why have there been no further development or changes if man's foot is the result of evolution? The difference between the mode of living of the savage and the civilized man ought to favor such evolution if that were the method by which the foot has come into being. But there are no such changes, and the foot has remained the same.

Would anyone say that the Golden Gate suspension bridge just happened? Of course not, if he were sane! But why do people assume that an even more intricate mechanism of the human foot could have just happened without design or the workmanship of a master engineer? To add to the wonders of the human foot we must also remember that it has been reproduced billions and billions of times in every human birth with exactly the same shape and form and with the same number of bones and tendons and nerves. And so we see that even the humble foot of man is one of the wonders of his body that glorifies the wisdom of the Creator who made it.

The Human Hand

Similar to the foot but infinitely more complex in design, construction, and function is the human hand.

Ordinarily we give little thought to the mechanism of the hand. We simply take it for granted. And yet, the hand is one of the most wonderful features of the human body. The hand is so unique and so wonderful in its construction and function that it alone marks man as apart and distinct from every other creature. No other creature in the world, not even the ape, is equipped with an instrument comparable to the human hand. Normal human life without the hand would be inconceivable; without it man could never have become what he is or could have achieved what he has accomplished. Without it our civilization would be impossible. In everything that man has created, his hands in one way or another have been involved.

Like the foot, so also the hand consists of a bony framework: muscles, tendons, fats, and nerve fibers. There are a total of 27 individual bones in the hand; 8 of these are in the wrist,

5 in the palm, and 14 in the fingers. The hand is so constructed that it lends itself to an unlimited variety of functions. But every act of the hand sets in motion a whole series of operations of the human mechanism. For example, to close the fist or make a simple grasping motion involves an array of muscles, joints, and tendons, all the way from the shoulder to the fingertips. Doing such a simple thing as lifting a spoonful of soup to one's mouth involves more than 30 joints and 50 muscles, all of them functioning together in perfectly synchronized order.

The five fingers of the hand determine the variety and character of the manual manipulations. The most important of these is the thumb. It is the strongest and has a wider sphere of motion than the rest of the fingers. It provides the base against which the hand can perform a grasping or a holding operation. The hand without a thumb has lost most of its usefulness, but the thumb with only two or even one finger is still an efficient mechanism.

While the hand is of greatest importance to everyone in normal life, it is especially important to such people as musicians, artists, craftsmen, physicians, engineers, machine operators and, of course, many others. The hand can be developed and trained to perform astonishing feats. For example, it is estimated that a master pianist can strike 120 notes a minute. The well-trained typist will accomplish a similar feat. With the fingers of the hands, the skilled surgeon is able to perform a delicate operation which requires the precision of a mechanical instrument. The trapeze artist can develop the comparatively small muscles of his hand to such a degree that he is able to hold with his hands and fingers many times his own weight and perform the most breathtaking stunts.

No other part of our body is so intimately associated with man's moods and general behavior. With our hands we work and play. We create and destroy, we sow and reap, we build and construct; with them we love and heal, we communicate and express our emotions, we write books and create works of art. With our clasped hands we express love, faith, and friendship, and with the clenched fist we threaten and attack. With the open hand we welcome friends and loved ones; the caressing hand expresses deep emotion and attraction, and with a handclasp we seal a solemn covenant. With our wringing hands we reveal the anguish of our soul, and with folded hands we express our devotion and reverence to our God.

The hand is a wonderful gift of the Creator to man. It is one of the seven wonders of the human body. Only an omnipotent and all-wise God could have designed and created the human hand.

So far in our examination of the physical side of man, we have concerned ourselves with the bony structure of his frame and with some external aspects of his body. But the wonders of man's being become even more wonderful and incomprehensible when we examine his internal organs, the mysterious functioning of his glands, and especially his brain and nervous system.

And so let us now turn to that phase of our subject.

The Digestive System

We shall begin by focusing our attention first on the miracle of his digestive system.

A medical dictionary defines digestion as "the process of converting food into material fit to be absorbed and assimilated."

The center of our digestive system is the stomach with its auxiliary organs, such as the salivary glands in the mouth, the liver and the pancreas in the abdominal cavity, the portions of the intestinal canal. This digestive system is the most wonderful chemical laboratory known to man. It converts plant and animal substances, such as vegetables of various kinds, cereals, fruits and nuts, and the flesh of different animals, birds, and fish, which man consumes as food, into human flesh and blood, bones and muscles, nerve and brain matter, and into the hair of the head, and the nails of his fingers and toes. In doing so it sustains life, creates energy, and engenders the required heat for the well-being of the body.

God formed man's body from the dust of the earth, says the sacred record. From chemical analysis we now know that man's body is composed of a number of carefully balanced elements and minerals, such as carbon, oxygen, nitrogen, hydrogen, chlorine, and five different minerals: namely, potassium, sodium, calcium, magnesium, and iron, plus sulphur and phosphorus. All of these elements and minerals, and others, are always found in a delicately proportioned balance. If this balance is disturbed one way or another, ill health or even death may result.

The life process of the body is maintained within the cell. The cell is composed of protoplasm, but the protoplasm is constantly breaking down in the process of digestion, and new protoplasm must take its place. The material from which the new cells are built is the food we eat. The used up remnants of the digestive process are excreted from the body through the skin, the kidneys, the bowels and the lungs.

This miracle of the constant repairing and rebuilding of the living cell is performed by the digestive system. Food is taken into the body, is crushed and ground into pulp by the teeth; then it is conveyed into the stomach by an ingenious muscular action we call swallowing; there it is dissolved and separated into its constituent elements. Then it is carried by the bloodstream to every part of the body and is assimilated to form the body substance. This process is controlled by the autonomic nervous system, which means that this very complicated process is automatic and operates day and night, whether we are awake or asleep, without our being conscious of the miracle that is being performed in our body.

If man abuses his digestive organs by placing too much or too little food or the wrong kind of food into his stomach, the system will rebel and will send up warning signals in the form of stomach cramps, nausea, headache, skin rash, or in still other ways.

And while the digestive system maintains the proper chemical balance in the body and repairs or rebuilds the living cells, it also produces bodily energy and the required body heat to make normal life possible. The cells in our body can live and can be in health only when the temperature of the body is close to 98.6°F. If it sinks below or rises above that figure, it is a signal for serious trouble. And the miracle of this automatic thermostat in our body is that it keeps the body at the same temperature at all times, in summer or in winter, in warm or in cold climates; and it operates the same in all races of men everywhere in the world. The body temperature of the fur-clad Eskimo on Herschel Island is the same as the body temperature of the naked Indian in the Amazon Basin.

Who can understand or fathom these mysteries and the wonders of our digestive system, that wonderful chemical laboratory which creates nourishment for our bodies? And who, when contemplating this wonder, is not constrained to confess with the ancient Magician of Pharaoh, "This is the finger of God"?

But that is not all. The human body is a veritable museum of science, full of God's creation wonders.

The Heart

Equally as miraculous in construction and function as the digestive system is the human heart. I spoke of the stomach and its auxiliary organs as the most wonderful chemical laboratory known to man. Here we can say that the heart is the most wonderful pumping machine found in the universe. No one knows the exact moment when it begins its operation in the fetus or what causes it to start there; but once started, it continues without interruption or rest for fifty, sixty, seventy, eighty, or even more years, pumping in perpetual rhythm the equivalent of about 75 gallons of blood through the body in every hour of man's life. The rate of this operation is about 70 strokes or beats per minute which adds up to approximately a hundred thousand beats for every 24 hours we live.

The heart is a comparatively small organ. Its size is about equal to the fist of the person to whom it belongs. It is located in the chest with its point to the left of the center. Its walls are formed of strong muscles, and its interior is divided into four chambers or cavities, two on each side. It functions in close cooperation with the lungs, another wonderful organ in our body.

The heart is the most powerful organ in the human system. Every day this mighty muscle, weighing only 12 ounces, pumps more than 1800 gallons of blood through miles of blood vessels to nourish the body's trillion cells.

The human body is composed, as we have seen, of billions and possibly trillions of individual cells. Every one of these cells requires a constant supply of nourishment and oxygen. And each cell must rid itself of waste material. The transportation system which performs this double function is the bloodstream. All through the body there is an intricate network of tubes and pipes we call blood vessels. It is estimated that the total length of these blood vessels literally adds up to thousands of miles—not feet, but actually miles. Night and day and every moment of our life the heart pumps blood through these endless miles of blood vessels, carrying to the cells the required food and oxygen and bringing back the discarded waste material.

The bloodstream is kept in perpetual motion by the heart. There are two types of blood vessels for this operation, the arteries and the veins. The arteries carry the blood from the heart to the cells, and the veins provide the return circuit. The large arteries which leave the heart send branches to all parts of the body, dividing themselves into ever smaller and smaller vessels in order to touch every cell of the body. Before each circuit is repeated, the blood passes through the lungs, where, by a most wonderful process of exhalation and inhalation, the waste material is removed, and the bloodstream is recharged with the fresh supply of oxygen. The pumping operation is produced by the contracting and relaxing of the heart muscles. And as every pump must have valves to keep its liquid from flowing backward, so the heart and the arteries are also supplied with a marvelous system of valves which automatically regulates the flow of the blood. The flow of blood through the vessels is very rapid, making the journey through the lungs in about 15 seconds and through the entire body in about one minute. By this perpetual steady operation of the heart, life is sustained. When it stops, death has set in.

The Blood

The whole mechanism of the heart with its life-preserving functions is so wonderful that we cannot understand it. But equally mysterious and marvelous is the blood itself that is being pumped through the body by the heart.

The blood is the life-stream in man. It is the physical carrier or seat of life itself. But that raises the perplexing question: What is life? How does it start? Why does it end?

The blood is composed of plasma and corpuscles. The plasma is the liquid part of the blood. In the plasma float millions of microscopic cells called corpuscles. The corpuscles are of two kinds, the red and the white. The red are the most numerous; millions of them are found in a single droplet of blood. The function of the red corpuscles is to carry food and oxygen to the cells and remove waste material. The white corpuscles are not as numerous; their function is to serve as bodyguards for the cells. It is their business to protect the cells against dangers that threaten them from invading disease germs. When these enemy germs enter the body, the white corpuscles rush automatically, like a fire department, to the spot thus threatened, surround the invading enemies, isolate them, and finally destroy them. When the number of white corpuscles is too low or out of balance, the disease germs multiply rapidly with serious results, which might prove fatal to the body.

There are other mysterious elements in our blood which even modern medical science does not as yet fully understand.

And so this, too, ought to convince every person of normal mentality to admit that only an omnipotent and all-wise God could have conceived, designed and created it, and that it is absurd, irrational, and ridiculous to assume the human heart and its blood vessels could have happened by chance in the process of blind, mechanical evolution.

The Kidney

The kidney is another organ in our body so mysterious in its function and so intricate in its mechanism that only bigotry and irrational opposition to the Biblical account of man's creation could lead men to assume that this marvelous mechanism developed by itself. This organ exists in a pair, one on each side of the spine, about the size of a human fist and shaped like a bean. It is the master chemist in our body, and with the intestinal tract, the main waste disposal system. All the blood of the body passes through the kidneys continually and is cleansed and filtered by them of waste material that would become deadly poison for the body. They maintain the chemical balance in the blood and help to produce the important red cells in the blood, regulate the water supply in the body, and perform so many functions for the health and well-being of man that life cannot last very long when they fail to function. This pair of organs weighs only 5 ounces but contains more than one million little filtering units, called tubules. These tubules stretched out in one long line would measure 70 miles. The kidney filters the total quantity of blood in the body every hour, and by an automatic process passes the waste into the bladder as urine, and from there passes it out of the body.

We are truly fearfully and wonderfully made. Only an omnipotent and all-wise master Mechanic could have created this wonderful organ.

But even that does not exhaust the number and greatness of the wonders we carry about us in our body, as we shall see when we move on to another incomprehensible wonder of man's life and contemplate the miracle of human conception and birth.

Reproductive System

Man begins his existence in the merger of two microscopic cells, the male spermatozoon and the female ovum or egg. These cells are derived by cell division in the testicles of the male and the ovaries of the female. Under the stimulus of hormones from the pituitary gland, the ovum ripens and separates itself in regular intervals from the ovary to begin its passage through the Fallopian tubes into the cavity of the uterus. The lining in the uterus is prepared by hormones from the ovaries, which receives and nourishes the newly arrived ovum. If the ovum has not been fertilized, it will be removed together with the lining of the uterus in the menstrual flow. If the ovum is fertilized it develops rapidly, and by the end of the first month this microscopic formless cell will already begin to assume a recognizable human form.

By a process of incredible precision, the fertilized egg is endowed by means of the chromosomes and genes with a chemical blueprint derived half from the mother and half from the father, which directs all the details of its further development. This blueprint composed of submicroscopic molecules determines how the cells will divide and multiply, how they will form into tissues and bones, limbs and organs, toes, teeth and fingers, and into all the other parts of the body. These invisible molecules will regulate the harmonious development of the body, will determine whether these cells will develop into a male or a female, have a white, black, or brown skin, be tall or small; or, in short, will select and combine those genes which make every human being different from every other human being in the world. The mother's body is the mold in which this miracle is performed. Her bloodstream provides the material from which this new body is being formed.

This stage of development is terminated at a fixed period of time, and then a miniature human being will leave its original habitat and a new child is born into the world. A new human personality who has not existed before has come into being and is endowed with an immortal soul and all those characteristics which distinguish it as a human being. His soul, that had its beginning in this process, will live on from this moment forever.

And while all this is happening, another remarkable miracle is performed in the body of the mother, giving her the power to provide the proper kind of nourishment for her newborn child from her own body. During the period of gestation, a miraculous change occurs in the body of the mother. Presently her mammary glands begin to develop, and at the precise moment when the child needs the food, these glands produce a nourishing milk that was not there before (which dries out when the child is no longer in need of it); and this milk is exactly the type of food that the newborn child requires for its normal development. All this is so marvelous that it is beyond understanding; neither an Aristotle nor an Einstein can explain or comprehend it. Thereafter, the growth and development of the human child continues for about 20 years, until he has reached the stage that we call "maturity." When maturity has been reached, this process comes to a stop. Why? Why does it not continue? Who has fixed the law to regulate it so?

Dr. Joseph Krimsky, a veteran medical practitioner for almost a half century, has witnessed this miracle of child birth again and again in his long professional career, and to him the birth of a child becomes more than a mere biological process. Every birth is an incomprehensible miracle in the presence of which he stands in awe and reverence. He expresses this awe and wonderment in a few beautiful paragraphs in his book, *The Doctor's Soliloquy*,[2] where he writes,

> The years of my life as a physician are filled with abundant testimony to the truth and estheticism of miracles. Conception and birth are miracles beyond our understanding, even though we can plot out the steps and stages in the process. The rapid movement of the microscopic spermatozoon towards the ovum, as if guided and directed by some impelling intelligence bent on the propagation and perpetuation of life—that is a miracle. And let not the materialistic skeptic prate of chemical and physical reactions.
>
> No amount of scientific rationalization can reveal the secret that shrouds the problem of beginning life, whether on earth or in the living womb. The very emotion of love and ecstasy that brings about the union of male and female germ cells is a mystery and an enigma that science cannot explain.
>
> Consider also how the seed is lodged in the womb; how cells and fibers, tissues and blood vessels are prepared to form the uteruarian nest. I am filled with wonder every time I see a bird building its nest. What foresight, what tender care, what clever and efficient use of materials! But, here in the womb of the human mother, the nest is built by some invisible and automatic force endowed by more than human intelligence or animal instinct. The newly fertilized egg, which by some strange magnetism has been drawn and propelled to its destination, is lodged in a wall of warm, palpitating, living flesh which is supplied with vital strength and nourishment.
>
> Reflect upon the wonder of harmony and adjustment that arouses every gland of the body to cooperate in a common effort for the security and growth of the tiny embryo. Think of the mystery of life in the womb; how here in a period of a few months the evolution—from the simple homogenous single-celled bit of protoplasma to the infinite complexity of structure and function in the child at birth.

[2] *The Doctor's Soliloquy*, by Dr. Joseph Krimsky, pp. 7-9.

The Darwinists tell us that it all came about through mutations and variations, through adaptation and selection. But science is learning that these mutations and combinations of mutations are not haphazard or accidental, not the product of blind chance. They occur in response to vital and functional needs. They emerge, or are evoked, whenever life has need of them for the more perfect and more efficient performance of its task. The bricks do not just spring up in place by a design and purpose; those who have eyes to see and a mind to understand must acknowledge with reverence and awe, though the great Architect is beyond the scope of mortal vision.

There are other wonders in our body too numerous to mention or to describe in detail in a treatise like this. In fact, the more we study the human anatomy, the more we are overwhelmed by the countless miracles which constitute our body, each of which is so great and so wonderful that all the superlatives of our language are inadequate to do justice to them.

The Glands

Among the most marvelous of the remaining wonders not yet mentioned is the system of glands in our body. Each one contributes an essential element in our total well-being.

These glands are divided into two groups, the duct and ductless:

1. *The duct glands*

The duct glands are those which are provided with a duct or a canal through which they discharge their secretion into the body. They are the salivary, gastric, and intestinal glands, the pancreas, liver, and kidneys; the tear, sweat, sebaceous, and reproductive glands. In some cases the name indicates the function of the respective glands. Some serve the digestive process; others produce blood cells and regulate the chemical content of the blood; still others separate waste material from the cells. The sebaceous glands lubricate the skin, the tear glands the eye, and the reproductive glands manufacture the male and female cells through which the human race is perpetuated.

Some glands produce more than one type of secretion, each for a separate purpose. All the glands are controlled by the autonomic nervous system and function automatically, each producing a specific type of secretion and an accurately balanced quantity necessary for the well-being of the whole body.

2. *The ductless glands*

But even more mysterious and wonderful than this group of glands are the ductless glands, also called the endocrine glands, which discharge their hormones directly into the bloodstream without the aid of a duct or canal. These glands are located in various parts of the body: two are in the brain, two in the throat, and the remaining four in different parts of the abdomen.

Most of these glands are quite insignificant in size, some even very small. But whether large or small, all of them are so important that without the functioning of any one of them, the body and mind of the individual cannot develop or remain normal.

The master gland of this group is the *pituitary gland*. It is located in the brain at the base of the skull, and in size is no larger than a pea. But even this tiny little gland is composed of three separate parts, each of which again secretes its own specific hormone, each with its own important function. The complete significance of this mysterious gland is not yet fully understood, but the following are some of its known functions:

It regulates the physical and mental development of the body. If one of the hormones is overactive, giantism results; if there is a deficiency, dwarfism may result. It affects the development of the sex organs and regulates the function of the sex glands. It has an influence on nutrition, regulates body temperature, stimulates the development of the mammary glands in the female and seems to be responsible for the growth of the beard and other masculine qualities in the male. It affects the physical and mental energy of the individual. It is intimately connected with, and affects the function of, all other glands, and for that reason it has been called the master gland.

This little, insignificant gland, the existence of which was not even known until modern times, is, therefore, of great importance in the normal development of a well-balanced human personality. Medical science is helpless when this gland fails to function properly.

The *thyroid gland* is located in front of the larynx and the windpipe. It, too, is a delicate organism. If overactive, it may grow into a goiter; if underactive, the result may be physical and mental retardation or serious mental and emotional disturbances. Imbedded in the lobes of this gland is a small separate gland called the *parathyroid gland*. Its secretion acts as a soother and regulates the calcium content in the blood. If removed or diseased, muscle spasms and death will eventually result.

The *gonads* produce the sex hormones. They are responsible for the masculinity and femininity of the individual. They account for the paternal, maternal, and homemaking instinct in the human being. It is the gland which affects the characteristic development of female form, the widening of the hips, and the development of the breasts.

All of these glands are important and deserve special mention, but we cannot discuss all of them. However, one more gland should be mentioned because of its importance; that is the *adrenal gland*. This gland is located in the upper end of the kidneys. It consists of two parts, each secreting its own hormone, each of which again has its own specific effect on the body. These hormones have a mysterious influence on the normal development of the individual. The output of one of these hormones seems to be stimulated by the emotion of anger. When one is angry, it causes the liver to discharge a greater amount of sugar into the bloodstream to provide the necessary emergency energy. It causes the blood to coagulate more readily. If it is overactive in childhood, it accelerates the approach of puberty. If it is out of proper balance in an adult woman, it may cause her to lose her normal sexual function and completely change her personality, bringing about the appearance of masculine characteristics such as a beard or voice change. The adrenal hormone is so potent that it functions normally when found in proportion of one part to a billion in the bloodstream. The delicacy of this balance is beyond comprehension.

There are other important endocrine glands in our body, all of which are of the greatest importance, and more should be said about them. But my purpose here is not to present an exhaustive physiological discussion of these glands, but only to say enough about them to emphasize their wonderful, mysterious, and delicate function in our bodies, and raise again and again the same old questions that I have raised before at every step in our analysis of the human body. That is, how could such a complex, delicate, and mysterious mechanism have happened without a divine, omnipotent and all-wise Creator as described in the first and second chapters of Genesis? Anyone assuming that this could have happened by accident or chance cannot be "deemed a rational being" as even the pagan Cicero says in his treatise on *De Natura Deorum*.

Sleep

And here the wonder and mystery of sleep should also be mentioned.

What is sleep?

Sleep can be defined as a state of quietness occurring periodically in man and animals, characterized by complete or partial unconsciousness, relaxation of body and mind, and a general diminution of vital functions. In animals it is sometimes much prolonged, as in hibernation. Sleep is as essential to life as food and drink. In fact, both animals and man can survive longer without food than without sleep. Sleep is irresistible. Soldiers on guard beyond endurance have been known to have gone to sleep, though they knew that they would be shot if found in this condition. Generals have lost battles, families have been disrupted, and people have even lost their minds because of loss of sleep.

But what is sleep? Why is it so irresistible? Why are we refreshed and our energies and vitality restored by sleep? No one knows the answer. Sleep is a miracle and a mystery. There is nothing that gives more satisfaction and pleasure than restful sleep when fatigued. Sleep is a wonderful gift and a profound blessing of the Creator to man.

And how would the evolutionist explain this miracle?

But all these wonders of the human body pale into insignificance when compared with the wonders of the soul, and the physical mechanism through which the soul functions.

19.

The Soul of Man

The Bible has different terms to express what we have combined in our English word "soul" or in the German "seele." The Greek New Testament has three terms for soul—namely, *psyche* ψυχή, *pneuma* πνεῦμα, *cardia* καρδία. And in the Hebrew there are three corresponding equivalents—namely, *nephesh* נֶפֶשׁ, *neshemah* נְשָׁמָה, and ruach רוּחַ. With some minor shades of difference in these three terms, the general meaning can be expressed by the words, soul, life, the principle of life, spirit, breath, living being, or the Latin *anima*.

The soul is a spiritual entity and therefore invisible and imperceptible to our senses. It resides in the body, permeates and animates the body, but is also affected by the body. Soul and body together constitute the human personality. On the basis of Genesis 9:4 and Leviticus 17:11, some would confine the soul to the bloodstream. The ancient Epicureans, modern evolutionists, and nearly all schools of psychology either deny the existence of the soul altogether or treat it as an open question. But the soul is a reality. It is the most important reality in man. It is the seat of the divine image in man. It is the real ego of man and the very essence of his personality.

The organ through which the soul functions and establishes contact with the world outside of itself is the body. Paul, writing to the Corinthians, says, "For we must all appear before the judgment seat of Christ; that everyone may receive the things done *in his body*, according to that he has done, whether it be good or bad" (2 Cor. 5:10). The English version has *in his body*; the Greek is *dia tou Somatos*, which means through or by means of the instrumentality of the body.

The Intimate Relation of Body and Soul

This soul permeates the body and the body affects the soul. This union of spirit and body is similar to the mysterious union of the divine and human in the person of Christ. Body and soul are so united that whatever affects the one also reacts on the other. Even a very simple act of the intellect requires the concurrence of the body, which is the instrument through which the soul functions. For example, physical fatigue will result from purely mental activity and vice versa; grief and sorrow or elation and joy will affect the body correspondingly.

The Nervous System

The mechanism in the body through which the soul functions is the nervous system, which reaches out to every part of the the body, to every organ and tissue of this physical being. It animates the body and governs all organic movements, voluntary or involuntary. There can be no communication or coordination in the body without this mechanism. There can be no consciousness, no sense impression, no knowledge, no feeling, and no willing without the nervous system.

The nervous system may be divided into three principal parts:

1. The central nervous system which comprises the brain and the spinal cord.
2. The peripheral nervous system, consisting of the nerve fibers running from the brain and the spinal cord to all parts of the body, carrying nerve impulses to and from the central nervous system to all parts of the body.
3. The autonomic nervous system which controls the vital organs such as the heart, the respiratory, circulatory and digestive systems.

The central nervous system consists of the brain and the spinal cord. The brain is the largest and most complex mass of nerve tissue in the body. It consists of two main parts, the cerebrum, which is the larger part of the entire brain and occupies the greater part of the skull, and the cerebellum. The cerebellum is located in the lower back part of the cerebrum.

The average weight of an adult brain is about fifty ounces for a man and forty-five for a woman, or just a little more than 2 percent of the weight of the entire body.

The brain is divided into two equal hemispheres by central fissures. The outer layer of the brain, about 1/8 of an inch in thickness, is called a cortex, or in popular language, the gray matter. The higher mental processes are centered in the cortex. The cortex is deeply grooved with fissures, thus increasing the cortical area. These fissures and ridges are called convolutions. The greater the number of convolutions, the greater the cortical area, and the greater the mental capacity.

The lower centers are found between the cerebral cortex and the spinal cord; they act independently of the higher processes and control the vital functions of the body.

The brain sends out twelve pairs of nerve strands whose fibers connect the sense organs, the muscles, the glands of the face, and of some of the vital organs.

The spinal cord issues thirty-one pairs of special nerve strands whose fibers connect the muscles and glands of the remaining parts of the body. The nerve fibers running to and from the central nervous system are nerve strands or a bundle of nerve fibers like a telephone cable line, each single nerve strand consisting of possibly a hundred thousand separate fibers.

According to their functions, both the cranial and spinal nerves are divided into three groups: the receptors, the connectors, and the affectors.

The Receptors

By *receptors* are meant the sense organs which receive stimuli from without. There are five sense organs: skin, tongue, nose, ear, eye. In addition to these highly specialized sense organs there are certain less clearly defined receptors in the vital organs, muscles, tendons, joints, and in the semicircular canal of the ear.

It is not within the scope of this treatise to describe in detail all the receptors and their functions. But because of the wonders of these organs of our soul, I feel that I should at least touch briefly upon some of them and then deal in greater detail with the two most important—namely, the ear and the eye.

1. *The skin*

The most widely diffused sense organ is found in the skin

and is scattered throughout the body in the sense of touch: It produces the four sensations of pressure, pain, cold, and heat.

By means of this organ we become aware of our physical environment and are able to touch and to hold things, are warned against danger threatening us through pain, and are protected against excessive heat and cold. It is estimated that at least three million of these receptors are scattered throughout the body and are so distributed that they are most numerous and most sensitive where they are most needed. The two most sensitive spots are the tip of the finger and the tip of the tongue; without the sense of touch normal life would be impossible.

2. *The tongue*

The sense of taste is located on the tongue, in the soft parts of the palate and in the throat. By means of these taste buds we are able to distinguish between the four basic tastes: namely, sweet, sour, salt and bitter, and the countless combinations of these basic tastes. The sense of taste also functions as a protection for man, but its chief purpose is to give pleasure and enjoyment to him. Taste is one of the foremost sources of human pleasure. The animal is attracted to certain foods, but animals in general are limited to a very narrow restriction in their choice of food.

3. *The nose*

The sense of smell is located in a very small area of the nose. The sense of smell is not as important nor as highly developed in man as it is in certain animals. But man is endowed with a wide variety of smell receptors. Smell enriches taste, but above all is a source of much pleasure. The varieties of pleasant odors we are able to receive are many. The sense of smell may arouse in us various emotions and affect our attitude. Certain odors cause nausea, disgust, and are repulsive; others give sheer enjoyment and have an aesthetic significance, or even arouse religious emotion. For man, the sense of smell is more of a luxury than an absolute necessity; for many animals it is essential for their very existence.

4. *The ear*

The human ear is a complicated organ. The odd-shaped shell to which the name "ear" is popularly applied is only an insignificant part of the organ of hearing. It merely collects the stimuli and directs them into the proper channels. The real hearing occurs inside the head. The receptor for hearing is divided into the outer, middle, and inner ear. The outer ear consists of a shell or concha, together with a tube about an inch long called "meatus," which leads into the head through an opening into the skull and ends in a vibrating membrane called the tympanic membrane, popularly known as the ear drum. The middle ear lies beyond the drum; it is a small cavity containing three small bones known as the hammer, anvil, and the stirrup. These take up and transmit the vibration of the drum. The middle ear cavity is the end of the passage. The eustachian tube, which opens into the back of the mouth, equalizes the air pressure on the eardrum. If the drum is pressed back too far into the inner ear cavity by a loud sound, we may remedy the trouble by swallowing, which forces air into the eustachian tube and thus again equalizes the pressure.

Since there is no air chamber on the inner side of the tympanic membrane, there must be some means of transmitting the vibration across the cavity to the inner ear. The means by which this is accomplished is a chain of three small bones called ossicles. The first is the malleus or hammer, which is attached by an arm to the middle of the tympanic membrane. The head of the malleus articulates with the head of the second bone called incus or anvil. One of the branches of the incus articulates with a stapes and thus transmits the vibration of the tympanic membrane to lymphatic fluid within the inner ear.

But this is not all. The real process of hearing takes place in the innermost ear. This inner ear or labyrinth is a very complicated structure, only part of which is concerned with hearing. A part of this cavity is the semicircular canal which helps to maintain the equilibrium of the body. The front part contains the spiral cochlea, which contains the real receptors of hearing. Between the canal and the cochlea lies the cavity called the vestibule. The inside of the cochlea is divided into two spiral tubes lying side by side, which run from the base to the tip of the cochlea. They are separated by a membrane.

Between these two tubes lies a small tube, the cochlea duct. Within the cochlea tube is a system of rods and hair cells called the organs of corti. These rods and hair cells connect with the fibers of the auditory nerves and are the real centers of hearing. The cells of the cochlea are set into vibration; these cells are of different lengths and each picks up waves of corresponding lengths, just as the strings of a piano vibrate and produce sounds of their own length.

When a wave of a given length is set into vibration, the appropriate rods or hair cells of the cochlea stimulate certain sets of fibers which carry the nerve impulses to the auditory nerve region of the brain.

The stimuli for hearing consist of vibrations of sound waves. These waves differ from light waves. They travel through the air at a uniform rate of approximately a thousand feet per second. Like light waves, they vary in length, and the longer the sound waves the fewer waves strike the ear drum in a given period of time. These are usually measured in frequency per second; the greatest frequency range that can be heard by the average man is about twenty-five thousand to fifty thousand per second. The average is placed at about thirty-two thousand.

The rate of vibration determines the quality of sensation. Sound waves differ not only in frequency but also in intensity. The same sound may be faint or strong, depending on the force of disturbance in the ear.

The ear is one of the most important organs given to man to enable him to communicate with his fellowman. The ability to hear and to speak are opposite sides of the same coin; the one presupposes the other.

The ear, with its intricate mechanism, is a miracle that no one can understand. But equally wonderful are the ability to speak and the gift of language. The human voice is produced by a mechanical process of the vocal cords. These cords are delicate membranes stretched across the windpipe in the throat and are set into vibration by air pressure from the lungs. But tongue, teeth and the palate are also essential for intelligible speech. Speech itself, the ability to produce articulate sounds, is an essential part of man's being, and therefore taken for granted. Few people ever think of the wonders of speech.

And when considering the gift of speech, we must also include the miracle of the human voice. What a marvelous gift to man is his voice! With our voice we communicate our thoughts and our deepest emotions. By the tone of our voice we command, we prod, we lament, we express grief, joy, anger and displeasure; the soothing voice of a mother heals the hurt and the fears of her infant child.

The voice produced by the silver-tongued orator of a Demosthenes and a William Jennings Bryan and the golden voice of a Marion Anderson, a Caruso and a galaxy of others similar to them, have stirred the souls of millions who have heard them perform in opera or sacred cantatas. And the wonder is that there are no two people with exactly the same voice. The human voice is as individual as is personality or character. And then to think that there are those who believe that this most varied and most beautiful, musical instrument just happened by itself!

But equally, or even more wonderful, is the gift of language.

What is language, we may ask? The idea of language is hard to define. The dictionary attempts to do so in various ways. It defines language as the expression of ideas by human words or again the words and combination of words formed, the means of communication among members of a single community, nation, or people.

But a close examination of these attempts at definitions of language reveals that they really do not explain the mystery of language. They merely speak of its function.

Language consists of a series of articulate sounds. These sounds produced by a delicate mechanism in the throat and in the mouth become words, and a word becomes a symbol of an object or an idea. And this is not a haphazard process, but words are combined according to very definite laws, laws as rigorous as any other law of nature. This is true of every language, even of the most primitive language of barbaric people. We call these laws "grammatical rules." These rules are not arbitrary, invented by the grammarian. The grammarian extracts them from the language itself, just as the chemist and the physicist deduce the laws from the sciences in which they are interested.

In his history of Shaka, the Zulu King of the early 1800's, author E. A. Ritter speaks of the Zulu language and writes: "The monumental dictionary of the Zulu language by Dr. A. T. Bryant contains 19,000 words. These 19,000 words were of necessity used by the Zulus in their daily talk; for being unwritten, they could not otherwise have been preserved. The Zulu language has eight different classes of nouns governing the inflection of each verb and adjective in one of the most complicated but exact grammars in the world. Although unwritten until the Europeans came, every Zulu, then as now, spoke with perfect grammatical exactitude, and ungrammatical speaking is utterly unknown to the Zulus." [1]

By means of language man is able to communicate with his fellowman. He can share with him his own experiences, his

[1] *Shaka Zulu*, by E. A. Ritter, pp. 77-78. Longmans, South Africa, Ltd.

joys and his sorrows, and reveal to him the innermost thoughts of his soul. Without such symbols as language man could not communicate with others and could not even think. Human society and civilization would be impossible without language; without language there would have been no literature, no books, no songs, and no communication between God and man.

By means of language the mother sings her soothing lullaby to her infant child; the teacher imparts knowledge to the young; the preacher exhorts, comforts, and inspires; and the statesman regulates society, sometimes by promulgating necessary laws, other times by arousing his nation to unified action for self-defense. Language is the means by which the poet produces his songs; these songs can then be converted into music. Music appeals to the whole order of man's emotions: stirs him, soothes him, comforts him, satisfies his aesthetic sense, or arouses him to sympathy, to anger, to hatred, to action. All of these mysteries are wonderful beyond comprehension, and contemplation of them ought to cause every normal human being, and especially every Christian, to say with the Psalmist again and again, "I will praise thee; for I am fearfully and wonderfully made: marvellous are thy works; and that my soul knoweth right well" (Ps. 139:14).

5. *The eye*

The ear and the faculty of hearing are wonderful gifts of God to man, but equally wonderful is the gift of sight made possible through the miracle of the human eye.

God gave man one nose and one mouth but two eyes and placed them in such array that they give balance and beauty to his appearance. They are the windows of his soul and an outlet for his emotions, and they are an important means man uses to adjust himself to his environment.

The eye has been quite properly compared with a camera. Just as the photographer's camera is equipped with a lens, a sensitive plate or film, and a diaphragm, so the human eye is provided with equivalent counterparts.

The lens is a double convex body filled with a liquid substance called aqueous humor, placed immediately between the lens and the cornea. Its function is to focus the light waves into the inner surface of the eyeball. The lens is held in position by a ring-shaped muscle which both contracts and expands the lens and thereby accommodates vision of distances. This adjustment is automatic.

The retina of the eye is the equivalent of the sensitive plate or film in a camera. The retina covers all the inner surface of the eyeball. It contains rods and cones which are the sensitive sense organs for the reception of light stimuli. It is estimated that there are 130 million rods and 7 million cones in the retina of the human eye. It is believed that the rods are the receptors for vision where illumination is low and the cones are the receptors of color and for vision in bright light and in daylight.

The iris is the equivalent of the diaphragm in the camera. Its function is to regulate the amount of light necessary for vision; this function is automatic.

The stimuli for the eye are light waves which travel at the rate of 186,000 miles per second. The eye is sensitive only to light waves which lie between infrared and ultraviolet. The light waves vary in length according to the color sensations they produce. Color itself is a phenomenon of nature we know to exist and to be a fact but which we cannot explain or understand.

Our visual sensations fall into two groups: namely, achromatic or colorless, and chromatic, that is the sensation of different colors. It is claimed that the normal adult eye can experience about 35,000 different color sensations.

Next to the vital organs, on which life itself depends, the eye is one of the most precious gifts of the Creator to man: It is the light of the body; it is the open window to the whole world outside of himself, and the means by which he can enjoy physical beauty. It is an important sense organ in the process of learning: eighty-three percent of normal learning takes place through the eye. The study of nouns in the English dictionary has revealed that 90 percent of them refer to something seen.

When we consider the wonders of the human eye, we realize again and again that all the superlatives of our language are insufficient to do justice to it or to make intelligible these wonders of our being. When we meditate on these wonders, we are again constrained to sing with the poet:[2]

> When all these wonders, O my God,
> My rising soul surveys,
> Transport with the view, I'm lost
> In wonder, love and praise.

---

[2] "When All These Wonders, O My God," by Joseph Addison, 1712, *Lutheran Hymnal*, No. 31.

Through all eternity to Thee
A joyful song I'll raise;
But, oh! eternity's too short
To utter all Thy praise!

May this suffice for our consideration of the receptors of our nervous system, but I must add a few brief paragraphs about the connectors, the second category in our nervous system.

The Connectors and Affectors

By the *connectors* are meant the nerve fibers which connect all parts of the body to the central nervous system. They carry the impulse received by the receptors to the brain and the spinal cord and from these centers to the *affectors*—that is, to the muscles and the glands. It is estimated that the central nervous system alone consists of 14 billion nerve units called "neurons" and that there are approximately 26 trillion nerve cells in the human body. Someone has calculated that if a person would attempt to count the neurons in the human body and he would count at the rate of two per second for eight hours a day and every day of the year, it would require at least a thousand years to complete this task!

The neuron system in the human body, brain, and spinal cord is so complex that it is altogether beyond comprehension or imagination. Robert C. Cook, in his book *Human Fertility, the Modern Dilemma*, New York 1941, describes the neurons as being essentially an electrical system, the complexity of which, he says, is beyond imagination. A building the size of the Pentagon in Washington, he claims, would not be large enough to house a computing machine with as many synapses as are found in the human brain. All the power developed by the Grand Coulee Dam would be required to operate such a "thinking factory"; all the waters of the Columbia River would be needed to dissipate the heat produced and keep the operation temperature down so that it would not burst into flames. And even such a machine would not perform such higher mental functions as imagination and intuition.

A neuron is a complex mechanism by which nerve energy is conducted from one part of the organism to another. It consists of a nerve cell with a nucleus, dendron, and axon. The impulse is received by the end of the dendron which transmits it to the nerve cell; there it is modified and recharged and then sent on its way through the axon by way of a synapse to the next neuron.

The working of the nervous system has been compared with the intricate wiring system of a modern telephone center. The brain may be compared with a battery or the source of electrical power. Inside the brain cells a chemical action takes place which goes on without interruption whether we are awake or asleep. This chemical action produces, so it is believed, electrical energy, and the electricity thus produced provides the energy for the impulse. The impulse is transmitted from the central nervous system to the nerve fibers which connect every organ and every cell of the human body with the central system.

As the electrical impulse is conducted to its destination by a system of wires, so the nerve impulse follows the nerve fibers to the *affectors*—that is, to the muscles and glands. There, at the contact with these organs is another wonderful mechanism which functions something like a transformer. It reconverts the nerve impulse into a chemical agent and this in turn becomes the stimulant to set muscles and glands into action to carry out what the brain had directed.

And all this is either automatic, as in the case of so-called reflex actions, or is the response to the command given by the will of the individual. If I wish to raise my hand to my mouth, a complex mechanism goes into action to carry out this command. If I wish to speak, to walk, to sit down, or to do any of the countless things I am able to do, millions and possibly billions of neurons are set into motion to make these actions possible. All this is so wonderful, so bewildering, so incomprehensible that man cannot even understand it himself. Man is the most wonderful and the most exalted creature in the universe. There is nothing in this visible world to compare with him. And therefore, if men would only contemplate their own being and thoughtfully consider the wonders of their own bodies, they could not possibly be deceived by the absurdities of the evolutionary theories and consider themselves the product of a blind mechanical process. They would instead give glory, praise and honor to God their Creator, who designed them in wisdom and power. And this happened when God said: "Let us make man in our image, after our own likeness."

20.

God Rested on the Seventh Day

> And on the seventh day God ended his work which he had made; and he rested on the seventh day from all his work which he had made.
>
> And God blessed the seventh day, and sanctified it: because that in it he had rested from all his work which God created and made. (Gen. 2:2-3)

The creation of man was God's final creative act. Man was the final touch and crown of all His works. With man, creation came to a close. Nothing new has been created since. That is the meaning of the words: "And on the seventh day God ended his work which he had made; and he rested on the seventh day from all his works which he had made."

God's relation to the world now is that of a Sustainer. He upholds all things by His omnipotent power. He has fixed immutable laws by which all things are ordered and by which all creation fulfills the purpose for which it was intended. He holds the earth suspended in space. There are no pillars or cables to support it. It rotates about its own axis and around the sun with absolute precision and regularity. Every man-made clock in the world is regulated by it. The millions and billions of stars that fill our universe move in their respective orbits with mathematical accuracy. Life in its myriads of forms and kinds perpetuates itself in strict conformity with the law of "after his kind." Day follows night and season follows season in regular succession. The sun continues to radiate light and life-producing energy to all creatures on the face of the earth and is not diminished in its heat and its power. And the moon follows with its gentle and mellow light to radiate beauty and serenity into the darkness of the night. The raven finds its food, and the beast of the forest and plains its prey, and the swallow continues to build its nest as its original parents did when they emerged from the hand of their Creator.

And so all things continue as God has ordained them to be. The laws by which the universe is sustained and regulated are as wonderful and incomprehensible as creation itself. Only those who willfully close their eyes to these wonders will fail to recognize in them the majesty and power of the eternal God.

> Thou, even thou, art Lord alone. Thou hast made heaven, the heaven of heavens, with all their host, the earth, and all things that are therein, the seas, and all that is therein, and *thou preservest them all.* (Neh. 9:6)

When God had completed the creation of heaven and earth, He inspected, as it were, the things He had made. And we read: "God saw everything that he had made, and behold, it was very good." "And God saw that it was good" had been the refrain at the end of every creation day, but at the end of it all He again said, "It was very good."

When God pronounced it "very good," it was good in the absolute, not only relatively good. God had created a perfect world, perfect in all its details. There were no thorns and thistles in that world. The earth brought forth abundantly of everything that was needful to provide for the wants, comforts, and pleasures of man. There was no struggle for existence by man or beasts. There were no Saharas, no barren wastes, no bleak and sterile hills, no rigors of the Arctic, and no disease-breeding marshlands of the tropics. The most enchanting islands of the South Seas today are but an imperfect replica of the world which had received the verdict "very good" from its Creator. In the earth there were no disorders, no earthquakes or tornadoes, no decay, and for man there was no aging process, no suffering and no death.

But something happened to this perfect creation of God. Sin with its curse and blighting effect entered this world. "By one man sin entered into the world, and death by sin" (Rom. 5:12). Through the disobedience of Adam and Eve the intimate fellowship of man with his Creator was broken, and disharmony and disorder in all creation followed in its wake. Since Adam had been given dominion over all things on earth, the consequences of his sin and the effect of its curse became a blight on all creation. Now the ground is cursed for his sake. It now brings forth thorns and thistles instead of nourishing food, and in the sweat of his brow man must now wrest from the earth his livelihood. Now there is sorrow and pain, aging, deterioration, and death in the world. And man eventually returns again to the elements from which his body was taken.

But even now, despite the curse and the blight of sin upon it, the world is still a wonderful world. The devil was not able to destroy it completely or rob it of all its beauty. It still proclaims the glory of the Maker:

> The heavens declare the glory of God,
> The firmament His power.
> Day unto day its story
> Repeats from hour to hour;
> Night unto Night replying,
> Proclaims in every land,
> O Lord, with voice undying
> The wonders of Thy hand.
>
> The sun with royal splendor
> Goes forth to chant Thy praise;
> And moonbeams soft and tender
> Their gentle anthems raise.
> O'er every tribe and nation
> That music strange is poured,
> The song of all creation,
> To Thee, creation's Lord.
>
> —Australian Lutheran Hymn Book, No. 186

The Mystery and Absurdity of Unbelief

It is difficult to understand how rational and otherwise intelligent human beings can become so irrational and spiritually blind as to believe that all this wonderful creation could have happened by chance or by itself, without an outside cause, or without the will of an all-wise and all-powerful Creator such as the Bible teaches us there is.

As an example of such willful blindness and intellectual dishonesty, Dr. Henry M. Morris quotes Julian Huxley, one of the world's foremost evolutionary biologists, as he expressed himself on this subject on a television panel discussion program with four other world-renowned scientists and notables, just prior to the famous Darwin Centennial Celebration at the University of Chicago, where Huxley is reported to have said:[1]

> Darwinism removed the whole idea of God as the Creator of organisms from the spheres of rational discussion. Darwin pointed out that no supernatural designer was needed. Since natural reactions could account for any known form of life, there was no room for any supernatural agency in its evolution.
>
> There was no sudden moment during evolutionary history, when "spirit" was instilled into life, anymore than than there was a single moment when it was instilled into you—I think we can dismiss entirely all idea of a supernatural, overriding mind being responsible for the evolutionary process.

And *Look* magazine quoted a modern theologian as saying:[2]

> Surely it is not possible for any responsible person to think that we can any longer know or experience God in nature, in history, in economics, or in political arenas, in the laboratory, or in anything which is genuinely modern; whether in thought or experience, wherever we turn in our experiences we experience the eclipse or silence of God.

Even the pagan Cicero knew better and called such a view the height of irrationality. Julian Huxley and modern theologians and all other devotees of the cult of evolution must know and should have the moral courage and the intellectual honesty to admit that they have no real scientific proof for the evolutionary theory, that Darwin's supposition on which he had based his origin of species has been shown to be erroneous, and that all other evolutionary theorists who put forth new attempts to establish their philosophy have also failed to provide scientific evidence for their faith. Just as the ancient Greek philosophers who knew not God tried to find a solution for the origin of the universe without God, so modern scientists who refuse to acknowledge God as the Creator try to find some other solution for the "Welt Rätsel" [riddle of the world]. But they are not always as honest as the groping pagan philosophers of Greece were in their attempt to prove their argument.

---

[1] Dr. Henry M. Morris, *The Twilight of Evolution*, p. 25. Grand Rapids, Michigan: Baker Book House.

[2] *Look* magazine, April 19, 1966, p. 70.

Christ und Welt, a popular German publication of December 3, 1953, reported that the geological division of the British Museum and the department of anatomy of Oxford University had discovered that the so-called Piltdown man was a fraud. But the evolutionists, who repudiate with contempt the faith of the Christian based on revelation, accepted by faith the hoax as scientific evidence for their theory. They have not repented for having been deceived, and they are still deceiving others; they continue to present their unscientific philosophy as fact and absolute truth.

In all its history, evolution has offered no rational solution for the basic problems of the universe. It has no answer for the origin of matter, nor for the origin of life; no answer for the magnificent order in the universe, nor for the immutable laws of nature by which all things are regulated.

Evolution cannot bridge the gulf between plant and animal life, nor can it account for the origin of the species and the fixity of their kind. Evolution has not found the link between the lower and the higher forms of plant and animal life and does not explain why there are no new creations appearing now, as there should be if its claim were true, or why none have appeared within historic times. Evolution has not produced a single missing link, and their number ought to be countless if its theory were a fact. Evolution cannot account for the wonders of the human body, much less for the miracle of the human mind. Evolutionists cannot explain why all living things deteriorate and eventually die, nor have they an answer for death itself. And there are thousands of other questions for which they have no answer, only wishful speculations.

They will not believe that the mere adding of more zeros to the supposed age of all things does not solve their problem. It is only an escape method and a device to becloud the issue or to impress the ignorant. Whether this universe, with all that is in it, had its origin 6,000 years or 6 billion years ago, it required an original cause; they fail to produce that cause.

And the great tragedy of our day is that so many craven theologians, the men who claim to be the spokesmen for God, yield to this diabolical deception and distort the clear, factual words of Genesis into meaningless poetry or allegory and hurry to join the crowds that worship at the new altar of Baal. They seek the honor of men rather than of God. They fear to be regarded as obscurantists, and want to be recognized as scholars, and so they become guilty of forgery, and in the name of scholarship distort the meaning of God's revelation which they claim to expound.

Why is this? Why do respectable churchmen act this way? Why do intellectual scientists, whose keenness of mind is so evident in every other respect, become so blind and irrational when they approach this question?

There is only one answer. It is the curse of sin and its blighting effect on the spiritual understanding of man. "But the natural man receiveth not the things of the Spirit of God: for they are foolishness unto him: neither can he know them, because they are spiritually discerned" (1 Cor. 2:14).

It is the power of Satan, active in and through the children of this world. When men refuse to submit to the authority of God, they become servants of the devil and obey him, and he delights to make fools of them. It is the "old serpent, called the Devil, and Satan, which deceiveth the whole world" (Rev. 12:9). He is the "father of lies" and causes men to believe the lie rather than the truth. He deceived Adam and Eve and caused them to mistrust the Word of God, and instead to believe his own lying promises that they would be like God.

And finally St. Paul gives us the ultimate reason for such irrationality. When men stubbornly refuse to accept divine truth, God will finally withdraw it from them and condemn them to accept their own folly and believe the lie rather than the truth. He writes: "Because they received not the love of the truth, that they might be saved. And for this cause God shall send them strong delusion, that they should believe a lie: that they all might be damned who believed not" (2 Thess. 2:10-12).

Is evolution science? No, and a thousand times no! Evolution, atheistic, theistic, or otherwise, is not science; neither is it chance, or accident, or the vagaries of godless men. The theory of evolution is a hoax of the devil and a delusion of Satan. It is blasphemy against God. It degrades man to an animal, man who was created in the image of God, and robs him of his dignity and honor. It destroys morality and denies man's responsibility to God. It destroys the very idea of sin and reduces the atonement of Christ to a meaningless martyrdom. It is the devil's most brazen affront on the majesty of God and the most diabolical attack on the Bible and all that the Christian religion stands for.

Therefore, let Christians beware lest they be deceived and be taken by the craftiness of the devil, because he is still their deadly adversary, as St. Peter writes, "Your adversary the devil, as a roaring lion, walketh about, seeking whom he may devour: whom resist steadfast in the faith" (1 Peter 5:8, 9). Christians need not be frightened by the bombastic pretense of great learning of these godless men: "For the wisdom of this world is foolishness with God" (1 Cor. 3:19).

Genesis is not a myth and not an allegory, but God's own revelation concerning the creation of heaven and earth. It is factual history presented in a highly condensed and telegraphic form. It is the only authentic source of knowledge we have of the beginning of all things. Christians will accept this as an article of faith, as the writer to the Hebrews says: "Through faith we understand that the worlds were framed by the word of God, so that things which are seen were not made of things which do appear" (Heb. 11:3).

And so they will continue to confess in all boldness and confidence with Luther:

> I believe that God has made me and all creatures, that He has given me my body and soul, eyes, ears, and all my members, my reason, and all my senses, and still preserves them. Also clothing and food, meat and drink, house and home, wife and children, fields, cattle, and all my goods. That He richly and daily provides me with all that I need to support this body and life, that He defends me against all danger and guards and protects me from all evil; and all this purely out of Fatherly, divine goodness and mercy, without any merit or worthiness in me; for all which it is my duty to thank and praise, to serve and obey Him. This is most certainly true.

And they will sing with the early Christian poet:

> At his word they were created;
> He commanded; it was done:
> Heaven and earth and depth of ocean
> In the three-fold order one; all that grows
> beneath the shining of the moon, and orbit sun.
> Evermore and evermore Thee let old men, Thee let
> young men, Thee let boys in chorus sing.
> Matrons, virgins, little maidens
> With glad voices answering;
> Let their guileless songs echo
> And the heart its music bring
> Ever more and ever more.
>
> —Aurelius Clemens Prudentius, 348-413

And so we shall conclude our meditation on the first two

chapters of Genesis, where we get a glimpse of the majesty, wisdom, power, and glory of our God, and join the Psalmist of old, praising God and saying:

> Bless the Lord, O my soul. O Lord my God, thou art very great; thou art clothed with honour and majesty.
>
> Who coverest thyself with light as with a garment; who stretchest out the heavens like a curtain:
>
> Who layeth the beams of his chambers in the waters; who maketh the clouds his chariot; who walketh upon the wings of the wind.
>
> Who maketh his angels spirits; his ministers a flaming fire:
>
> Who laid the foundations of the earth, that it should not be removed for ever.
>
> Thou coveredst it with the deep as with a garment: the waters stood above the mountains.
>
> At thy rebuke they fled; at the voice of thy thunder they hasted away.
>
> They go up by the mountains; they go down by the valleys unto the place which thou hast founded for them.
>
> Thou hast set a bound that they may not pass over; that they turn not again to cover the earth.
>
> He sendeth the springs into the valleys, which run among the hills.
>
> They give drink to every beast of the field: the wild asses quench their thirst.
>
> By them shall the fowls of the heaven have their habitation, which sing among the branches.
>
> He watereth the hills from his chambers: the earth is satisfied with the fruit of thy works.
>
> He causeth the grass to grow for the cattle, and herb for the service of man: that he may bring forth food out of the earth;
>
> And wine that maketh glad the heart of man, and oil to make his face to shine, and bread which strengtheneth man's heart.
>
> The trees of the Lord are full of sap; the cedars of Lebanon, which he hath planted;
>
> Where the birds make their nests: as for the stork, the fir trees are her house.
>
> The high hills are a refuge for the wild goats; and the rocks for the conies.
>
> He appointed the moon for seasons: the sun knoweth his going down.
>
> Thou makest darkness, and it is night: wherein all the beasts of the forest do creep forth.
>
> The young lions roar after their prey, and seek their meat from God.

The sun ariseth, they gather themselves together, and lay them down in their dens.

Man goeth forth unto his work and to his labour until the evening.

O Lord, how manifold are thy works! in wisdom hast thou made them all: the earth is full of thy riches.

So is this great and wide sea, wherein are things creeping innumerable, both small and great beasts.

There go the ships: here is that leviathan, whom thou hast made to play therein.

These wait all upon thee; that thou mayest give them their meat in due season.

That thou givest them they gather: thou openest thine hand, they are filled with good.

Thou hidest thy face, they are troubled: thou takest away their breath, they die, and return to their dust.

Thou sendest forth thy spirit, they are created: and thou renewest the face of the earth.

The glory of the Lord shall endure forever: the Lord shall rejoice in his works.

He looketh on the earth, and it trembleth: he toucheth the hills, and they smoke.

I will sing unto the Lord as long as I live: I will sing praise to my God while I have my being.

My meditation of him shall be sweet: I will be glad in the Lord.

Let the sinners be consumed out of the earth, and let the wicked be no more. Bless thou the Lord, O my soul. Praise ye the Lord.

—Psalm 104

And Christians everywhere will join the chorus of saints and angels and sing with awesome wonderment:

O Lord my God! When I in awesome wonder
Consider all the worlds Thy hands have made,
I see the stars, I hear the rolling thunder,
Thy power throughout the universe displayed!

Then sings my soul, my Saviour God, to Thee:
How great Thou art, how great Thou art!
Then sings my soul, my Father God to Thee:
How great thou art, how great thou art!

When through the woods and forest glades I wander
And hear the birds sing sweetly in the trees;
When I look down from lofty mountain grandeur
And hear the brook and feel the gentle breeze;

And when I think that God His Son not sparing,

Sent Him to die, I scarce can take it in;
That on the cross, my burden gladly bearing,
He bled and died to take away my sin.

When Christ shall come with shout of acclamation
And take me home, what joy shall fill my soul!
Then I shall bow in humble adoration,
And there proclaim, my God, how great Thou art!

Then sings my soul, my Saviour God to Thee:
How great Thou art, how great Thou art!
Then sings my soul, my Father God to Thee:
How great thou art, how great Thou art!

—How Great Thou Art!, Carl Boberg

APPENDIX

Some suggestions for use of the material are offered here in this book for study groups, adult Bible classes, and classes in religious courses in Christian high schools and colleges.

The study of Genesis has become most important for Christians in our day because of the devastating effect of the theory of evolution taught as scientific truth in practically all our schools from kindergarten to graduate school.

To get the maximum benefit of the material here offered, I would suggest the following additional activities:

A. Memory work

1. All members of the group ought to endeavor to memorize at least the following selections:
   a) All of Genesis chapter one
   b) Psalm 8
   c) Psalm 19:1-6
   d) Romans 1:18-25
   e) Romans 2:14,15
   f) Psalm 139:14
   g) Hymn 43 (Lutheran Hymnal)

B. Additional Reading

1. My book, *The Flood.* This will be helpful for a better understanding of the geological conditions of our world today without the millions and billions of years postulated by the evolutionary geologist.
2. *The Age of the Earth: Chronology of the Bible*, also by myself. This will give the reader an interpretation

of the remarkable genealogical tables found in our Bible, on the basis of which the approximate age of the earth can be calculated. These two books, together with the present volume, constitute a trilogy which provides a Biblical answer to the question of the origin and age of the universe and a reasonable explanation for the physical condition of our world today. All three of these books are available at Concordia Publishing House, St. Louis, Missouri, and almost all Christian bookstores.

3. *Darwin, Evolution, and Creation.* A symposium of Lutheran scholars on the topics as indicated in the title of the book, edited by Dr. Paul Zimmerman, available at Concordia Publishing House, St. Louis, Mo.
4. *Genes, Genesis and Evolution*, by Dr. John W. Klotz, available at Concordia Publishing House. This book deals with the subjects of creation and evolution from the scientific point of view.
5. *The Twilight of Evolution*, by Dr. Henry M. Morris, Baker Book House, Grand Rapids, Michigan. The author is a professor of civil engineering, but a staunch believer in the Biblical creation account.
6. *Biblical Cosmology and Modern Science*, by the same author. Craig Press, Nutley, New Jersey.
7. For a general survey of natural science on the level of elementary school children, *Nature and Nature's God*, by Herman W. Schaars, Department of Christian Education, South Wisconsin District, 8100 West Capitol Drive, Milwaukee, Wisconsin 53222. This is delightful and interesting reading.
8. *Luther's Commentary on Genesis*, Luther's Works, Vol. I, pages 1 to 140. Concordia Publishing House.
9. *Why I Accept the Genesis Record,* by John Raymond Hand, Back to the Bible Broadcast, Lincoln, Nebraska, Box 232. Pamphlet, excellent.
10. *Evolution on Trial*, Cora Reno, The Moody Bible Institute of Chicago, a textbook for high school students.
11. Subscribe to the publications of Bible Science Association, Inc., Box 1016, Caldwell, Idaho 83605.

Members of a study group are encouraged to gather other helpful materials on this subject from books, magazine articles or reports that appear in the daily press or elsewhere.

For further study of the subject, I would suggest the following:

Some standard commentary on Genesis

Luther's commentary on Genesis

The Flood, by myself

Darwin, Evolution, and Creation, by Paul Zimmerman, *et al.*

The Twilight of Evolution, by Henry M. Morris, Baker Book House, Grand Rapids, Michigan

Why I Accept the Genesis Record, by John Raymond Hand, Back to the Bible Broadcast, Lincoln, Nebraska, Box 233, pamphlet

From the Greeks to Darwin, by Henry Fairfield Osborn, Charles Scribner & Sons, New York

The Tower of Babel, by Andre Parrot, Philosophical Library, New York

The Five Books of Moses, by Oswald T. Allis, The Presbyterian and Reformed Publishers, Co., Philadelphia, Pa., 1949

A Short Introduction to the Pentateuch, by G. H. Aalders, Th.D., The Tyndale Press, 39 Bedford Square, W. C.

Fossils, Flood, and Fire, by Harold W. Clark, published by Outdoor Pictures, Escondido, California

The Babylonian Genesis, by Alexander Heidel, The University of Chicago Press, Chicago, Ill., 1950

The Divine Worker—Creation and Providence, by Oswald Dykes, M.A., D.D., T. and T. Cork, Edinburgh, 1900

The Six Creation Days, by L. Franklin Gruber, D.D., L.L.D., Lutheran Literary Board, Burlington, Iowa, 1941

The Age of the Earth and the Chronology of the Bible, by myself, Lutheran Publishing House, Adelaide, South Australia (Also available from Concordia Publishing House, St. Louis.)

INDICES

Index of Scripture Passages

Index of Authors

Index of Subjects

ABOUT THE AUTHOR
Alfred Martin Rehwinkel, B.A., B.D., M.A., LLD., DDD.

Dr. Rehwinkel is a scholar, in the best sense of the word. But he is not addicted, as are so many, to the notion that to be erudite is to be obscure. The result is refreshing . . . he gets through to you.

He received his training at an impressive succession of schools, beginning at Concordia College of Milwaukee, Concordia Seminary of St. Louis, and continuing to the University of Alberta for both his B.A. and M.A. degrees. He then received a bachelor of divinity from St. Stephen College of Edmonton, and did a great deal of further graduate work at four other institutions from 1931 to 1944.

He was a pastor for about twelve years and then a professor at Concordia College in Alberta, Canada. Then followed eight years as president of St. John's College in Kansas, and 29 years as professor at Concordia Seminary, St. Louis. From 1944 to 1954 he served the seminary in important additional capacities.

He has held a number of offices in the Missouri Synod throughout his ministry, and has been a prolific writer on a variety of significant themes ranging from the Reformation to Christian Ethics.

In addition to all these qualifications Dr. Rehwinkel has been president of Kappa Delta Pi, and an esteemed member of the Academy of Political Science and other learned societies.

He has been in great demand as a lecturer and preacher in both this country and Canada, as well as overseas. For twenty years he travelled from twenty to forty thousand miles per year filling speaking engagements.

His journeys have taken him across much of the world, and he has done intensive research abroad, particularly in Bible lands.

His additional labors in various fields are too numerous to recount here.

Perhaps his most notable previous book was entitled, *The Flood*, which has been reprinted eleven times and translated into six languages in complete or condensed versions, and also into Braille.